Sixth Workshop on the Use of Computational Methods in the Study of Endangered Languages (computel 2023)

Online
5-6 March 2023

ISBN: 978-1-7138-9029-4

Printed from e-media with permission by:

Curran Associates, Inc.
57 Morehouse Lane
Red Hook, NY 12571

CURRAN ASSOCIATES INC.
proceedings
.com

Some format issues inherent in the e-media version may also appear in this print version.

Printed with permission by Curran Associates, Inc. (2024)

For permission requests, please contact the Association for Computational Linguistics at the address below.

Association for Computational Linguistics
209 N. Eighth Street
Stroudsburg, Pennsylvania 18360

Phone: 1-570-476-8006
Fax: 1-570-476-0860

acl@aclweb.org

Additional copies of this publication are available from:

Curran Associates, Inc.
57 Morehouse Lane
Red Hook, NY 12571 USA
Phone: 845-758-0400
Fax: 845-758-2633
Email: curran@proceedings.com
Web: www.proceedings.com

computel 2023

Sixth Workshop on the Use of Computational Methods in the Study of Endangered Languages

Proceedings of the Workshop

March 5-6, 2023

Introduction

We are excited to welcome you to the 6th Workshop on the Use of Computational Methods in the Study of Endangered Languages. This year it is going to be held as a virtual event from March 5-6, 2023, and co-located with the 8th International Conference on Language Documentation and Conservation (ICL-DC).

As the name implies, this is the sixth workshop held on the topic—the first meeting was co-located with the ACL main conference in Baltimore, Maryland in 2014 and the second, third, and fourth ones in 2017, 2019, and 2021 were co-located with the 5th, 6th, and 7th editions of the International Conference on Language Documentation and Conservation (ICLDC) at the University of Hawaii at Mānoa. The fifth iteration of the workshop was held in 2022 alongside the 60th Association of Computational Linguistics (ACL) conference in Dublin, Ireland. This is the fourth time this workshop has been co-located with the ICLDC, and it enhances the conference's 2023 theme of justice. The workshop covers a wide range of topics relevant to the study and documentation of endangered languages, ranging from technical papers on working systems and applications, to reports on community activities with supporting computational components. This year, the workshop held a special session centering work on justice and equity in language technology as a part of ICLDC 8.

The purpose of the workshop is to bring together computational researchers, documentary linguists, and people involved with community efforts of language documentation and revitalization to take part in both formal and informal exchanges on how to integrate rapidly evolving language processing methods and tools into efforts of language description, documentation, and revitalization. The organizers are pleased with the range of papers, many of which highlight the importance of interdisciplinary work and interaction between the various communities that the workshop is aimed towards.

We received 24 submissions as papers or extended abstracts. After a thorough review process, 17 submissions were selected to be published in the ACL Anthology. In addition to these papers, we had four oral presentations that made up our special session on justice.

The Organizing Committee would like to thank the Program Committee for their thoughtful review of the submissions. We are also grateful to the Social Sciences and Humanities Research Council (SSHRC) of Canada for supporting the workshop through their Partnership Grant 895-2019-1012. We would moreover want to acknowledge the support of the organizers of ICLDC 8.

Organizing Committee

Organizers

Atticus Harrigan, University of Alberta, Canada
Aditi Chaudhary, Google Research, USA
Shruti Rijhwani, Google Research, USA
Sarah Moeller, University of Florida, USA
Antti Arppe, University of Alberta, Canada
Alexis Palmer, University of Colorado Boulder, USA
Ryan Henke, University of Wisconsin-Madison, USA
Daisy Rosenblum, The University of British Columbia, Canada

Program Committee

Program Committee

Aditi Chaudhary, Google Research, USA
Atticus Harrigan, University of Alberta
Shruti Rijhwani, Google Research, USA
Daisy Rosenblum, The University of British Columbia
Ryan Henke, University of Wisconsin-Madison
Robert Forkel, Max Planck Institute for Evolutionary Anthropology
Anna Kazantseva, National Research Council Canada
Antti Arppe, University of Alberta
Vera Ferreira, Centro Interdisciplinar de Documentação Linguística e Social
Daan van Esch, Google
Jeff Good, University at Buffalo
Matthew Kelley, University of Washington
Alexis Palmer, University of Colorado Boulder
Michael Maxwell, University of Maryland
Jordan Lachler, University of Alberta
Emily M. Bender, University of Washington
František Kratochvíl, Palacký University
Martin Benjamin, Kamusi Project International
Olivia Sammons, First Nations University of Canada
Gary Simons, SIL International
Yves Scherrer, University of Helsinki
Conor Snoek, University of Lethbridge
Steven Bird, Charles Darwin University
Roland Kuhn, National Research Council Canada
Andrea Berez-Kroeker, University of Hawaii at Mānoa Department of Linguistics
Richard Sproat, Google
Fei Xia, University of Washington
Kevin Scannell, Saint Louis University
Harald Hammarström, MPI Nijmegen
Paul Trilsbeek, Max Planck Institute for Psycholinguistics
Atticus Harrigan, University of Alberta
Olga Lovick, University of Saskatchewan
Sarah Moeller, University of Florida
Lori Levin, Carnegie Mellon University
W N Martin, University of Virginia
Dorothee Beermann, Norwegian University of Science and Technology

Table of Contents

Program

Sunday, March 5, 2023

10:30 - 10:40	*Day-1 Welcome + Introduction*
10:40 - 13:30	*Special Session Justice through Technology*
16:00 - 17:45	*Session 1*
	User-Centric Evaluation of OCR Systems for Kwak'wala Shruti Rijhwani, Daisy Rosenblum, Michayla King, Antonios Anastasopoulos and Graham Neubig
	Towards a finite-state morphological analyser for San Mateo Huave Francis M. Tyers and Samuel Herrera Castro
	A morphological analyzer for Huasteca Nahuatl Ana Tona, Guillaume Thomas and Ewan Dunbar
16:45 - 17:15	*Day-1 Break*
17:00 - 17:30	*Session 2*
	LSDT a Dependency Treebank of Lombard Sinti Marco Forlano and Luca Brigada Villa
	Towards Universal Dependencies in Cook Islands Māori Sarah Karnes, Rolando Coto-Solano and Sally Akevai Nicholas

Monday, March 6, 2023

09:00 - 09:45 *Session 1*

Leveraging supplementary text data to kick-start automatic speech recognition system development with limited transcriptions
Nay San, Martijn Bartelds, Blaine Billings, Ella de Falco, Hendi Feriza, Johan Safri, Wawan Sahrozi, Ben Foley, Bradley McDonnell and Dan Jurafsky

Studying the impact of language model size for low-resource ASR
Zoey Liu, Justin Spence and Emily Prud'Hommeaux

Speech-to-text recognition for multilingual spoken data in language documentation
Lorena Martín Rodríguez and Christopher Cox

09:45 - 10:00 *Break*

10:00 - 10:45 *Session 2*

FileLingR An R Script validation tool for depositors and users of digital language collections
Irene Yi and Claire Bowern

Investigating Speaker Diarization of Endangered Language Data
Gina-Anne Levow

From Raw Data to Acoustic Analysis A Roadmap for Acquaviva Collecroce
Simon Gonzalez

10:45 - 11:45 *Midday Break*

11:45 - 14:15 *Session 3*

A Survey of Computational Infrastructure to Help Preserve and Revitalize Bodwéwadmimwen
Robert Lewis

12:30 - 13:15 *Break*

Monday, March 6, 2023 (continued)

12:30 - 13:15 *Session 4*

Challenges and Issue of Gender Bias in Under-Represented Languages An Empirical Study on Inuktitut-English NMT
Ngoc Tan Le, Oussama Hansal and Fatiha Sadat

A text-to-speech synthesis system for Border Lakes Ojibwe
Christopher Hammerly, Sonja Fougère, Giancarlo Sierra, Scott Parkhill, Harrison Porteous and Chad Quinn

Text normalization for low-resource languages the case of Ligurian
Stefano Lusito, Edoardo Ferrante and Jean Maillard

13:15 - 13:30 *Day-2 Break*

13:30 - 14:15 *Session 5*

Morphological Data Generation from FLEx
Shengyu Liao, Beth Bryson and Sarah Moeller

Using LARA to rescue a legacy Pitjantjatjara course
Manny Rayner and Sasha Wilmoth

Applications of classification trees for endangered language description Finite verb morphology in Kolyma Yukaghir
Albert Ventayol-Boada

14:15 - 15:15 *SIGEL Business Meeting*

Leveraging supplementary text data to kick-start automatic speech recognition system development with limited transcriptions

Nay San[1], Martijn Bartelds[2], Blaine Billings[3], Ella de Falco[4], Hendi Feriza, Johan Safri, Wawan Sahrozi, Ben Foley[5], Bradley McDonnell[3], Dan Jurafsky[1]
[1]Stanford University; [2]University of Groningen; [3]University of Hawai'i at Mānoa; [3]University of Washington; [5]University of Queensland
nay.san@stanford.edu

Abstract

Recent research using pre-trained transformer models suggests that just 10 minutes of transcribed speech may be enough to fine-tune such a model for automatic speech recognition (ASR) — at least if we can also leverage vast amounts of text data (803 million tokens). But is that much text data necessary? We study the use of different amounts of text data, both for creating a lexicon that constrains ASR decoding to possible words (e.g. **dogz* vs. *dogs*), and for training larger language models that bias the system toward probable word sequences (e.g. *too dogs* vs. *two dogs*). We perform experiments using 10 minutes of transcribed speech from English (for replicating prior work) and two additional pairs of languages differing in the availability of supplemental text data: Gronings and Frisian (~7.5M token corpora available), and Besemah and Nasal (only small lexica available). For all languages, we found that using only a lexicon did not appreciably improve ASR performance. For Gronings and Frisian, we found that lexica and language models derived from 'novel-length' 80k token subcorpora reduced the word error rate (WER) to 39% on average. Our findings suggest that where a text corpus in the upper tens of thousands of tokens or more is available, fine-tuning a transformer model with just tens of minutes of transcribed speech holds some promise towards obtaining human-correctable transcriptions near the 30% WER rule-of-thumb.

1 Introduction

Automatic speech recognition (ASR) systems can help speed up the labour-intensive process of transcribing speech by providing human-correctable first-pass transcriptions. The Catch-22, however, is that some speech must first be manually transcribed in order to develop a sufficiently performant ASR system. As such, recently developed pre-trained transformer models for speech such as wav2vec 2.0 (Baevski et al., 2020) have spurred on much experimentation to leverage them to accelerate transcription workflows in language documentation contexts (e.g. Coto-Solano et al., 2022; Guillaume et al., 2022; Macaire et al., 2022; San et al., 2022; Zhang et al., 2022), given a much reduced upfront cost in terms of transcribed speech.

Impressively, Baevski et al. (2020) showed that a wav2vec 2.0 model pre-trained on 960 hours of untranscribed English speech required just 10 minutes of transcriptions to yield competitive results on the LibriSpeech ASR benchmark (Panayotov et al., 2015). This result, however, also leveraged the official LibriSpeech lexicon and language model derived from the entire 803 million token text corpus based on 14.5k public domain books.[1] However, an in-domain text corpus of such size is not within immediate reach for many other languages. In this paper, we investigate the real-world ASR performance achievable with 10 minutes of transcribed speech along with more tenable amounts of supplemental text data.

We first replicated the wav2vec 2.0 experiments on LibriSpeech and then extended them by creating lexica and language models using reduced amounts of supplemental text data (8M, 80k, and 8k tokens) from both the in-domain LibriSpeech text corpus and an out-of-domain corpus composed of web-scraped text (Common Crawl: Buck et al., 2014). Our experiments showed that first-pass transcriptions within the 20-30% word error rate (WER) rule-of-thumb (Gaur et al., 2016; Sperber et al., 2016) can indeed be obtained with just 10 minutes of transcribed speech if supplemented with a lexicon and language model derived from a corpus with at least 80k tokens.

We then performed analogous experiments with two pairs of languages differing in the availability of supplemental texts: Gronings and Frisian (two Germanic languages for which a modest amount of external text-only data can be sourced), and

[1]https://www.openslr.org/11/

Besemah and Nasal (two Malayo-Polynesian languages for which the documentation projects' own materials constitute the only available text data). For these experiments, we used 10 minutes of audio from each of the languages to fine-tune the multilingual wav2vec 2.0 XLS-R model (Babu et al., 2021) that is pre-trained on 450k hours of speech from 128 languages.

For all four languages we found that using only a lexicon to restrict ASR system output to possible words did not appreciably reduce the WER. For Gronings and Frisian, where there was sufficient text data to derive both lexica and language models from various samples (~7.5M, 80k, and 8k tokens), we found that those derived from 80k tokens of text reduced the WER to 34.9% for Gronings and 43.0% for Frisian (mean: 39.0%).

While these error rates are above the 20-30% rule-of-thumb for first-pass transcriptions (Gaur et al., 2016; Sperber et al., 2017), it is worth noting that the multilingual XLS-R model used for Gronings and Frisian was not pre-trained on the target datasets. This is in contrast to the English wav2vec 2.0 model, which was pre-trained on all 960 hours of the target LibriSpeech dataset. Thus, if combined with a domain adaptation technique (e.g. continued pretraining: Gururangan et al., 2020), our results suggest that where 80k or more of supplementary text is available, fine-tuning a pre-trained model with just tens of minutes of transcribed speech could help kick-start a virtuous cycle of data collection and training for ASR system development.

2 Motivations

2.1 Related work

As mentioned above, there have been several recent studies appraising the utility of pre-trained transformers for ASR in language documentation settings. Coto-Solano (2022) reported that the XLS-R model fine-tuned with 4 hours of transcribed speech from Cook Islands Māori yielded a WER of 22.9% without using a language model (LM). Similarly, Guillaume et al. (2022) found that the XLS-R model fine-tuned with 10 hours of transcriptions from Japhug yielded a WER of 18.5% also without a LM. Notably, both these studies explicitly mentioned that the system outputs (~20% WER) did indeed appear suitable as first-pass transcriptions for their respective projects and that LM integration is a clear next step.

Of the two studies that have examined the use of a LM with a fine-tuned wav2vec 2.0 model for language documentation projects (Macaire et al., 2022; San et al., 2022), a common theme has been to examine the effect of varying amounts of transcribed speech (e.g. 10–70 minutes) with and without the use of a LM trained on the full corpus (e.g. 74.5k tokens of text). Similarly, the original wav2vec 2.0 experiments by Baevski et al. (2020) also only examined the use of different amounts of fine-tuning data (10 minutes to 960 hours), with or without the use of LMs trained on an 803M token corpus.

Given the broader community interest in using fine-tuned wav2vec 2.0 models with LM integration, we undertook a series of experiments holding constant the amount of fine-tuning data (i.e. 10 minutes) while varying the amount of LM training text (e.g. 8k–8M tokens) to complement the aforementioned studies.

2.2 Language projects

For Besemah, Nasal, and Gronings, the motivation for the development of ASR systems is to help derive first-pass transcriptions and hence accelerate the process of indexing a large collection of audiovisual materials. Besemah (ISO 639-3: pse) and Nasal (ISO 639-3: nsy) are two Malayo-Polynesian languages spoken in Sumatra, Indonesia. For both languages, approximately 45 hours of informal conversations have been collected as part of fieldwork by author BM. Part of these collections have been transcribed by author BM and collaborators from the Besemah (author HF) and Nasal communities (authors JS and WS). The collections are managed by authors BB and EF and are accessible at PARADISEC (McDonnell, 2008, 2019).

Gronings (ISO 639-3: gos) is a Low Saxon language variant spoken in the province of Groningen in the Netherlands. An ongoing language documentation project (of which author MB is part) has so far recorded approximately 15 hours of speech, with more being continually gathered. The materials will be used to create ASR and text-to-speech systems to be made available through an online cultural portal.[2] For an additional point of comparison in our experiments, we also included West Frisian (another minority language spoken in the Netherlands; ISO 639-3: fry), using data from the FAME! ASR corpus (Yilmaz et al., 2017).

[2] `https://www.woordwaark.nl`

3 Method

For English, we used the '1h/0' ten minute training set defined in Libri-Light (Kahn et al., 2020) to approximate the fine-tuning experiments in Baevski et al. (2020). As supplementary text data, we used the official normalised LibriSpeech as the in-domain corpus and Common Crawl (Buck et al., 2014) as the out-of-domain corpus.

For Besemah, Nasal, Gronings and Frisian, we constructed comparable 4-hour datasets for our broader set of ASR experiments. Each dataset is composed of an 80/10/10 train/dev/test split, approximately 24 minutes for each of the dev and test sets and 3.2 hours for training set, from which we sampled 10 minutes for the experiments reported here. As supplementary text data, we sourced two 9.5k word lists for Nasal and Besemah from project materials and remaining transcriptions not included in the ASR corpora. For Gronings and Frisian, we sourced two ~7.5M corpora used in de Vries et al. (2021).

For English, we used the monolingual English wav2vec 2.0 model (Baevski et al., 2020). For the other four languages, we used the multilingual XLS-R model (Babu et al., 2021). For fine-tuning these models, we used the HuggingFace Transformers library (Wolf et al., 2019). For beam search decoding with a lexicon and language model, we used the torchaudio implementation of the Flashlight decoder (formerly wav2letter: Kahn et al., 2022) used in the original paper. We fine-tuned each model for 12k steps and then selected the best checkpoint based on the dev set WER using greedy decoding (for Besemah and Nasal) or beam search decoding with fixed parameters (language model weight: 2, word insertion penalty: -1). We then performed a parameter search with the best checkpoint to further optimise the dev set WER. We repeated the decoding experiments with 5 different random samples of each size of sub-corpora. All our experiment code is available on GitHub.[3]

4 Results and discussion

The results from our experiments are collated in Table 1. For English, we found that fine-tuning with 10 minutes of transcribed speech yielded a test set WER of 40.2 (Row E1) without the use of supplementary texts and a WER of 14.2 (Row E3) using a lexicon and language model derived from the full 803M LibriSpeech text corpus. These WERs are consistent with those reported by Baevski et al. (2020, Table 9), respectively: 45.3 and 13.1, allowing for some error likely from differences in the 10 minute samples.[4]

For all languages, we found that using only a lexicon did not appreciably reduce the WER. For example, for English, the test set WER remained practically the same with or without a lexicon (Row E1 vs. E2: 40.2 vs. 40.5). For Nasal, the test set WER increased from 70.7 without a lexicon (Row N1) to 75.1 when using a small 9.5k token lexicon (Row N2), which led to many erroneous substitutions from the combination of an already high WER and high out-of-vocabulary rate.

For English, Gronings, and Frisian, we found that using lexica and language models derived from 80k of out-of-domain supplementary texts appreciably reduced the mean test set WER. For English, the test set WER was reduced from 40.2 (Row E1) to 27.7 (Row E8). For Gronings, the test set WER was reduced from 44.0 (Row G1) to 34.9 (Row G4). For Frisian, the test set WER was reduced from 53.1 (Row F1) to 43.0 (Row F4). These results suggest that where supplemental texts in the upper tens of thousands or more are available, fine-tuning a wav2vec 2.0 model with just tens of minutes of speech holds promise for deriving first-pass transcriptions near the 20-30% rule-of-thumb.

For English, the acceptably low sub-30% WER likely reflect an idealised set of circumstances in that the wav2vec 2.0 model used was pre-trained on the target dataset and that the genre of the audio is read speech. Regarding genre, the higher proportion of read speech in the Gronings dataset likely reflects its lower WER compared to Frisian, which has mainly news and radio broadcasts. Regarding pre-training, the multilingual XLS-R model used for Gronings and Frisian was not pre-trained on these datasets. This disadvantage could be partially overcome by a domain adaptation technique such as continued pre-training (Gururangan et al., 2020) or by using a wav2vec 2.0 model pre-trained on a similar language such as Dutch (Bartelds and Wieling, 2022). Macaire et al. (2022) report a 5–9% reduction in WER when using a wav2vec 2.0 model pre-trained on French over a multilingual model when fine-tuning for ASR on Gwadloupéyen and Morisien, two French-based creole languages.

[3] https://github.com/fauxneticien/w2v2-10min-exps/

[4] There was no indication as to which of the six 10-minute Libri-Light training sets were used in the original experiments.

wav2vec 2.0 model (Fine-tuning data, 10 mins)	Language model (Text corpus size, no. of tokens)	Mean WER (SD)		Mean CER (SD)	
		dev	test	dev	test
LS-960 (English)	E1. None	40.4	40.2	13.0	12.8
	E2. None, lexicon only (973k)	40.1	40.5	12.3	12.2
	LibriSpeech (in-domain)				
	E3. 4-gram, full corpus (803M)	13.4	14.2	6.51	6.75
	E4. 4-gram, subset (8M)	15.9 (0.09)	16.6 (0.07)	7.41 (0.05)	7.58 (0.07)
	E5. 3-gram, subset (80k)	23.5 (0.13)	24.1 (0.12)	10.5 (0.07)	10.6 (0.10)
	E6. 3-gram, subset (**8k**)	**36.5** (0.20)	**36.8** (0.34)	17.1 (0.09)	17.0 (0.15)
	CommonCrawl-En (out-of-domain)				
	E8. 3-gram, subset (**80k**)	**27.7** (0.13)	**27.7** (0.10)	12.1 (0.13)	12.0 (0.13)
	E9. 3-gram, subset (8k)	39.8 (0.12)	39.8 (0.24)	18.5 (0.19)	18.3 (0.22)
XLS-R (Gronings)	G1. None	43.8	44.0	11.2	11.3
	G2. None, lexicon only (216k)	41.4	40.7	10.5	10.3
	G3. 4-gram, full corpus (7.6M)	23.4 (0.22)	22.3 (0.22)	7.61 (0.62)	7.44 (0.71)
	G4. 3-gram, subset (**80k**)	**35.6** (0.30)	**34.9** (0.51)	11.8 (0.28)	11.4 (0.34)
	G5. 3-gram, subset (8k)	45.6 (0.41)	46.3 (0.24)	16.9 (0.67)	16.7 (0.43)
XLS-R (Frisian)	F1. None	55.1	53.1	18.6	18.3
	F2. None, lexicon only (251k)	53.8	51.7	17.9	17.6
	F3. 4-gram, full corpus (7.4M)	36.7	35.2	16.3	15.9
	F4. 3-gram, subset (**80k**)	**44.4** (0.37)	**43.0** (0.22)	20.3 (0.16)	19.9 (0.22)
	F5. 3-gram, subset (8k)	54.2 (0.39)	52.2 (0.29)	26.2 (0.30)	26.0 (0.25)
XLS-R (Besemah)	B1. None	62.3	62.1	21.4	21.2
	B2. None, lexicon only (9.5k)	59.9	62.2	20.1	21.2
XLS-R (Nasal)	N1. None	67.2	70.7	23.1	25.5
	N2. None, lexicon only (9.5k)	70.1	75.1	24.1	26.1

Table 1: Results of fine-tuning wav2vec 2.0 models (LS960: pre-trained on 960 hours of English; XLS-R pre-trained on 400k hours of speech from 128 languages) for automatic speech recognition (ASR) using only 10 minutes of transcribed speech from a target language and with varying amounts of reliance on supplementary text data. ASR performance measured by word error rate (WER) and character error rate (CER). For subset experiments, reported means and standard deviations (in parentheses) were derived across 5 runs with different samples of the text corpus. Alphanumeric labels (E1–N1) used to assist with in-text references to results. Highlighted numbers indicate the smallest supplementary text corpus size which yielded an appreciably lower WER.

For languages where tens of thousands of tokens in supplementary texts are not available, we suspect it remains unavoidable for the time being that more than 10 minutes of transcribed speech is required to begin ASR system development. For reducing the out-of-vocabulary rate with lexica and LMs derived from small text corpora, decomposing words into sub-word units (e.g. syllables) may be worth investigating. In trialling an interactive transcription app for Kunwinjku, Le Ferrand et al. (2022) report that incorporating syllable unigram frequencies derived from a word list improved the word retrieval performance by 4% (F-score).

5 Conclusion

We investigated the real-world performance obtainable when leveraging various amounts of supplemental text data to help kick-start automatic speech recognition (ASR) system development with only a limited amount of transcribed speech. Our results suggest that fine-tuning a pre-trained transformer model with just 10 minutes of transcribed speech may hold some promise for deriving human-correctable first-pass transcriptions if the ASR system can incorporate a lexicon and language model derived from a 'novel-length' corpus with at least 80,000 tokens or more of text.

Acknowledgements

We would like to thank people from the Nasal and Besemah communities who took part in these documentation projects, especially Anton Supriyadi, Sarkani, Asfan Fikri Sanaf, and Kencana Dewi as well as collaborators on the Nasal project, including Yanti and Jacob Hakim. We are also grateful to the Ministry of Research and Technology in Indonesia for providing permissions for research on Besemah and Nasal as well as the Center for Culture and Language Studies at Atma Jaya Catholic University of Indonesia for sponsoring this research. This material is based upon work supported by the National Science Foundation under Grant No. (1911641). Any opinions, findings, and conclusions or recommendations expressed in this material are those of the author and do not necessarily reflect the views of the National Science Foundation.

References

Arun Babu, Changhan Wang, Andros Tjandra, Kushal Lakhotia, Qiantong Xu, Naman Goyal, Kritika Singh, Patrick von Platen, Yatharth Saraf, Juan Pino, et al. 2021. Xls-r: Self-supervised cross-lingual speech representation learning at scale. *arXiv preprint arXiv:2111.09296*.

Alexei Baevski, Yuhao Zhou, Abdelrahman Mohamed, and Michael Auli. 2020. wav2vec 2.0: A framework for self-supervised learning of speech representations. In *Advances in Neural Information Processing Systems*, volume 33, pages 12449–12460. Curran Associates, Inc.

Martijn Bartelds and Martijn Wieling. 2022. Quantifying language variation acoustically with few resources. In *Proceedings of the 2022 Conference of the North American Chapter of the Association for Computational Linguistics: Human Language Technologies*, pages 3735–3741, Seattle, United States. Association for Computational Linguistics.

Christian Buck, Kenneth Heafield, and Bas van Ooyen. 2014. N-gram counts and language models from the common crawl. In *Proceedings of the Language Resources and Evaluation Conference*, Reykjavik, Iceland.

Rolando Coto-Solano. 2022. Evaluating word embeddings in extremely under-resourced languages: A case study in Bribri. In *Proceedings of the 29th International Conference on Computational Linguistics*, pages 4455–4467, Gyeongju, Republic of Korea. International Committee on Computational Linguistics.

Rolando Coto-Solano, Sally Akevai Nicholas, Samiha Datta, Victoria Quint, Piripi Wills, Emma Ngakuravaru Powell, Liam Koka'ua, Syed Tanveer, and Isaac Feldman. 2022. Development of automatic speech recognition for the documentation of Cook Islands Māori. In *Proceedings of the Thirteenth Language Resources and Evaluation Conference*, pages 3872–3882, Marseille, France. European Language Resources Association.

Wietse de Vries, Martijn Bartelds, Malvina Nissim, and Martijn Wieling. 2021. Adapting monolingual models: Data can be scarce when language similarity is high. In *Findings of the Association for Computational Linguistics: ACL-IJCNLP 2021*, pages 4901–4907, Online. Association for Computational Linguistics.

Yashesh Gaur, Walter S Lasecki, Florian Metze, and Jeffrey P Bigham. 2016. The effects of automatic speech recognition quality on human transcription latency. In *Proceedings of the 13th International Web for All Conference*, pages 1–8.

Séverine Guillaume, Guillaume Wisniewski, Cécile Macaire, Guillaume Jacques, Alexis Michaud, Benjamin Galliot, Maximin Coavoux, Solange Rossato, Minh-Châu Nguyên, and Maxime Fily. 2022. Fine-tuning pre-trained models for automatic speech recognition, experiments on a fieldwork corpus of Japhug (Trans-Himalayan family). In *Proceedings of the Fifth Workshop on the Use of Computational Methods in the Study of Endangered Languages*, pages 170–178.

Suchin Gururangan, Ana Marasović, Swabha Swayamdipta, Kyle Lo, Iz Beltagy, Doug Downey, and Noah A Smith. 2020. Don't stop pretraining: adapt language models to domains and tasks. *arXiv preprint arXiv:2004.10964*.

Jacob Kahn, Morgane Rivière, Weiyi Zheng, Evgeny Kharitonov, Qiantong Xu, Pierre-Emmanuel Mazaré, Julien Karadayi, Vitaliy Liptchinsky, Ronan Collobert, Christian Fuegen, et al. 2020. Libri-light: A benchmark for asr with limited or no supervision. In *ICASSP 2020-2020 IEEE International Conference on Acoustics, Speech and Signal Processing (ICASSP)*, pages 7669–7673. IEEE.

Jacob D Kahn, Vineel Pratap, Tatiana Likhomanenko, Qiantong Xu, Awni Hannun, Jeff Cai, Paden Tomasello, Ann Lee, Edouard Grave, Gilad Avidov, et al. 2022. Flashlight: Enabling innovation in tools for machine learning. In *International Conference on Machine Learning*, pages 10557–10574. PMLR.

Éric Le Ferrand, Steven Bird, and Laurent Besacier. 2022. Fashioning local designs from generic speech technologies in an Australian aboriginal community. In *Proceedings of the 29th International Conference on Computational Linguistics*, pages 4274–4285, Gyeongju, Republic of Korea. International Committee on Computational Linguistics.

Cécile Macaire, Didier Schwab, Benjamin Lecouteux, and Emmanuel Schang. 2022. Automatic speech recognition and query by example for creole languages documentation. In *Findings of the Association for Computational Linguistics: ACL 2022*, pages 2512–2520, Dublin, Ireland. Association for Computational Linguistics.

Bradley McDonnell. 2008. Besemah. PARADISEC Collection BJM01.

Bradley McDonnell. 2019. Documentation of the multilingual linguistic practices of the Nasal speech community. PARADISEC Collection BJM02.

Vassil Panayotov, Guoguo Chen, Daniel Povey, and Sanjeev Khudanpur. 2015. LibriSpeech: an ASR corpus based on public domain audio books. In *2015 IEEE international conference on acoustics, speech and signal processing (ICASSP)*, pages 5206–5210. IEEE.

Nay San, Martijn Bartelds, Tolulope Ogunremi, Alison Mount, Ruben Thompson, Michael Higgins, Roy Barker, Jane Simpson, and Dan Jurafsky. 2022. Automated speech tools for helping communities process restricted-access corpora for language revival efforts. In *Proceedings of the Fifth Workshop on the Use of Computational Methods in the Study of Endangered Languages*, pages 41–51, Dublin, Ireland. Association for Computational Linguistics.

Matthias Sperber, Graham Neubig, Satoshi Nakamura, and Alex Waibel. 2016. Optimizing computer-assisted transcription quality with iterative user interfaces. In *Proceedings of the Tenth International Conference on Language Resources and Evaluation (LREC'16)*, pages 1986–1992, Portorož, Slovenia. European Language Resources Association (ELRA).

Matthias Sperber, Graham Neubig, Jan Niehues, Satoshi Nakamura, and Alex Waibel. 2017. Transcribing Against Time. *Speech Communication*, 93C:20–30.

Thomas Wolf, Lysandre Debut, Victor Sanh, Julien Chaumond, Clement Delangue, Anthony Moi, Pierric Cistac, Tim Rault, Rémi Louf, Morgan Funtowicz, et al. 2019. Huggingface's transformers: State-of-the-art natural language processing. *arXiv preprint arXiv:1910.03771*.

Emre Yilmaz, Jelske Dijkstra, H Velde, H Heuvel, and DA van Leeuwen. 2017. Longitudinal speaker clustering and verification corpus with code-switching Frisian-Dutch speech. *INTERSPEECH*.

Shiyue Zhang, Ben Frey, and Mohit Bansal. 2022. How can NLP help revitalize endangered languages? a case study and roadmap for the Cherokee language. In *Proceedings of the 60th Annual Meeting of the Association for Computational Linguistics (Volume 1: Long Papers)*, pages 1529–1541, Dublin, Ireland. Association for Computational Linguistics.

Applications of classification trees for endangered language description: Finite verb morphology in Kolyma Yukaghir

Albert Ventayol-Boada
University of California, Santa Barbara
aventayolboada@ucsb.edu

Abstract

This study investigates the use of the finite verb-focus forms *-jə* and *-mə* in Kolyma Yukaghir. These forms are described in terms of valency: *-jə* is the intransitive form, and *-mə* is the transitive. In this study, I revise this analysis by using decision tree modeling on five monologic texts annotated for different discourse and morphological factors. The results show that 1) valency alone cannot account for the distribution of the finite verb-focus forms in discourse, and 2) speakers are sensitive to different discourse factors and use *-jə* and *-mə* to achieve different communicative goals. In short, this study demonstrates how machine learning methods like classification decision trees can offer a more nuanced picture of the choices speakers make at the discourse level and help the language description process.

1 Introduction

Finite verb morphology in the endangered language of Kolyma Yukaghir (Yukaghiric; Russia) has a four-way distinction from which language users choose when making an assertion (Krejnovich, 1982; Maslova, 1997, 2003, 2008; Nagasaki, 2010, 2018). These four forms are said to represent the grammaticalization of the "information structure status" of core participants (Nikolaeva, 2005) and are classified according to valency (i.e., intransitive vs. transitive) and as to whether they highlight the event (i.e., verb-focus) or the event participants (i.e., subject-focus or object-focus). This description, however, fails to account for a significant number of utterances in spontaneous discourse, since examples of verbs with the 'intransitive' verb-focus form *-jə* are attested with two participants (1), and the 'transitive' verb-focus *-mə* also occurs with a single participant (2).

(1) *опольэ мэткэлэ монну*ŋ*ий,*
opoll'ə met-kələ mon-nu-ŋi-**j**,
later 1SG-ACC say-IPFV-PL-**JƏ**.3
'Later they told me' ("Tobacco," 34:13)

(2) *и*ŋ*эртэм и*ŋ*эртэм,*
iŋer-tə-**m** iŋer-tə-**m**,
hole-?-**MƏ**.3SG hole-?-**MƏ**.3SG
'He dug, he dug' ("The felt boots," 13:21)

An alternative view is to consider the choice over the four finite forms as carrying out different discourse functions (Nagasaki, 2018), and thus being sensitive to different discourse and pragmatic factors. In this view, explanations for speakers' choices can be found in a more dynamic view of transitivity in which events do not have an inherent amount of participants (Hopper and Thompson, 1980; Diver et al., 2012), as well as the accessibility of the referents (Ariel, 2001), and the different degrees of attention-worthiness placed onto the participants and the event (Diver and Davis, 2012).

The goal of this study is to investigate these factors in concert in order to understand what communicative goals the two verb-focus forms (i.e., 'intransitive' *-jə* and 'transitive' *-mə*) fulfill, with a study of the less common subject-focus and object-focus forms to follow. Ultimately, the objective is to improve current descriptions of Kolyma Yukaghir through a multifactorial analysis of spontaneous discourse in a context where recording additional linguistic materials is difficult due to language endangerment.

2 Data

I analyzed 5 of the 40 monologic texts collected in the late 20th century (Nikolaeva and Mayer, 2004). These five texts were narrated by the same person, but differ slightly in terms of genre: there is a personal story ("Tobacco"), a fantastical story ("Elizar"), the description of a game played between two people with their hands ("A game"), the depiction of a yearly meeting among the Yukaghirs ("Yearly meetings"), and an account of the fortune telling practice to predict the ethnic group a woman will marry into ("Fortune telling").

I first divided each text into intonation units (IUs; Chafe, 1979, 1994; Du Bois et al., 1993) and then extracted all 135 verb-focus finite forms (88 -jə's and 47 -mə's). Afterwards, I manually annotated in a table each token for linguistic features that have been shown to correlate with accessibility and attention-worthiness: number of overt participants (Huffman, 2001) and their linguistic encoding (Ariel, 2009), case-marking and co-occurrence with the finite form in the same IU (Himmelmann, 2022), the grammatical persons involved in the event (Contini-Morava, 1983), polarity (Diver, 2012), and aspect (Reid, 1976; Gorup, 1987). Below I list the predictors I used in the study and their levels.

First, the number of overt (i.e., explicitly-mentioned) participants contains three levels: 0, 1, and 2. Additionally, I created a separate variable with the total number of participants (i.e., including covert, contextual-inferred participants that are not explicitly mentioned). For example, verbs of transfer like 'give' only appear with one or two explicit participants but never three, although these are often thought of involving three participants (Haspelmath, 2004).

Second, the linguistic encoding of participants generates two predictors, one for each participant. Both include five levels: lexical, pronoun, and quantifier (for overt participants), and mentioned and implicit (for covert participants). The last two categories capture the distinction between covert participants of a finite verb appearing as overt participants of a preceding non-finite verb (but with case-marking assigned by the finite verb), and covert participants of a finite verb appearing as overt participants of a preceding finite verb.

Third, case marking on overt first participants contains two levels (i.e., predicative and no case marking), and three levels for overt second participants (i.e., accusative, predicative and no case marking). Similarly, I included another predictor for the case markings of non-core arguments (i.e., ablative, dative, instrumental, lative, locative, and prolative). Fourth, the co-occurrence of overt participants with the finite form in the same IU generates two predictors, one for each participant. Both predictors have two levels: co-occurring in the same IU and not co-occurring in the same IU.

Fifth, the grammatical persons involved in the event is a single predictor with 14 levels: five with a single participant (1SG, 1PL, 2SG, 3NPL, 3PL), seven with two participants (1SG > 3NPL, 1SG > 3PL, 3NPL > 1SG, 3NPL > 3NPL, 3NPL > 3PL, 3PL > 1SG, 3PL > 3NPL), and two with three participants (1SG > 3NPL > 3NPL, 1SG > 3NPL > 3PL). Other combinations of grammatical persons are not attested in the data.

Sixth, polarity is operationalized as the co-occurrence of the negative proclitic *əl* with the finite verb form. This predictor has two levels: co-occurring and not co-occurring.

Finally, aspect in Kolyma Yukaghir includes several categories that occupy different slots in the finite verb template and can co-occur; these are: habitual, inchoative, imperfective, iterative, noniterative, resultative, and perfective. I also annotated the data for three additional morphemes that can appear in the morphological template and co-occur with aspect: future tense, causative and evidential. Each of these categories is treated as a separate predictor with a binary choice, i.e., whether they co-occur or not with the finite verb form.

Table 1 summarizes the list of predictors and their levels. In total, the data was annotated for 21 independent variables that include a variety of morphological and discourse factors, and I used the choice of the verb-focus form (i.e., *-jə* vs. *-mə*) as the dependent variable.

3 Methods

In order to investigate speakers' choices of the verb-focus forms at the discourse level, I used a classification decision tree. Tree-based methods have gained popularity in linguistics research over the past decade (Tagliamonte and Baayen 2012; Wiechmann and Kerz 2013; Bernaisch et al. 2014; Hundt 2018, among others), but studies applied to languages other than English have mostly focused on NLP applications rather than linguistic analyses (but see Klavan et al. 2015). Tree-based modeling, however, is particularly suitable for grammatical analyses in endangered languages, as it is applicable to small-*n* large-*p* (i.e., few data points, many predictors) scenarios, and it avoids problems of collinearity (Strobl et al., 2009; Gries, 2021).

A classification decision tree is an effective method to investigate the choice of verb-focus forms. As mentioned, current descriptions of Kolyma Yukaghir describe the use of *-jə* vs. *-mə* as depending only on valency (intransitive vs. transitive). In machine learning terms, this characterization can be formulated as a decision tree with a single split based on transitivity: if intransitive, pre-

Predictor	Levels
Number of overt ppts	0, 1, 2
Number of covert ppts	0, 1, 2, 3
Encoding of 1st & 2nd ppts	lexical, pronoun, quantifier, mentioned, implied
Case marking on 1st ppt	bare, predicative
Case marking on 2nd ppt	bare, predicative, accusative
Other referents	ablative, dative, instrumental, lative, locative, prolative
Co-occurrence with 1st ppt in IU	yes, no
Co-occurrence with 2nd ppt in IU in IU	yes, no
Grammatical persons	1SG, 1PL, 2SG, 3NPL, 3PL, 1SG > 3NPL, 1SG > 3PL, 3NPL > 1SG, 3NPL > 3NPL, 3NPL > 3PL, 3PL > 1SG, 3PL > 3NPL, 1SG > 3NPL > 3NPL, 1SG > 3NPL > 3PL
Co-occurrence with negative *əl*	yes, no
Co-occurrence with habitual, imperfective, evidential...	yes, no

Table 1: Predictors and their levels used to annotate each token of *-jə* and *-mə*

dict *-jə*; if not intransitive, predict *-mə*. Thus, any alternative decision tree configuration from the supervised model (i.e., either with more leaves or a single split with a different predictor) would suggest that speakers are sensitive to the morphological and discourse factors listed above.

4 Findings

Due to the imbalanced distribution of the two forms, the baseline/no-information rate accuracy of the classification model is already at 65.2%. Rather than a training-testing split, a leave-one-out cross-validation method was used instead, given that some predictors (e.g., grammatical persons) had too few observations for some levels to make predictions with a testing set. The model performs with an 81.5% true prediction accuracy. A test-is-training model, however, outperforms the cross-validation model with 89.6% accuracy ($p_{binomial\ test} = 0.006$). Figure 1 shows the classification tree from the test-is-training model.

The results show that the choice of verb-focus forms is most sensitive to the grammatical persons involved in the event. Two-participant events with two third persons are favored by the form -*mə* (3), whereas single-participant events and two-participant events with a speech-act participant (i.e., first-person or second-person) are favored by *-jə* (4). Examples (3) and (4) both display a two-participant event with an implicit first participant and a mentioned second participant (i.e., 'pipe' and 'strap' appear as overt participants of a preceding non-finite verb), but they differ in the grammatical persons involved: (3) only involves third persons, whereas (4) involves a speech-act participant.

(3) *табаах пиэдэттэллэ хаӈсаа*
tabaaq peedə-t-təllə qaŋsaa
tobacco burn-?-CVB.SEQ pipe
пиэдэттэллэ оожаануннуӈаа.
peedə-t-təllə oož-aa-nun-nu-**ŋaa**.
burn-?-CVB.SEQ drink-INCH-HAB-IMPF-**MƏ.3PL**
'After kindling the tobacco, after kindling the pipe, they used to smoke (it)' ("Tobacco," 34:8)

(4) *льамкапки лончииллэ*
l'amka-p-ki lon-čii-llə
strap-PL-3POSS take.down-ITER-CVB.SEQ
иркилльэӈоон ултэсь.
irkill'ə-ŋoo-n ultə-**s'**.
together-COP-LNK tie-**JƏ.1SG**
'After taking down their straps, I tied (them) together' ("Tobacco," 34:34)

The exceptions to this pattern are single-participant events with a first-person plural, and three-participant events with a third-person non-plural recipient. These, however, only have 3 observations each, so the algorithm might be picking up on idiosyncrasies of these examples; in comparison, two-participant events with two third persons make up around 20% of the data—or 31 observations of the total 135.

Additionally, the results show that two-participant events with a speech-act participant are favored by *-mə* if there are two or more overt participants (5). The form *-mə* is also

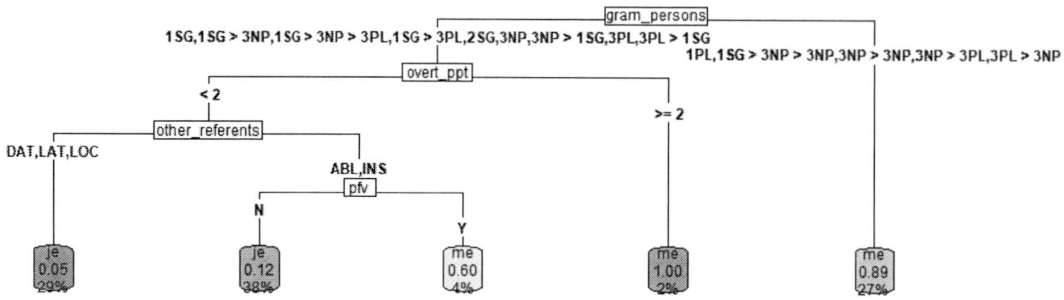

Figure 1: Classification tree from the test-is-training model

predicted for single-participant events and for two-participant events with a speech-act participant in co-occurrence with the perfective marker and an additional referent in ablative or instrumental (6).

(5) *мэт табаах өнмэгэ эйтэ,*
met tabaaq önmə-gə ej-tə-**Ø**,
1SG tobacco mind-LOC get-?-**Mə.1SG**

'I remembered the tobacco' ("Tobacco," 34:44)

(6) *пиэдисьэлэ.*
peedis'ə-**lə**.
finger-**INS**

'With (his) finger'

льэнульэлум
l'ə-nu-l'əl-u-m
PH-IMPF-EV-(EP)-Mə.3SG
*ньум**шэш**нульэлу**м**.*
ɲum-**šə**-š-nu-l'əl-u-**m**.
press-**PFV**-CAUS-IMPF-EV-(EP)-**Mə.3SG**

'He whatchamacallit, he presses' ("A game," 43:10)

5 Discussion & Conclusion

The findings suggest that valency alone cannot account for the choices speakers make between the two verb-focus forms at the discourse level, as it is argued in current descriptions of Kolyma Yukaghir. The form *-mə* is used in events that might look "transitive," but the configuration of the participants involved is relevant: *-mə* is overwhelmingly preferred with two third-person participants. These events differ from other events (i.e., single-participant events and two-participant events with a speech-act participant) in that they involve more discourse referents. Thus, a potential interpretation of this skewing is that *-mə* might be cuing speakers to a higher potential for reference tracking problems, while *-jə* might signal a lower probability of problems in reference tracking.

Marginally, *-mə* is also preferred in two additional contexts: in two-participant events with a speech-act participant when both are overtly specified (i.e., lexically or pronominally), and in perfective events with one or two participants and a referent in locative or instrumental. These configurations are in line with the idea that 1) perfective aspect is used in discourse to foreground important events (Hopper and Thompson, 1980), and 2) the higher the number of explicitly-mentioned participants, the more thematic importance of the event (Diver and Davis, 2012). As a result, *-mə* can be seen as highlighting events worthy of more attention, whereas *-jə* is used for events with lower attention-worthiness.

Overall, the results suggest that speakers choose the verb-focus forms depending on different discourse factors and may use *-jə* and *-mə* to achieve different communicative goals: cuing the addressee to a higher potential of reference problems, and highlighting important events in the discourse. In order to validate these results, a follow-up study with random forests will also be carried out. In sum, this study demonstrates how machine learning methods like decision trees can offer a more accurate picture of the choices speakers make at the discourse level and can help documentary efforts in the description process. Tree-based approaches are especially well-suited for endangered languages, as they can model linguistic input and make predictions with a relatively small number of examples.

Acknowledgements

This publication resulted (in part) from research supported by the Columbia School Linguistic Society. I want to thank Prof. Ellen Contini-Morava for her invaluable insight and continuous feedback from the early stages of this project. I am also thankful to Prof. Joseph Davis and Prof. Ricardo Otheguy for their comments and questions to refine the ideas presented here.

Abbreviations

1	first person	IPFV	imperfective
2	second person	ITER	iterative
3	third person	JƏ	-jə
ACC	accusative	LNK	linker
CAUS	causative	LOC	locative
COP	copula	MƏ	-mə
CVB	converb	NPL	nonplural
EP	epenthesis	PFV	perfective
EV	evidential	PH	placeholder
HAB	habitual	PL	plural
IMPF	imperfective	POSS	possessive
INCH	inchoative	SEQ	sequential
INS	instrumental	SG	singular

References

Mira Ariel. 2001. Accessibility theory: an overview. In Ted Sanders, Joost Schilperoord, and Wilbert Spooren, editors, *Text Representation: Linguistic and Psycholinguistic Aspects*, pages 29–87. John Benjamins Publishing Company, Amsterdam, Philadelphia.

Mira Ariel. 2009. Discourse, grammar, discourse. *Discourse Studies*, 11(1):5–36.

Tobias Bernaisch, Stefan Th. Gries, and Joybrato Mukherjee. 2014. The dative alternation in South Asian English(es). *English World-Wide. A Journal of Varieties of English*, 35(1):7–31.

Wallace L. Chafe. 1979. The Flow of Thought and the Flow of Language. In Talmy Givón, editor, *Discourse and Syntax*, pages 159–181. Brill, New York.

Wallace L. Chafe. 1994. *Discourse, Consciousness, and Time*. The University of Chicago Press, Chicago, London.

Ellen Contini-Morava. 1983. Ranking of Participants in Kinyarwanda: The Limitations of Arbitrariness in Language. *Anthropological Linguistics*, 25(4):425–435.

William Diver. 2012. The system of Relevance of the Homeric Verb. In Alan Huffman and Joseph Davis, editors, *Language: Communication and Human Behavior*, pages 135–159. Brill, Leiden.

William Diver and Joseph Davis. 2012. Latin voice and case. In Alan Huffman and Joseph Davis, editors, *Language: Communication and Human Behavior*, pages 194–245. Brill, Leiden.

William Diver, Joseph Davis, and Wallis Reid. 2012. Traditional Grammar and Its Legacy in Twentieth-century Linguistics. In Alan Huffman and Joseph Davis, editors, *Language: Communication and Human Behavior. The Linguistic Essays of William Diver*, pages 371–443. Brill, Leiden.

John W. Du Bois, Stephan Schuetze-Coburn, Susanna Cumming, and Danae Paolino. 1993. Outline of Discourse Transcription. In Jane A. Edwards and Martin D. Lampert, editors, *Talking data: Transcription and coding in discourse research*, pages 45–89. Lawrence Erlbaum Associates Publishers, Hillsdale.

Radmila J. Gorup. 1987. *The Semantic Organization of the Serbo-Croatian Verb*. Verlag Otto Sagner, Munich.

Stefan Th. Gries. 2021. *Statistics for linguistics with R: A practical introduction*, 3rd editio edition. De Gruyter Mouton, Berlin.

Martin Haspelmath. 2004. Explaining the Ditransitive Person-Role Constraint: A usage-based approach. *Constructions*, 2:1–71.

Nikolaus P. Himmelmann. 2022. Prosodic phrasing and the emergence of phrase structure. *Linguistics*, 60(3):715–743.

Paul J. Hopper and Sandra A. Thompson. 1980. Transitivity in Grammar and Discourse. *Language*, 56(2):251–299.

Alan Huffman. 2001. The linguistics of William Diver and the Columbia school. *Word*, 52(1):29–68.

Marianne Hundt. 2018. It is time that this (should) be studied across a broader range of Englishes. In Sandra C. Deshors, editor, *Modeling World Englishes. Assessing the interplay of emancipation and globalization of ESL varieties*, pages 217–244. John Benjamins Publishing Company, Amsterdam.

Jane Klavan, Maarja Liisa Pilvik, and Kristel Uiboaed. 2015. The use of multivariate statistical classification models for predicting constructional choice in spoken, non-standard varieties of Estonian. *SKY Journal of Linguistics*, 28(2015):187–224.

Eruxim A. Krejnovich. 1982. *Issledovanija i materialy po jukagirskomu jazyku*. Akademia Nauk SSSR, Moscow.

Elena S. Maslova. 1997. Yukagir focus in a typological perspective. *Journal of Pragmatics*, 27(4):457–475.

Elena S. Maslova. 2003. *A Grammar of Kolyma Yukaghir*. Mouton de Gruyter, Berlin, New York.

Elena S. Maslova. 2008. Case in Yukaghir languages. In Andrej L. Malchukov and Andrew Spencer, editors, *The Oxford Handbook of Case*, pages 789–796. Oxford University Press, Oxford.

Iku Nagasaki. 2010. Kolyma Yukaghir. In Yasuhiro Yamakoshi, editor, *Grammatical Sketches from the Field*. Research Institute for Languages and Cultures of Asia and Africa (ILCAA), Tokyo.

Iku Nagasaki. 2018. The Focus Construction in Early Modern Kolyma Yukaghir. *Gengo Kenkyu (Journal of the Linguistic Society of Japan)*, 154(C):123–152.

Irina Nikolaeva. 2005. Review of *A grammar of Kolyma Yukaghir* by Elena S. Maslova. *Linguistic Typology*, 9:299–325.

Irina Nikolaeva and Thomas Mayer. 2004. Online Documentation of Kolyma Yukaghir.

Wallis Reid. 1976. *The human factor in linguistic analysis: The passé simple and the Imparfait*. Phd dissertation, Columbia University.

Carolin Strobl, James Malley, and Gerhard Tutz. 2009. An Introduction to Recursive Partitioning: Rationale, Application, and Characteristics of Classification and Regression Trees, Bagging, and Random Forests. *Psychological Methods*, 14(4):323–348.

Sali A. Tagliamonte and R. Harald Baayen. 2012. Models, forests, and trees of York English: Was/were variation as a case study for statistical practice. *Language Variation and Change*, 24(2):135–178.

Daniel Wiechmann and Elma Kerz. 2013. The positioning of concessive adverbial clauses in English: Assessing the importance of discourse-pragmatic and processing-based constraints. *English Language and Linguistics*, 17(1):1–23.

Using LARA to rescue a legacy Pitjantjatjara course

Manny Rayner
FTI/TIM
University of Geneva, Switzerland
Emmanuel.Rayner@unige.ch

Sasha Wilmoth
University of Melbourne and
ARC Centre of Excellence for the
Dynamics of Language, Australia
sasha.wilmoth@unimelb.edu.au

Abstract

Learning resources for endangered languages are rare, and good ones may remain relevant for a long time. They will however be much more attractive if they can be repackaged in a modern format. Here, we describe a case study where we used the open source LARA platform to transform a substantial course for the Australian Indigenous language Pitjantjatjara, developed in the 1960s, into a web-compatible multimodal format. The transformation process required about two person-months of effort and produced a resource, freely available on the web, containing about 4.7 hours of Pitjantjatjara audio. The methods are simple and general, and could easily be used to update other legacy resources of this nature. Online documentation is provided.

1 Introduction and background

Endangered languages are almost invariably low-resource languages, and this particularly applies to learning resources. A good learning resource may remain relevant for a long time. However, the format will typically have dated so much that the resource can be hard to use in practice. It is thus interesting to explore methods that can be used to update legacy learning resources into formats appropriate to the twenty-first century.

In this short paper, we present a case study where we used the open source LARA toolkit to transform a substantial course, developed in the 1960s for the Central Australian Indigenous language Pitjantjatjara, into a multimodal web format. We briefly present background on Pitjantjatjara and LARA, describe a simple extension we added to LARA to support incorporation of legacy audio, and outline how we used it to convert the course. Links are given to the result, which is freely available on the web, and to relevant online documentation.

1.1 Pitjantjatjara

Pitjantjatjara is a Pama-Nyungan language spoken in Central Australia. It is one of the most widely spoken Australian Indigenous languages, with over 3,000 speakers as of the 2016 census (Department of Infrastructure, Transport, Regional Development and Communications et al., 2020). It is spoken particularly in the A<u>n</u>angu Pitjantjatjara Yankunytjatjara (APY) Lands in the far north of South Australia, but also in other communities in the neighbouring regions of the Northern Territory and Western Australia, and some communities further south in South Australia (such as Yalata). There are also substantial numbers of Pitjantjatjara speakers in urban centres such as Adelaide and Alice Springs. It is still being acquired as a first language by children, and in most Pitjantjatjara-speaking communities, English is learned as an additional language at school, and is mostly used in interactions with government services such as education and health. While there is copious description and documentation of the language by professional linguists, there are fewer publicly available options for learning the language. This is particularly an issue for non-Indigenous people living and working with A<u>n</u>angu[1]. The University of South Australia offers a Pitjantjatjara/Yankunytjatjara Language and Culture Program (`https://study.unisa.edu.au/short-courses/pitjantjatjara-yankunytjatjara-language/`; see Gale et al. 2020 for more information). For those who cannot enrol in these courses, options are more limited. *Wangka Wi<u>r</u>u* (Eckert and Hudson, 1988) is a detailed grammatical description aimed at non-specialist language learners, however, it is not a language course as such, and does not include audio. The same applies to other resources such as dictionaries (Goddard and Defina, 2020, for example). Two courses with audio have been developed, one in the 1960s at the University of Adelaide (Downing et al. 1967; see details in Amery 2020, p. 492 and §3 immediately below), and *Wangka Kulintjaku* (Kirke, 1985). Neither are

[1] *A<u>n</u>angu* literally means "person/people" but is used in the region in both Pitjantjatjara and English to mean "Aboriginal person", particularly an Aboriginal person from the Western Desert. Compare with *Inuit*.

```
@Once upon a time@ there were#be# four little Rabbits#rabbit#,
and their names#name# were#be# Flopsy#Flopsy#, Mopsy#Mopsy#,
Cotton-tail#Cottontail#, and Peter#Peter#.||

They lived#live# with their Mother in a sand-|bank, underneath
the root of a very big fir-|tree.||
```

Figure 1: Example of text (first page of *Peter Rabbit*) with LARA markup. Segment boundaries are marked by double vertical bars (||). Words marked as consisting of more than morpheme are subdivided by single vertical bars (|). Inflected words are tagged with a morpheme enclosed in hashes (# . . . #)

easily available for purchase.

While this is more than exists for many other Australian Indigenous languages, there is still a need for Pitjantjatjara language-learning materials—particularly with audio—to be more accessible, for both non-Indigenous people working and living with A<u>n</u>angu, and A<u>n</u>angu who grew up speaking English and are looking to reconnect with their heritage language.

1.2 LARA

LARA (Akhlaghi et al. 2019; `https://www.unige.ch/callector/lara/`) is an open source platform, under development since 2018 by an international consortium with partners in countries including Australia, Iceland, Iran, Ireland, Israel, the Netherlands, Poland, Slovakia and Switzerland. The goal of the project is to develop tools that support the conversion of texts into a multimodal annotated form which supports learner readers. Annotations typically include audio, translations, and a concordance. Text is divided into longer units (typically, but not always, sentences), and then into smaller units (typically, but not always words). Audio and translation annotations can be attached at either level (i.e. sentence or word), and are accessed by clicking or hovering. The LARA examples page (`https://www.unige.ch/callector/lara-content`) contains links to LARA texts in many languages. The LARA tools can be downloaded and used from the command-line, as described in the online documentation (Rayner et al., 2020). Much of the functionality is also available through an online portal; however, the new functionality described here is currently only available in the command-line version. Though not originally designed for this purpose, LARA has turned out to be a good fit to the requirements of endangered languages. Initial work is described in papers presented at the last two ComputEL workshops (Zuckerman et al., 2021; Bédi et al., 2022).

In the present paper, we will be mostly concerned with the process of adding audio and translation annotations to LARA texts. In previous LARA projects, the workflow to do this has been as follows. First, the text is marked up to add segment and morpheme boundaries; Figure 1 illustrates. Second, a script is invoked to create files listing the audio and translation annotations that need to be created. Third, the files from the second step are used to create the required annotations. This can be done in several ways, as described in the documentation. In particular, lists of missing audio annotations can either be passed to an online recording tool or to a TTS engine; both services are integrated with LARA. Finally, another script is called to combine all the pieces and create the multimedia document.

2 Importing legacy audio into LARA

The above workflow was designed for the case where audio is to be created for an existing LARA resource, but does not fit the situation we are interested in here, where audio already exists and we are cutting it up to add it to the LARA resource. We developed a simple method to address these requirements and integrated it into LARA. As usual with such tasks, the challenge is to make the workflow straightforward and efficient; the central question is how to review the audio to find the cutting points. We quickly ascertained that it would be difficult or impossible to implement something better than the popular Audacity audio editor[2], so we organised the process around that. Starting with the audio file and a piece of LARA source text marked up as in Figure 1, the process is as follows:

1. Run a script which transforms the marked up

[2] `https://www.audacityteam.org/`.

```
<i>Now you'll hear a sentence of the type "the man made a boomerang
for me", first in the long form, followed by the short form.</i>||
wati|ngku#-ngku# ngayuku#ngayulu# kali palyanu#palyani#||
wati|ngku#-ngku#|tju#ngayulu# kali palyanu#palyani#||
wati|ngku#-ngku# nyuntumpa#nyuntu# kali palyanu#palyani#||
wati|ngku#-ngku#|nku#nyuntu# kali palyanu#palyani#||
```

(a) Marked-up LARA text.

```
Now you'll hear a sentence of the type "the man made a boomerang
for me", first in the long form, followed by the short form.|3641|
watingku ngayuku kali palyanu|3642|
watingkutju kali palyanu|3643|
watingku nyuntumpa kali palyanu|3644|
watingkunku kali palyanu|3645|
```

(b) Text with numbered labels.

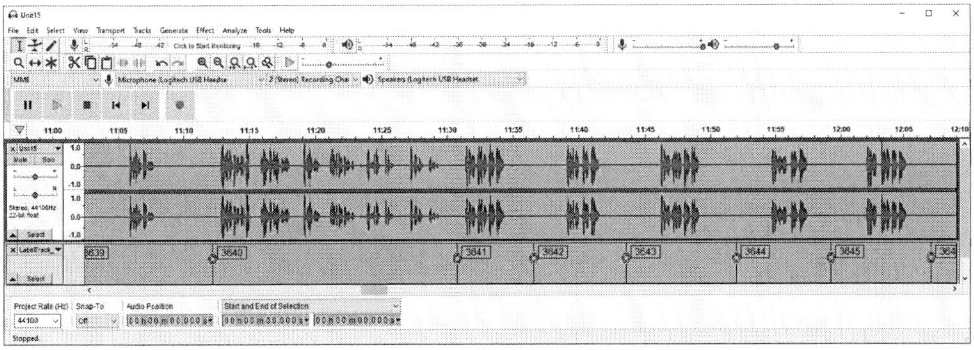

(c) Matching labels to audio in Audacity tool for passage in (a) and (b).

```
{ "audio_file":  "extracted_file_ch15_3753.mp3",
"label_file":  "LabelTrack_extracted_file_ch15_3753.txt",
"labelled_text":  "|1|wati|2| |3|pulka|4|ngku|5|",
"relevant_word":  "ngku" }
```

(d) Generated metadata to extract morpheme-level audio for sample morpheme *-ngku*.

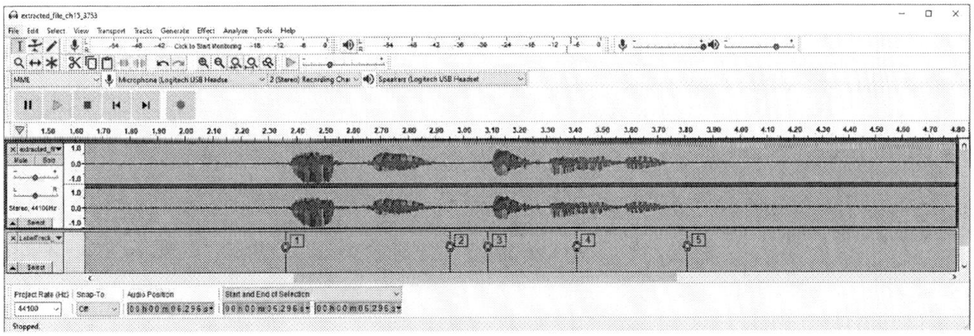

(e) Matching labels to audio in Audacity tool for segment in (d).

Figure 2: Different processing stages for converting a short section of the Pitjantjatjara course.

LARA source text into a version where each segment boundary is labelled with a number.

2. Use Audacity to add a "label track" where the labels are placed at the points in the audio corresponding to marked segment boundaries.

Figure 3: Screenshot showing the short section of the Pitjantjatjara course used in Figure 2, as it appears in the final LARA document. Clicking on an audio control plays the preceding segment. Hovering over a morpheme highlights it and shows a popup gloss: thus, for example, in the word *watingkunku* it is possible to hover over any of the three component morphemes *wati* ("man"), *-ngku* (ergative case suffix) and *-nku* ("for you"). Clicking on a morpheme plays audio and shows a concordance in the other pane. Here, the user has clicked on *palyanu* ("made"). The document is freely available online, a link is given in §4.

3. Export the label track from Audacity.

4. Run a second script, which uses the labelled source text and the Audacity label track to extract relevant segments of audio and save them together with associated metadata. The extraction is performed using `ffmpeg`[3].

5. Optionally run a third script to create labelled data for further cutting up of segment audio into audio for individual words, and repeat steps (2)–(4) for each segment using word-level versions of the segment-level scripts.

Figure 2 illustrates. In practice, it is common to find errors in the segmentation while carrying out step (2). When this happens, the annotator corrects the errors, reruns step (1), and continues. As described below, the process works well enough that it is practically feasible to create LARA documents based on several hours of audio.

3 Rescuing the 1960s course

The Pitjantjatjara course (Amery, 2012) was developed at Adelaide University between 1966 and 1968 by Jim Downing, Ken Hale and Gordan Ingkatji. Pitjantjatjara audio was recorded by Gordon Ingkatji, a Pitjantjatjara native speaker, and two unknown female speakers, one a native Pitjantjatjara speaker, the other a non-native speaker with a strong Australian English accent.[4] The course consists of 28 units, of which the first 16 are designated as the "Elementary" course, and the remaining 12 as the "Advanced" course. There is a Xeroxed text handout of 3–6 pages and a recorded audio segment of 15–35 minutes for each unit; the text is approximately, though not exactly, a transcript of the audio. Materials for the course were digitised by Paul Eckert and Mary-Anne Gale, and have been preserved by the Australian Society for Indigenous Languages (AuSIL)[5], who distribute them on USB sticks sold through outlets including Red Kangaroo Books[6] and the Goldfields Aboriginal Language Center[7]. The USB stick is accompanied by a printed notice saying that the material is "now out of print, so legally copied".[8]

The emphasis in the "Elementary" course is on basic Pitjantjatjara grammar, introduced through various kinds of drill exercises. The main topics are demonstratives, common and proper nouns, singular, dual and plural pronouns in both the "long" and the "short" forms[9], present, past, future

[3] `https://ffmpeg.org/`.

[4] We have reached out to many people who might have been able to identify the female Pitjantjatjara speaker, without success.

[5] `https://ausil.org.au/`

[6] `https://redkangaroobooks.com/`

[7] `https://wangka.com.au/`

[8] According to Paul Eckert (personal communication), he and Mary-Anne Gale made extensive attempts to determine whether any person or institution had ever claimed copyright, concluding that no one had done so.

[9] Most pronouns in Pitjantjatjara have a "long" form (free pronoun) and "short" form (a second position clitic which can be attached to any part of speech).

and imperative forms of verbs, ergative, locative, allative, ablative, and genitive/dative case markers, YN- and WH-questions, and conjunctions. About 115 lemmas of basic vocabulary are presented.

The "Advanced" course alternates grammar units with ones organised around short stories; there are six of each. The main topics in the grammar units are the past continuous, habitual, serial, participle, purposive, nominalized, imperfective imperative and negated forms of verbs, locative and reflexive pronouns, and the avoidance case marker. The story units become successively longer as the course progresses, starting at about 75 words and ending at about 240 words. About 190 more lemmas of vocabulary are presented, giving a total of about 305 lemmas.

To convert the course to LARA form, we first ran the text content though an English OCR site[10] and then cleaned up the output manually. After adding LARA markup, we followed the workflow outlined in §2 to cut up and attach the audio (cf. Figure 2), and added word glosses. End-to-end, a unit typically required 6–12 person-hours of effort to convert, the most laborious part of the process being the manual audio annotation. The main work was carried out by the first author, a person who had extensive LARA experience but no prior exposure to Pitjantjatjara, and then corrected by the second author, a linguist with expertise in the language. Typical issues corrected in this stage included the segmentation, lemmatisation, glossing, and spelling of particular words.

An unforeseen complication resulted from the presence of audio recorded by the non-native speaker. After reviewing the initial draft of the course, we decided that the difference in quality, compared to the two native speakers, was so marked that it was necessary to minimize her contribution. We addressed this issue by manually labelling her audio segments and dispreferring them when attaching audio for individual words, adding generic infrastructure to support these tasks.

4 Accessing the course and the tools

The finished LARA version of the course, which contains a total of about 4.7 hours of Pitjantjatjara audio, is freely available online.[11] A sample passage from the "Elementary" course is shown in Figure 3.

The online LARA documentation (Rayner et al., 2020) describes how to use the tools. The details of the annotation process from §2 are presented in the section "Creating segment audio by cutting up MP3s".[12]

5 Summary and further directions

We have described a simple and general method, implemented within the open source LARA platform, which allowed us to transform a substantial legacy course for Pitjantjatjara into a modern multimedia format. The conversion process required about two person-months of effort.

The course was put online in early November 2022, and so far we only have a small amount of feedback from users. Anecdotally, the response is quite positive. In particular, AuSIL immediately asked us for permission to distribute the new version of the course in the same USB packaging as the original one, since many of their clients do not have good internet. We expect this to be available through their usual resellers by the time of the conference.

It is to be noted that the process of cutting up legacy audio and incorporating it into a LARA document can be performed much more efficiently when an adequate speech recogniser is available for the language in question, making it possible to use automatic alignment methods; we present initial results in a recent paper (Rayner et al., 2022). At the moment, no such recogniser exists for Pitjantjatjara, but it is not out of the question that one could be trained.

Acknowledgements

We would very much like to thank Paul Eckert for providing us with the background to the 1960s course and generally giving us the benefit of his enormous experience with the Pitjantjatjara language and community.

References

Elham Akhlaghi, Branislav Bédi, Matthias Butterweck, Cathy Chua, Johanna Gerlach, Hanieh Habibi, Junta Ikeda, Manny Rayner, Sabina Sestigiani, and Ghil'ad Zuckermann. 2019. Overview of LARA:

[10] https://ocr.space/

[11] https://www.issco.unige.ch/en/research/projects/callector/pitjantjatjara_courses_1_and_2vocabpages/_hyperlinked_text_.html. View in Chrome or Firefox.

[12] https://www.issco.unige.ch/en/research/projects/callector/LARADoc/build/html/cutting_up_audio.html

A learning and reading assistant. In *Proc. SLaTE 2019: 8th ISCA Workshop on Speech and Language Technology in Education*, pages 99–103.

Rob Amery. 2012. The history of Aboriginal languages and linguistics at the University of Adelaide. In Nick Harvey, Jean Fornasiero, Greg McCarthy, Clem Macintyre, and Carl Crossin, editors, *A History of the Faculty of Arts at the University of Adelaide: 1876-2012*, pages 265–298.

Rob Amery. 2020. Teaching Aboriginal Languages at University: To What End? In Jean Fornasiero, Sarah M. A. Reed, Rob Amery, Eric Bouvet, Kayoko Enomoto, and Hui Ling Xu, editors, *Intersections in Language Planning and Policy: Establishing Connections in Languages and Cultures*, Language Policy, pages 475–489. Springer International Publishing, Cham.

Branislav Bédi, Hakeem Beedar, Belinda Chiera, Nedelina Ivanova, Christèle Maizonniaux, Neasa Ní Chiaráin, Manny Rayner, John Sloan, and Ghil'ad Zuckermann. 2022. Using LARA to create image-based and phonetically annotated multimodal texts for endangered languages. In *Proceedings of the Workshop on Computational Methods for Endangered Languages*.

Department of Infrastructure, Transport, Regional Development and Communications, Jacqueline Battin, Jason Lee, Douglas Marmion, Rhonda Smith, Tandee Wang, Yonatan Dinku, Janet Hunt, Francis Markham, Denise Angelo, Emma Browne, Inge Kral, Carmel O'Shannessy, Jane Simpson, and Hilary Smith. 2020. National Indigenous Languages Report. *https://www.arts.gov.au/what-we-do/indigenous-arts-and-languages/national-indigenous-languages-report.*

Jim Downing, Ken Hale, and Gordon Ingkatji. 1967. Pitjantjatjara language course materials for use at the University of Adelaide.

Paul Eckert and Joyce Hudson. 1988. *Wangka Wiṟu: A Handbook for the Pitjantjatjara Language Learner*. South Australian College of Advanced Education, Underdale, S. Aust.

Mary-Anne Gale, Dan Bleby, Nami Kulyuṟu, and Sam Osborne. 2020. The Pitjantjatjara Yankunytjatjara Summer School: Kulila! Nyawa! Arkala! Framing Aboriginal Language Learning Pedagogy within a University Language Intensive Model. In Jean Fornasiero, Sarah M. A. Reed, Rob Amery, Eric Bouvet, Kayoko Enomoto, and Hui Ling Xu, editors, *Intersections in Language Planning and Policy*, volume 23, pages 491–505. Springer International Publishing, Cham.

Cliff Goddard and Rebecca Defina. 2020. *Pitjantjatjara/Yankunytjatjara to English Dictionary*, 2nd rev. ed., updated edition. IAD Press, Alice Springs, N.T.

Brian Kirke. 1985. *Wangka Kulintjaku: Talk so as to Be Understood. Introductory Self-Instruction Course in Basic Conversational Pitjantjatjara*. Faculty of Education and Humanities, South Australian College of Advanced Education.

Manny Rayner, Belinda Chiera, and Cathy Chua. 2022. Using public domain resources and off-the-shelf tools to produce high-quality multimedia texts. In *Proceedings of the 20th Annual Workshop of the Australasian Language Technology Association*, Adelaide, Australia.

Manny Rayner, Hanieh Habibi, Cathy Chua, and Matt Butterweck. 2020. *Constructing LARA content*. `https://www.issco.unige.ch/en/research/projects/callector/LARADoc/build/html/index.html`. Online documentation.

Ghil'ad Zuckerman, Sigurður Vigfússon, Manny Rayner, Neasa Ní Chiaráin, Nedelina Ivanova, Hanieh Habibi, and Branislav Bédi. 2021. LARA in the service of revivalistics and documentary linguistics: Community engagement and endangered languages. In *Proceedings of the Workshop on Computational Methods for Endangered Languages*, volume 1, pages 13–23.

User-Centric Evaluation of OCR Systems for Kwak'wala

Shruti Rijhwani,[1] **Daisy Rosenblum,**[2] **Michayla King,**[3]
Antonios Anastasopoulos,[4] **Graham Neubig**[1]
[1]Language Technologies Institute, Carnegie Mellon University
[2]University of British Columbia
[3]K̲'wa̲la Language Program
[4]Department of Computer Science, George Mason University
srijhwan@cs.cmu.edu, daisy.rosenblum@ubc.ca, michayla.g3@gmail.com
antonis@gmu.edu, gneubig@cs.cmu.edu

Abstract

There has been recent interest in improving optical character recognition (OCR) for endangered languages, particularly because a large number of documents and books in these languages are not in machine-readable formats. The performance of OCR systems is typically evaluated using automatic metrics such as character and word error rates. While error rates are useful for the comparison of different models and systems, they do not measure whether and how the transcriptions produced from OCR tools are useful to downstream users. In this paper, we present a human-centric evaluation of OCR systems, focusing on the Kwak'wala language as a case study. With a user study, we show that utilizing OCR reduces the time spent in the manual transcription of culturally valuable documents – a task that is often undertaken by endangered language community members and researchers – by over 50%. Our results demonstrate the potential benefits that OCR tools can have on downstream language documentation and revitalization efforts.[1]

1 Introduction

Documentation and revitalization efforts for endangered languages frequently lead to the creation of textual documents in these languages. These include cultural materials such as folk tales and poetry; linguistic documentation like speech transcriptions and vocabulary lists; and other archival material (Himmelmann, 1998; Grenoble and Whaley, 2005). However, even though a substantial number of such documents have been created for endangered languages around the globe, the vast majority are not widely accessible because they exist only as printed books and handwritten notes.

[1]Code, models, and datasets are available at https://shrutirij.github.io/ocr-el/.

Although some of these documents are digitally available as scanned images, the text contained in the images is not machine-readable, inhibiting several use cases that are important to communities that speak endangered languages. For example, (1) the text is not searchable for speakers and researchers of these languages; (2) it cannot be reformatted, indexed, or adapted to various needs; and (3) it cannot be used to build datasets for training NLP models. Machine-readable transcriptions of documents are typically produced by a human transcriber, who looks at the document and retypes the text present in it. Like other manual transcription tasks (e.g., speech transcription), this process is time-consuming and requires significant effort.

That said, there are computational approaches to producing machine-readable text from scanned documents, specifically through optical character recognition (OCR). Training a high-performance OCR system is challenging given the small amount of data that is typically available in endangered languages. However, there has been recent interest (Rijhwani et al., 2020, 2021; Tjuatja et al., 2021; Disbray et al., 2022) in improving OCR even in very low-resourced settings using the technique of *automatic post-correction*. Post-correction models correct errors in existing OCR transcriptions (Kolak and Resnik, 2005; Dong and Smith, 2018; Krishna et al., 2018). The post-correction methods presented in Rijhwani et al. (2021) demonstrated substantial performance gains for multiple low-resourced endangered languages – reducing character error rates (CER) by 32–58% and word error rates (WER) by 29–59% relative to off-the-shelf OCR systems.[2]

[2]Character error rate (CER) and word error rate (WER) are based on edit distance and are standard metrics for evaluating OCR systems (Berg-Kirkpatrick et al., 2013; Schulz and Kuhn, 2017). CER is the edit distance between the predicted and

While error rates are useful to quantify the performance of various OCR technologies, they do not measure whether the produced transcriptions are useful to the primary audience for these transcriptions: community language learners, teachers, and researchers. In this paper, we look beyond error rates and take a human-centered approach to evaluating OCR and understanding whether the automatically produced transcriptions are beneficial to downstream users. More specifically, we analyze whether OCR is effective in lowering the time and effort spent in manually creating accurate transcriptions of scanned documents which, as discussed above, is a task that is frequently undertaken in language documentation and preservation programs.

As a case study, we focus on Kwak'wala, an endangered language spoken in North America, because of its long tradition of written documentation and active community engagement in accessing the knowledge contained in these texts (detailed in Section 2). We conduct a user study where we compare the time spent by human transcribers on producing an accurate transcription of typewritten Kwak'wala documents with and without the use of an OCR system.[3] We demonstrate that there is a statistically significant reduction in the time needed for manual transcription when an OCR system is used beforehand. Our results indicate that further research and development of improved OCR tools for endangered languages can add valuable efficiency to language preservation and revitalization efforts.

2 Documents in the Kwak'wala Language

To conduct our proposed human-centric evaluation of OCR, we focus on documents in the Kwak'wala language, while noting that our user study does not involve any language-specific components and can be extended to other languages.

Kwak'wala is a member of the Wakashan language family spoken on the Northwest North American Coast. Heritage learners and teachers are actively engaged in the revitalization of Kwak'wala. Written documentation of the language extends back over 120 years, including a collection of documents produced by anthropologist Franz Boas in collaboration with George Hunt, a native speaker of Kwak'wala (Boas, 1897; Boas and Hunt, 1902; Boas, 1911; Boas and Hunt, 1921; Boas, 1934, *inter alia*). The Hunt-Boas documents include 14 published volumes and several more unpublished manuscripts. The documents encompass a grammar of the language; word lists; stories; recipes; procedural texts; descriptions of practices, beliefs, and customs; descriptions of dialectal differences; maps and lists of placenames; and more. For Kwak'wala communities and language researchers today, these texts are rich troves containing knowledge that has special value to community-led projects focused on teaching, learning, strengthening, and reclaiming their language, cultural practices, and territorial sovereignty (Lawson, 2004).

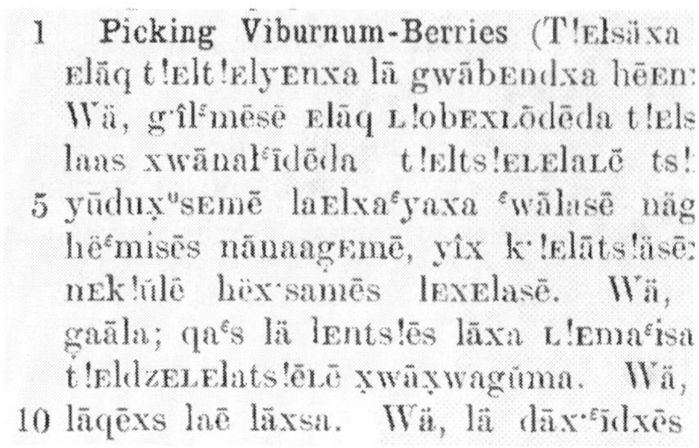
1 Picking Viburnum-Berries (T!ᴇlsäxa ᴇlāq t!ᴇlt!ᴇlyᴇnxa lā gwābᴇndxa hēᴇn: Wä, g·îlᵋmēsē ᴇlāq ʟ!obᴇxʟōdēda t!ᴇls laas xwānalᵋîdēda t!ᴇlts!ᴇʟᴇlaʟē ts! yūduxᵘsᴇmē laᴇlxaᵋyaxa ᵋwālasē nāg hēᵋmisēs nānaagᴇmē, yîx k·!ᴇlāts!äsē: nᴇk!ūlē hēx·samēs lᴇxᴇlasē. Wä, gaāla; qaᵋs lā lᴇnts!ēs lāxa ʟ!ᴇmaᵋisa t!ᴇldzᴇʟᴇlats!ēʟē xwāxwagūma. Wä, lāqēxs laē lāxsa. Wä, lā dāx·ᵋîdxēs

Figure 1: An excerpt from the Hunt-Boas publications documenting the community's method for picking viburnum berries. As seen, the Hunt-Boas orthography is complex – it uses several digraphs and diacritics that are challenging for an OCR system to recognize.

However, to the extent the Hunt-Boas documents have been digitized, they are still 'trapped' in scanned images. The texts are not searchable and researchers potentially need to look at tens or hundreds of images to locate relevant information. Moreover, the Hunt-Boas orthography is technical and somewhat idiosyncratic and is primarily used in archival research contexts – because the texts are not machine-readable, they cannot be automatically transliterated to modern, community-preferred orthographies. Researchers who draw on these materials often resort to retyping excerpts (sometimes into a different writing system), a time-consuming process that introduces a tight bottleneck to sharing

the gold transcriptions of the document, divided by the total number of characters in the gold transcription. WER is similar but is calculated at the word level.

[3]Similar user studies have been carried out to determine the effectiveness of machine translation in reducing human post-editing effort (Specia and Farzindar, 2010; Gaspari et al., 2014; Koponen, 2016), but none for OCR or endangered languages, to the best of our knowledge. Kettunen et al. (2022) measure user-perceived (qualitative) utility of OCR transcripts based on information gain, as opposed to our quantitative study on reducing transcription time.

and accessing this knowledge.

Therefore, extracting the Hunt-Boas texts into a machine-readable format can serve the community in many ways. Our user study, thus, focuses on evaluating the utility of existing OCR techniques as applied to these culturally important documents. We select OCR systems based on the experiments in Rijhwani et al. (2021) which describe two models that worked particularly well on the challenging Hunt-Boas orthography (Figure 1 has an example):

- **Ocular** is an unsupervised OCR system that uses a generative model to transcribe scanned documents (Berg-Kirkpatrick et al., 2013; Garrette et al., 2015). Ocular's transcription model relies on a character n-gram language model trained on the target language. Rijhwani et al. (2021) use a small amount of Kwak'wala text data to train the language model and show that Ocular's OCR system resulted in a CER of 7.90% and a WER of 38.22% on the Hunt-Boas texts.

- **Post-correction** involves correcting the errors made by an existing OCR system to improve overall accuracy. Rijhwani et al. (2021) present a neural encoder-decoder model (Bahdanau et al., 2015) trained with semi-supervised learning to improve post-correction performance in low-resource scenarios. Relative to Ocular, the post-correction method reduces the CER by 52% and the WER by 41% on the Kwak'wala data.

In the following sections, we describe a user study focused on evaluating the two OCR pipelines (Ocular and post-correction) to understand whether the automatically produced transcriptions are beneficial to downstream users that access the information in the Hunt-Boas publications.

3 Evaluation with a User Study

Traditionally, accurate transcriptions of the Hunt-Boas documents are produced by a human transcriber (often a Kwak'wala community member, linguistic researcher, or archivist). The transcriber looks at the scanned image of each document and types out the text present in it – a time-consuming process. To evaluate the utility of the outputs from OCR models, we conduct a user study where we compare the time spent by transcribers on producing an accurate transcription in various settings with and without the use of an OCR system. We attempt to answer two primary questions:

1. Is it faster for a human transcriber to correct the errors in an OCR output as compared to typing out the text from scratch?

2. Does adding a post-correction model affect transcription speed beyond existing off-the-shelf OCR tools such as Ocular?

We design controlled experiments to measure human transcription speed on a subset of images from the Hunt-Boas texts and evaluate how the speed is affected in various settings to understand whether there is utility in introducing OCR into the process. Additionally, we obtain subjective feedback on how having OCR outputs affected the transcription task through a survey sent to participating transcribers after tasks were completed.

3.1 Participants

We employed nine participants for the user study, all of whom had some transcription experience. Of the nine, two participants had familiarity with the Kwak'wala language as well as the Hunt-Boas texts and the orthography – one is a heritage Kwak'wala language learner and the other is an academic linguist working with Kwak'wala language materials.

We also employed seven participants that had no experience or familiarity with Kwak'wala. Three of these participants are computer science graduate students at a university and four participants were employed through Upwork,[4] a marketplace for freelance professionals. We selected them based on prior transcription experience, knowledge about data annotation for machine learning, and linguistic training as well as a high job success rate on the Upwork platform.[5] Including participants with varying degrees of prior knowledge of the Kwak'wala language also allowed us to evaluate whether this is a factor that affects transcription speed and the overall experience with the user study tasks.

3.2 Transcription Interface and Keyboard

We use Label Studio,[6] an open-source data annotation interface for setting up transcription tasks for the user study. We customized the interface for the

[4] `https://www.upwork.com/`

[5] Full IRB approval was obtained for the user study; all participants signed a consent form before working on the transcription tasks; and all data collected was anonymized.

[6] `https://labelstud.io`

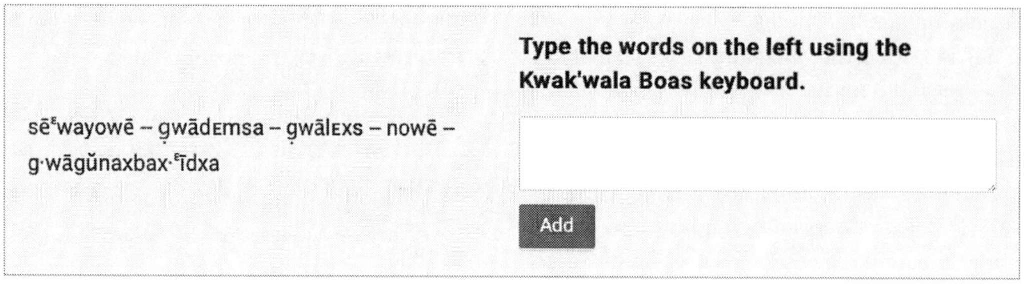

Figure 2: Practice task for transcribers to become familiar with the Boas keyboard. We included eight practice tasks in the Label Studio interface to cover all special character combinations in the Boas orthography multiple times. Users could repeat tasks as many times as they wanted to before moving on to the main transcription task.

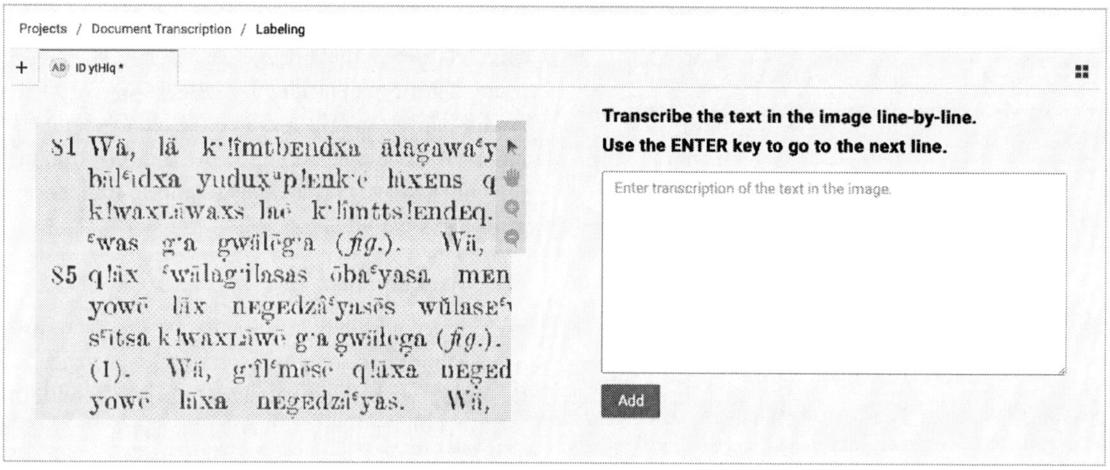

Figure 3: Transcription task interface, designed in Label Studio. The interface displays the image of a page and a text box to enter the transcription. It also has zoom and pan tools for the image, allowing users to zoom in on characters that might be hard to identify. The figure depicts a cropped image for clarity. When an OCR system is used before the manual transcription task, the text box on the right is pre-filled with the output transcription from the model and the user's task is to correct any remaining errors.

transcription task and additionally modified it to record information necessary for our analysis of transcription speed, including timestamps for when transcribers operate on each task.

Many characters and diacritics in the Hunt-Boas orthography are not present on a standard computer keyboard. To increase transcription efficiency, we used Keyman Developer[7] (an open-source toolkit) to create a keyboard for representing the characters in the orthography. The keyboard maps standard US English keyboard keystrokes to characters in the Hunt-Boas orthography. A detailed description of the keyboard layout and usage is in Section A.1. All participants were required to use this virtual keyboard to ensure consistency in terms of typing efficiency across all transcribers.

To train participants before the user study experiments, we designed a keyboard practice task, which presents a few sentences of text in the Hunt-Boas orthography that the transcriber has to type using the keyboard. The practice texts were selected such that all the different diacritic and digraph keystroke combinations were covered multiple times. The practice tasks were also added to the Label Studio web interface – a screenshot of the interface for the practice task is shown in Figure 2. Participants were able to repeat the practice tasks as many times as needed to gain familiarity with the keyboard. Additionally, we added keystroke mapping information to the interface for all tasks (transcription and practice tasks) for users to quickly reference.

3.3 Transcription Task Settings

The primary objective for the participants was to produce an accurate transcription of the image presented to them in each task. In the Label Studio interface, as seen in Figure 3, the image is dis-

[7]https://keyman.com/developer/

played alongside a text box for the user to enter the transcription. To evaluate whether using OCR is useful in reducing transcription speed, we have three different setups for the tasks:

- **Baseline**: This setup does not include the use of any OCR system. The transcriber must type out the text seen in the image from scratch – they are presented with the image and an empty text box in the interface (see Figure 3). This setup represents our baseline for measuring transcription speed, as this is the method currently used by Kwak'wala researchers and community members.

- **Ocular**: In this setup, we use the off-the-shelf OCR tool Ocular on the image for each task before manual annotation. The transcriber is presented with the image and a text box containing the OCR output – that is, the text box on the right in Figure 3 will be pre-filled with the OCR output. The task here involves looking at the text present in the image (which is the target text) and editing the OCR output in the text box to correct all the errors and produce an accurate transcription.

- **Post-correction**: This is similar to the previous setup, but we use a pipeline that includes applying the OCR post-correction method from Rijhwani et al. (2021), and as described in Section 2), it improves OCR performance (CER and WER) on Kwak'wala text as compared to Ocular. The transcriber is presented with the image alongside a text box containing the post-corrected transcription. The task is to correct any remaining errors.

3.4 Experiment Design

While measuring transcription speed for a single page is relatively straightforward, determining whether there is a statistically significant difference in speed between the three different setups described above requires consideration of several factors. For example, a single transcriber cannot be assigned the same page multiple times with different setups as they would become familiar with the page's content, potentially leading to incorrect estimation of speed differences. Additionally, some participants may be faster at transcription in general and some pages in the document may be more challenging than others – these factors need to be accounted for when measuring transcription time across the task setups.

A	B	C	D
B	C	D	A
C	D	A	B
D	A	B	C

A	B	C	D
B	A	D	C
C	D	B	A
D	C	A	B

Figure 4: Two 4x4 Latin Squares. Each symbol appears only once in each row and each column. The number of symbols is the same as the number of rows and columns. Figure adapted from Dean and Voss (1999).

In statistics, such factors are known as sources of variability (or nuisance factors). We design the transcription tasks to control the variability introduced by these factors using the Latin Square Design (Dean and Voss, 1999) to assign tasks to each transcriber. The Latin Square has the same number of rows and columns (square-shaped), with a specific symbol appearing exactly once in each row and exactly once in each column; Figure 4 shows two examples of a Latin Square design that has 4 rows and 4 columns. This design allows control of two sources of variability – one along the rows and one along the columns.

Since we have three task setups, we choose a 3x3 Latin Square – each setup appears only once in each row and column. The two sources of variability we control are (1) the user doing the transcription and (2) the page being transcribed. We randomly divide the nine participants into three groups of three users each (to fit the 3x3 square) and choose a fixed set of nine pages from the documents that all participants will transcribe in their tasks. For each group of three users, we form three squares (since we have nine pages). The task setups – i.e., baseline, Ocular, post-correction – are randomly assigned within the Latin Square constraints. Adding randomization for all factors (user, page, task setup) is aimed at spreading out the effect of undetectable or unsuspected characteristics. An example of task setup assignments for one group of three users for the nine pages is in Figure 5.[8]

Therefore, each user has nine transcription tasks with the task setups evenly distributed so all users are sufficiently timed on each setup. The user does not transcribe the same page more than once, but all users transcribe the same set of nine pages (with

[8]We follow `https://online.stat.psu.edu/stat503/lesson/4/4.4` and randomize Latin Squares separately for each group of users and each set of pages, so task setup assignments may not look identical across groups.

	page1	page2	page3
user1	ocu	base	post
user2	post	ocu	base
user3	base	post	ocu

page4	page5	page6
ocu	post	base
base	ocu	post
post	base	ocu

page7	page8	page9
post	ocu	base
base	post	ocu
ocu	base	post

Figure 5: Task setup assignments for a group of three users using the Latin Square design. We use 3x3 Latin Squares because we have three task setups: Baseline (*base*), Ocular (*ocu*), and post-correction (*post*). We need three squares for each group of users because we have nine pages for transcription. All users transcribe the same set of pages, but with the Latin Square framework, they have different task setups for each page which helps control sources of variability. All user identifiers and page identifiers are randomized before applying the Latin Square design.

varied task setups). The Latin Square Design, thus, introduces randomness across the factors to reduce variance and improve the generalization of the statistical analysis.

Dataset selection We selected nine pages from the Hunt-Boas volumes for the user study experiments, which were randomly chosen from a larger subset of 50 pages that community-based researchers deemed representative of the volumes and important to transcribe.

3.5 Evaluation Procedure

The nine transcription tasks were designed to take approximately 7 hours to complete. The participants accessed the Label Studio interface remotely through any web browser and first completed the keyboard practice tasks described above. Then, the participants began the transcription tasks and the interface recorded all timestamps for when transcriptions were edited and submitted. After the participants completed all tasks, we collected the timestamp information and computed how long it took to complete each task – with nine users transcribing nine pages each, we have 81 measurements of transcription speed to be used for quantitatively evaluating the utility of the OCR systems. We also calculated the character error rate (CER) of each transcription with respect to the transcription for the same page by our most experienced participant (a Kwak'wala heritage language learner who is very familiar with the orthography and had transcribed parts of the Hunt/Boas volumes before the user study), and discarded time measurements for transcriptions with CER $\geq 1\%$. Across all 81 transcriptions, only one had an error rate higher than this threshold, and thus, the quantitative analysis below is conducted with 80 time measurements.[9]

We also obtained qualitative feedback through a short survey that the participants filled out after completing the transcriptions. The survey asked several questions about the experience with the user study, including if the transcribers found specific tasks more difficult than others, whether they preferred typing from scratch or correcting OCR outputs (and which they thought was faster) as well as general feedback on the task and interface.

3.6 Quantitative Analysis

To quantify the effect of introducing OCR into the transcription process, we analyze the measurements of transcription speed that were collected from the user study tasks. As stated previously, we cannot use the time values directly to make a generalized conclusion because transcription time is not independent of the sources of variability. Instead, we use the statistical technique of Linear Mixed Effects (LME) modeling (Bates, 2007) to describe the relationship between the response variable (the transcription time) and the factors that contribute to variance. The term "mixed effects" refers to a combination of random effects and fixed effects. We have two random effects:

1. *transcriber identity*, which can take values from user1 to user9;
2. *page number*, which can take values from page1 to page9.

We also have two fixed effects:

1. *transcriber group*, which can either be yes or no indicating prior familiarity with the Kwak'wala language or not;
2. *task setup*, which can be one of the three setups described above – baseline, Ocular, or post-correction.

[9]There was no statistical difference between character error rates of from-scratch and corrected transcriptions as well as between participants with and without prior knowledge of Kwak'wala. The participants chosen for the user study had experience in transcription tasks, and all except one transcription were highly accurate (CER $< 1\%$).

Task Setup	Time Est. (*min.*)	p-value
Baseline	61.65	3.04e-07 *
With OCR	28.21	4.80e-08 *

Table 1: Per-page transcription time estimates in minutes from the LME model comparing the baseline, which does not use any OCR, with the task setups that use some form of OCR (either Ocular or post-correction). The time estimate for producing an accurate transcription of a page is reduced by 33.44 minutes when OCR technologies are used beforehand. The p-value is < 0.05, indicating statistical significance (*).

Task Setup	Time Est. (*min.*)	p-value
Ocular	31.67	2.55e-05 *
Post-correction	24.98	0.0121 *

Table 2: Per-page transcription time estimates in minutes from the LME model comparing task setups using an off-the-shelf OCR system (Ocular) with an OCR post-correction method. The time estimate is reduced by 6.69 minutes for a page, indicating the utility of post-correction to downstream users over using Ocular. The p-value is < 0.05, indicating statistical significance (*).

The LME estimation models the transcription time as a function of the above random and fixed effects. Using the estimations, our primary analysis attempts to identify whether the task setup affects transcription time in a statistically significant manner. We additionally look at whether the transcriber group (i.e., whether the participant has prior knowledge of Kwak'wala) plays a role in how fast the user completes tasks.

Does having some form of OCR help reduce transcription time? In Table 1, we present transcription time estimates from the LME model comparing two settings: (1) the baseline setup which does not use any OCR and the user types the transcription from scratch, and (2) having some form of OCR before the transcription process which the user can correct to produce error-free text (either Ocular or post-correction). As is evident from the results, having some form of OCR greatly improves transcription speed, reducing the time estimate by over 50% (from 61.65 to 28.21 minutes) and consequently, reducing the manual effort needed to produce an accurate machine-readable version of the documents.

Does post-correction help reduce transcription time beyond using an off-the-shelf OCR tool?

Group	Time Est. (*min.*)	p-value
Not familiar	43.60	8.12e-05 *
Familiar	25.74	0.228

Table 3: Per-page transcription time estimates in minutes from the LME model comparing transcribers that had prior familiarity with Kwak'wala with those that did not. The time estimate is reduced by 17.86 minutes for a page when the user is familiar with Kwak'wala, indicating that target knowledge language might be useful to have in image transcription tasks. The p-value is > 0.05 for the estimate, which indicates that it is not statistically significant, likely because we only had two users that were familiar with the language.

From the previous results, it is evident that using OCR is beneficial in reducing manual transcription time. We also evaluate whether using the post-correction model is useful or just using an off-the-shelf tool like Ocular is sufficiently useful for transcribers. The LME model estimates for this comparison are in Table 2. We see that using post-correction, as proposed in Rijhwani et al. (2021), in the transcription pipeline reduces manual correction time by 21%, indicating its utility to the downstream task of manually correcting the text.

Does prior familiarity with Kwak'wala and the Boas script affect transcription time? Beyond our primary analysis of the effect of using OCR, we also try to evaluate the extent to which the user's knowledge of the Kwak'wala language affects the speed of transcription. Table 3 demonstrates this comparison with results across all three task setups. The estimates show that this factor does play a role with the LME model estimate with a 40% reduction in transcription time for the group familiar with Kwak'wala. However, the p-value of this estimate is > 0.05, indicating that the result is not statistically significant – this is likely because only two transcribers in the user study had prior knowledge of the language and more data is needed to draw a statistically significant conclusion.

3.7 Subjective Feedback

After participants completed the transcription tasks, we asked them to fill out a short survey to describe their experience with the task. Note that, to avoid any bias, the participants were not told which OCR setup (Ocular or post-correction) was used for each task. Therefore, the survey focused on understanding whether users observed any differences between typing from scratch or correcting transcriptions, but the questions did not distinguish between the two OCR-based setups. The full list of questions contained in the survey is in Section A.2.

We asked which of the setups led to faster completion of the tasks, and 100% of the participants perceived that correcting an OCR output was faster than typing the transcription from scratch. Some participants also provided feedback:

> *"Correcting is faster, as there is much less typing involved which requires most of the time"*
> (user7, from Upwork, not familiar with Kwak'wala)

> *"Correcting felt far more efficient!"*
> (user2, linguistic researcher, familiar with Kwak'wala)

However, even though it was slower, two out of the nine participants preferred typing out the text without the aid of an OCR output:

> *"I preferred typing the text from scratch, as searching for any editable text is difficult. You need more effort for editing."*
> (user8, from Upwork, not familiar with Kwak'wala)

However, the remaining seven transcribers provided strong feedback that correcting OCR outputs was the preferable task setup, for various reasons:

> *"I vastly preferred correcting OCR outputs. It was so much faster, and also required less investment of attention."*
> (user2, linguistic researcher, familiar with Kwak'wala)

> *"I preferred correcting text - it's much faster. I can spend more mental energy making sure the characters are correct rather than wasting time on transcribing trivially-easy letters."*
> (user5, computer science student, not familiar with Kwak'wala)

> *"I prefer correcting text because typing from scratch is somehow tricky to follow line by line."*
> (user9, from Upwork, not familiar with Kwak'wala)

Overall, transcribers participating in the user study identified a reduction in time spent when the OCR outputs were utilized and the majority preferred the task setup not only because of the speed improvement but also because the OCR outputs allowed them to zoom in and fix specific errors rather than spending time on the entire image.

Additionally, we asked participants if any tasks seemed to be easier or more difficult than others. While several described correction as easier than typing from scratch, some transcribers focused on interesting language-specific and document-specific challenges:

> *"A few alphabets were difficult to annotate from the images. For example, it was difficult to differentiate between l and ł."*
> (user6, from Upwork, not familiar with Kwak'wala)

> *"image text was with small fonts."*
> (user4, computer science student, not familiar with Kwak'wala)

> *"the hardest thing for me was identifying a particular character (ł) that is very faint in the original PDF. It is often difficult to tell if a character is ł or l. Because I have some knowledge of the language, I relied on that background knowledge at times, but this slowed down the correction process."*
> *(user2, linguistic researcher, familiar with Kwak'wala)*

In giving feedback about the keyboard practice tasks, all participants indicated that the practice task helped them learn the Hunt-Boas orthography and the keystroke mappings. Moreover, 100% of the participants stated that as they completed more tasks, they became faster at transcription. One participant (user7, from Upwork, not familiar with Kwak'wala) stated *"After transcribing a few pages, I became faster at typing with the keyboard and noticing the different accents and letters."* While the ordering of the tasks was not taken into account in our LME model because of the small amount of data in the current user study, we hope to understand the effect of task order on transcription time in future, larger-scale research.

4 Conclusion

In this paper, we evaluate the utility of OCR and post-correction models in a user-centric manner. We conduct a case study on Kwak'wala, an endangered language with a long history of written documentation that is currently not widely accessible to community-based speakers and researchers. With a user study, we highlight the utility of incorporating OCR to make these texts easier to manually transcribe into machine-readable formats. Our statistical analysis shows that OCR can reduce the time taken by a human transcriber in producing an accurate retyping of the texts by over 50%. While we focus on a single language in this case study, our results demonstrate the immense potential impact that OCR technologies can have on global language documentation and revitalization efforts. Our work, however, is limited in scale and scope – we do not make statistically significant conclusions on the effect of prior knowledge of the language; whether the order of pages transcribed has an impact on measured time; and the effect of general familiarity with computers and technology. In the future, we hope to conduct a larger-scale evaluation that accounts for these factors; includes transcriptions from a variety of state-of-the-art OCR systems; and expands to more languages, documents, and orthographies.

Acknowledgements

This work was supported by the US National Endowment for the Humanities grant PR-276810-21 (*"Unlocking Endangered Language Resources"*) as well as the Government of Canada Social Sciences and Humanities Research Council Insight Development grant GR002807 *"Ḵ'a̱nḵ'otłax̱a̱nts A̱wi'nag̱wis (Knowing our land)"*. We are very grateful to the transcribers for their participation in the user study and to the reviewers for their helpful feedback.

References

Dzmitry Bahdanau, Kyunghyun Cho, and Yoshua Bengio. 2015. Neural machine translation by jointly learning to align and translate. In *3rd International Conference on Learning Representations, ICLR 2015*.

Douglas Bates. 2007. Linear mixed model implementation in lme4. *Manuscript, University of Wisconsin*, 15.

Taylor Berg-Kirkpatrick, Greg Durrett, and Dan Klein. 2013. Unsupervised transcription of historical documents. In *Proceedings of the 51st Annual Meeting of the Association for Computational Linguistics (Volume 1: Long Papers)*, pages 207–217, Sofia, Bulgaria. Association for Computational Linguistics.

Franz Boas. 1897. *The Social Organization and the Secret Societies of the Kwakiutl Indians: Smithsonian Institution. United States National Museum. By Franz Boas. With 51 Plates.* Washington: G.P.O.

Franz Boas. 1911. *"Kwakiutl." Pp. 423–557 in Handbook of American Indian Languages, vol. 40.1, Bureau of American Ethnology Bulletin, edited by Franz Boas.* Washington: G.P.O.

Franz Boas. 1934. *Geographical Names of the Kwakiutl Indians.* New York: Columbia University Press.

Franz Boas and George Hunt. 1902. *Kwakiutl Texts.* Leiden, New York: E.J. Brill; G.E. Stechert & Co.

Franz Boas and George Hunt. 1921. *Ethnology of the Kwakiutl: Based on Data Collected by George Hunt.* Washington: G.P.O.

Angela Dean and Daniel Voss. 1999. *Design and analysis of experiments.* Springer.

Samantha Disbray, Ben Foley, Shruti Rijhwani, and Meladel Mistica. 2022. Reading it right: A case study in pintupi-luritja. In *Digital Approaches to Multilingual Text Analysis.*

Rui Dong and David Smith. 2018. Multi-input attention for unsupervised OCR correction. In *Proceedings of the 56th Annual Meeting of the Association for Computational Linguistics (Volume 1: Long Papers)*, pages 2363–2372, Melbourne, Australia. Association for Computational Linguistics.

Dan Garrette, Hannah Alpert-Abrams, Taylor Berg-Kirkpatrick, and Dan Klein. 2015. Unsupervised code-switching for multilingual historical document transcription. In *Proceedings of the 2015 Conference of the North American Chapter of the Association for Computational Linguistics: Human Language Technologies*, pages 1036–1041, Denver, Colorado. Association for Computational Linguistics.

Federico Gaspari, Antonio Toral, Sudip Kumar Naskar, Declan Groves, and Andy Way. 2014. Perception vs. reality: measuring machine translation post-editing productivity. In *Proceedings of the 11th Conference of the Association for Machine Translation in the Americas*, pages 60–72, Vancouver, Canada. Association for Machine Translation in the Americas.

Lenore A Grenoble and Lindsay J Whaley. 2005. *Saving languages: An introduction to language revitalization.* Cambridge University Press.

Nikolaus P Himmelmann. 1998. Documentary and descriptive linguistics.

Kimmo Kettunen, Heikki Keskustalo, Sanna Kumpulainen, Tuula Pääkkönen, and Juha Rautiainen. 2022. Ocr quality affects perceived usefulness of historical newspaper clippings–a user study. *arXiv preprint arXiv:2203.03557*.

Okan Kolak and Philip Resnik. 2005. OCR post-processing for low density languages. In *Proceedings of Human Language Technology Conference and Conference on Empirical Methods in Natural Language Processing*, pages 867–874, Vancouver, British Columbia, Canada. Association for Computational Linguistics.

Maarit Koponen. 2016. Is machine translation post-editing worth the effort? a survey of research into post-editing and effort. *The Journal of Specialised Translation*, 25:131–148.

Amrith Krishna, Bodhisattwa P. Majumder, Rajesh Bhat, and Pawan Goyal. 2018. Upcycle your OCR: Reusing OCRs for post-OCR text correction in Romanised Sanskrit. In *Proceedings of the 22nd Conference on Computational Natural Language Learning*, pages 345–355, Brussels, Belgium. Association for Computational Linguistics.

Kimberley L. Lawson. 2004. *Precious fragments: First Nations materials in archives, libraries and museums*. Ph.D. thesis, University of British Columbia.

Shruti Rijhwani, Antonios Anastasopoulos, and Graham Neubig. 2020. OCR Post Correction for Endangered Language Texts. In *Proceedings of the 2020 Conference on Empirical Methods in Natural Language Processing (EMNLP)*, pages 5931–5942, Online. Association for Computational Linguistics.

Shruti Rijhwani, Daisy Rosenblum, Antonios Anastasopoulos, and Graham Neubig. 2021. Lexically aware semi-supervised learning for OCR post-correction. *Transactions of the Association for Computational Linguistics*, 9:1285–1302.

Sarah Schulz and Jonas Kuhn. 2017. Multi-modular domain-tailored OCR post-correction. In *Proceedings of the 2017 Conference on Empirical Methods in Natural Language Processing*, pages 2716–2726, Copenhagen, Denmark. Association for Computational Linguistics.

Lucia Specia and Atefeh Farzindar. 2010. Estimating machine translation post-editing effort with hter. In *Proceedings of the Second Joint EM+/CNGL Workshop: Bringing MT to the User: Research on Integrating MT in the Translation Industry*, pages 33–43.

Lindia Tjuatja, Shruti Rijhwani, and Graham Neubig. 2021. Explorations in transfer learning for ocr post-correction. In *Fifth Widening Natural Language Processing Workshop (WiNLP)*.

A Appendix

A.1 Keyboard for the Boas/Hunt Orthography

For the user study described in Section 3, we designed a keyboard for the Boas/Hunt orthography to make transcription more efficient.

The keyboard is developed using open-source software Keyman[10] and it maps characters in the Boas orthography to the user's computer keyboard. Keyman also provides an on-screen keyboard to see the mapped layout. We briefly describe the layout and usage of the keyboard below:

- Standard English keyboard alphabet and numbers remain in the same position (A-Z, a-z, 0-9) because the Boas orthography uses several Latin script characters.
- The special characters, diacritics, and digraphs of the Boas orthography have been assigned to various punctuation keys according to their frequency of use, estimated with a small sample of manually transcribed text (10 pages from Boas and Hunt (1921)).
- All accents are typed after the base character. Examples are shown below:
  - ⋆ ä is typed *a then square bracket]*
  - ⋆ k· is typed *k then slash /*
  - ⋆ ō is typed *o then single quote '*
  - ⋆ â is typed *a then shift + comma ,*
  - ⋆ ă is typed *a then shift + period .*
  - ⋆ g̣ is typed *g then shift + square bracket]*
  - ⋆ q´ is typed *q then option (alt key) + 1*
- Other special characters are:
  - ⋆ ᴇ is assigned to *semicolon ;*
  - ⋆ ł is assigned to *square bracket [*
  - ⋆ Ł is assigned to *shift + square bracket [*
  - ⋆ $^{\varepsilon}$ is assigned to *option (alt key) + e*
  - ⋆ ^{u} is assigned to *option (alt key) + u*
  - ⋆ ʟ is assigned to *option (alt key) + l*
- All changed punctuation keys can type their original value by holding down the Alt or Option key. For example, to get the original value of the square bracket [, type *Alt + [* (Windows) or *Option + [* (Mac).

[10] https://keyman.com/developer/

A.2 Kwak'wala Transcription: Post-Completion Survey

In Section 3, we describe a user study to evaluate the utility of OCR and post-correction models in reducing the time and effort needed for manual transcription. After participants completed transcriptions tasks, we also asked them to fill out a survey to get subjective feedback on their experience with the tasks. Discussion and analysis of the answers from the survey are in Section 3.7. We provide a complete list of the questions asked in the survey here:

1. Were there specific tasks you found easier or more difficult to annotate?
2. Did you prefer typing the text from scratch or correcting predictions from a model? Why?
3. If you are a Kwak'wala language learner, did the annotation help your language learning? How?
4. Did the practice task help you become familiar with the keyboard?
5. After annotating a few pages, do you feel like you become faster at annotation?
6. Which do you feel is faster: typing from scratch or correcting predictions?
7. Any other feedback or thoughts on the task?

Towards a finite-state morphological analyser for San Mateo Huave

Francis M. Tyers
Department of Linguistics
Indiana University
Bloomington, IN
ftyers@iu.edu

Samuel Herrera Castro
Instituto de Investigaciones Antropológicas
Universidad Autónoma de México
México D.F.
sherrera@unam.mx

Abstract

This paper describes the development of a free/open-source computational morphological description for San Mateo Huave, language spoken in the state of Oaxaca in Mexico. The language is of the agglutinative morphological type, with both prefixing and suffixing morphology. Both the nominal and verbal morphology are moderately complex. Huave is under-resourced and this is the first publication describing a computational tool for the language. We use the Helsinki Finite-State Toolkit (HFST) for implementing the finite-state transducer. An automatic evaluation of the coverage of our implementation shows that the coverage is adequate, between 80% and 93% on range of freely available corpora. Both the analyser and the hand-annotated test set are available under a free/open-source licence.

1 Introduction

Mexico is home to 68 languages, 63 of them Indigenous languages. This paper concerns Huave, particularly the variety (ISO-639: huv) spoken in San Mateo del Mar (Oaxaca), referred to as *ombeayiiüts* [o^{m}b^{j}ajiːt͡s] 'our (incl.) speech' by its speakers. Unlike most of the Indigenous languages of Mexico, in San Mateo del Mar at least, Huave is still widely spoken by adults and children alike. It is worth noting however that the language is seriously under-resourced and this paper is the first published computational tool for the language.

Huave is an agglutinative language where much meaning is expressed via combinations of stems and prefixes and suffixes. For example the word *tatajtüw* /t-a-tajt-üw/ "they cleaned (it)" is composed as follows *t-* 'PAST', *a-* 'SG3', *tajt* < *taad* 'clean' and *-üw* 'PL. Words may also be contracted with each other, for example *timikambajaats* /ti-mi-kambaj-aats/ "in our (incl.) village" is composed of the preposition *ti-* < *tiül* 'in', *mi-* 'POSS.3', *kambaj* 'village', and *-aats* 'POSS.PL-IN'.

This means that for most natural language processing applications an important first step is tokenisation and morphological analysis. Where large amounts of data are available, unsupervised corpus-based approaches can be used, however for Huave, as with all of the Indigenous languages of Mexico, there is a dearth of data, corpus-based or otherwise.

An alternative approach, and one with a long pedigree, is to use finite-state transducers to model tokenisation and morphology (Beesley and Karttunen, 2003). A finite-state morphological analyser returns, for a given surface form, a set of all possible valid analyses. Each analysis is formed of a lemma and sequence of morphological tags. For example given the surface form *iüm* it would return, `ij<num><c4>` 'two-CLF', `iüm<n>` 'door' and `<pres><sg2>üm<v><iv>` 'you weigh'.[1]

Analysers of this type exist for many languages, including for many languages of the Americas, for example Yupik (Chen and Schwartz, 2018), Arawak (Ingunza et al., 2021), K'iche' (Richardson and Tyers, 2021) and Western Sierra Puebla Nahuatl (Pugh et al., 2021) and given an existing grammatical description and lexicon one can be built comparatively rapidly (Washington et al., 2014). An additional benefit of these analysers is that they can be used to generate training data for supervised data-driven morphological models, cf. (Moeller et al., 2018).

The morphological analyser in this paper is based on the Helsinki Finite-State Toolkit (Lindén et al., 2011) due to its support for weighted finite-state transducers and the `twol` formalism (Koskenniemi, 1983).[2] We chose the formalism to avoid issues with intermediate forms and rule-ordering in rewrite approaches.

[1]The tags are as follows: `<num>` 'numeral', `c4` 'type-4 classifier', `<n>` 'noun', `<pres>` 'present tense (atemporal)', `<sg2>` '2nd person singular', `<v>` 'verb', `<iv>` 'intransitive'.

[2]The `twol` formalism is equivalent in descriptive power to the more familiar `xfst` rewrite rule formalism (Karttunen, 1993).

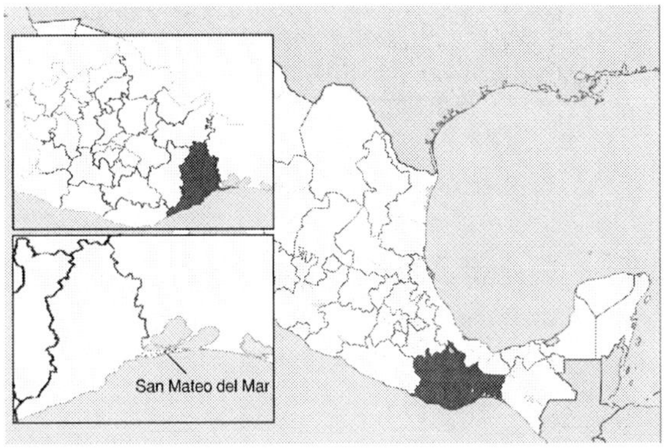

Figure 1: A map of Mexico (background) indicating the state of Oaxaca and the district of Tehuantepec (top left). The town of San Mateo del Mar is located on the Isthmus of Tehuantepec (bottom left). It is labelled on the map with other dots indicating outlying villages where the same variety of Huave is also spoken.

The remainder of the paper is laid out as follows: section 2 gives an overview of the sociolinguistic situation and typological features of San Mateo Huave, section 3 describes prior linguistic work, section 4 describes the methodology of completing the analyser, section 5 provides an evaluation of the analyser, and looks qualitatively at the remaining issues. Sections 6 and 7 describe some future directions and offer some concluding remarks.

2 Huave

Huave is a linguistic grouping that is spoken in four municipalities in the districts of Tehuantepect and Juchitán in the state of Oaxaca in the south of Mexico: San Mateo del Mar, Santa María del Mar, San Francisco del Mar, and San Dionisio del Mar. According to *Instituto Nacional de Lenguas Indígenas de México* (INALI; National Institute of Indigenous Languages) there are two principal languages in the grouping: Eastern Huave and Western Huave (INALI, 2016). The Eastern variant includes the languages spoken in the towns of San Francisco del Mar and San Dionisio del Mar, the Western includes the languages spoken in the towns of San Mateo del Mar (see Figure 1) and Santa María del Mar. By far the municipality with the largest number of speakers is San Mateo del Mar.

As of 2020, the total population of San Mateo del Mar was 15,571 with 15,538 living in households classified as Indigenous and 14,034 speakers over the age of three (INEGI, 2020). The language is widely spoken both at home and in public places. It is used in primary education alongside Spanish, in which the vast majority of speakers are bilingual. In recent years incipient language shift has been seen with a recent survey of secondary school pupils showing only half are speakers of Huave.

Constituent order is flexible (Stairs and Hollenbach, 1981; Herrera Castro, 2010), the object usually follows the verb in transitive clauses, but the subject can appear either before the verb (Subject–Verb–Object) or after the object (Verb–Object–Subject). The difference in order can also have different phonological properties (Pak, 2014). Intransitive verbs prefer the subject to appear after the verb (Verb–Subject). On verbs, tense, aspect and modality is indicated by suffixes or auxiliary words, while person/number is indicated by combinations of prefixes and suffixes. Nouns may be possessed.

Person and number in both the possessive and verbal system has eight combinations as indicated in the following list using: First person singular [+I, -You, -Other] 'SG1'; First person dual [+I, +You, -Other] 'DU1'; Second person singular [-I, +You, -Other] 'SG2'; Third person singular [-I, -You, +Other] 'SG3'; First person plural (inclusive) [+I, +You, +Other] 'PL1.INCL'; First person plural (exclusive) [+I, -You, +Other] 'PL1.EXCL'; Second person plural [-I, +You, -Other] 'PL2'; Third person plural [-I, -You, +Other] 'PL3'.

The second and third person singular and plural functions broadly as in other languages, the function of the first person agreement (SG1, DU1, PL1.INCL, PL1.EXCL) is illustrated with the present tense forms of the verb *w* 'go out' in (1).

(1) a. *saw*
sa-w
1-go.out
'I'm going out (me)'

b. *awar*
a-w-ar
3-go.out-DU
'We're going out (me and you)'

c. *awaats*
a-w-aats
3-go.out-PL.INCL
'We're going out (me, you and them)'

d. *sawan*
sa-w-an
1-go.out-PL.EXCL
'We're going out (me and them, not you)'

Verbs are marked for subject agreement, and rarely a limited form of object agreement.

2.1 Orthography

There have been a number of orthographic proposals for the language, the most notable being the form used by the translation of the New Testament and the Huave–Spanish dictionary of Stairs and Stairs (1981). This orthography uses Spanish-style orthographic conventions to represent /g/, /gw/, /kw/ and /k/, for example *qui* for /ki/ and *cua* for /kwa/ (cf. *miquiej* /mikieh/ 'his blood' and *cuane* /kwane/ 'what').

More recent texts produced by speakers have replaced these with *k* for /k/ and *kw* for /kw/, resulting in *mikiej* 'his blood' and *kwane* 'what', but texts with *k* and *ku* are also found. In this work we have used the recent orthography as proposed and used by speakers themselves.

3 Prior work

One of the earliest published descriptive linguistic works on Huave is a grammar sketch by Belmar (1901). There are no full length grammars, but an technical report was done by Stairs and Stairs (1983) which includes a large number of elicited example sentences and a grammar sketch (Stairs and Hollenbach, 1981) as part of a bilingual Huave–Spanish dictionary (Stairs and Stairs, 1981).

Much existing work has been done on the system of verbal morphology, including a study by Stairs and Hollenbach (1969) which looked at the verbal system from an item-and-arrangement view and an alternative word-and-paradigm model by Matthews (1972). A certain subclass of verbal affixes in Huave are *mobile* meaning that they can appear as prefixes or suffixes. This phenomenon has been studied by Noyer (1993) in the framework of Optimality Theory.

A study of the morphosyntax of the verbal system was published by Herrera Castro (2010) looking particularly at morphosyntactic alignment, person-number marking and valency changing operations (such as causative and reflexive/reciprocal).

Two other relevant works are Noyer (2013), who gives a comprehensive analysis of word-level phonology and Herrera Castro (2016) who makes a detailed study of the semantics of argument noun phrases.

There are two main published dictionaries, the first is a Huave–Spanish dictionary (Stairs and Stairs, 1981) and the second is an etymological dictionary of the Huave languages (Noyer, 2012). The latter dictionary includes reconstructed forms along with attested forms in the contemporary languages and translations in Spanish and English.

4 Methodology

There are three main components to a finite-state transducer: the lexicon (containing the lexemes and their paradigms, or continuation classes); the morphotactic rules which are implemented as continuation classes; and the morphophonological rules. This section deals with each component in turn.

4.1 Lexicon

The lexicon consists of 1,455 lexemes which were added in frequency order (calculated using the New Testament) and with reference to the two available dictionaries (Stairs and Stairs, 1981; Noyer, 2012) for part-of-speech classification. The lexicon has been created in the `lexc` formalism, which is standard in HFST.

Each entry consists of four parts. The first two are a lemma and a morphotactic stem. The lemma comes first, before the colon and is always the dictionary form of the word. The stem, which appears after the colon can contain formal symbols to simplify the writing of phonological rules. For example the transitive verb *taad* 'clean' and the noun *chiig* 'little brother' would have the following entries:

```
taad:ta{:}d V-TV ; ! "limpiar"
chiig:chi{:}g N-mi-A ; ! "hermano menor"
```

Where the IPA length symbol, {:} stands in for either the long vowel itself, *a* as in *tataad* 'He cleaned it' or the aspiration after shortening *j* /h/ as in *tatajtüw* 'They cleaned it'. The underlying form of the stem is defined as ta{:}d and the length symbol can be realised as either a copy of the vowel, in this case *a* /a/ or as the aspiration *j* /h/.

After the lemma and stem comes a continuation class, this is a classification of the entry by part of speech and morphology. In this case the verb *taad* 'to clean' has the class V-TV, indicating transitive verb and the noun *chiig* 'younger brother' has the class N-mi-A for a noun taking the *mi* set of possessive prefixes and the *A* set of suffixes. Finally, after the exclamation mark, which indicates a comment, comes a gloss in Spanish.

	P	C	PN	N
1	*xi-*, *sa-*, *na-*, *-Vs*			*-Vn*
2	*i-*, *r-*			*-Vn*
3	*a-*			*-Vw*
DU		*a-*	*-Vr*	
1.INCL		*a-*	*-VVts*	

Table 1: Affixes for subject agreement in Huave. These are marked with a hyphen following for prefixes and a hyphen preceeding for suffixes. The uppercase V indicates a vowel governed lexically or phonologically. In the column headings, *P* stands for person, *C* for clusivity and *N* for number.

4.2 Morphotactics

In addition to the lexemes, the lexicon also contains 70 *continuation lexica* which model the morphotactics of the language. Morphemes can appear as prefixes, suffixes and infixes. In our description of morphotactics we follow the examples in the available descriptions (Stairs and Hollenbach, 1981; Herrera Castro, 2010, 2016).

4.2.1 Verbs

As mentioned in §2, verbs inflect for eight combinations of person and number: First person singular, dual, inclusive plural and exclusive plural; second person singular and plural and third person singular and plural. Agreement is for the subject of the sentence.

There are five inflectional markers of tense-aspect-mood, including punctual in *l-*, past in *t-*, progressive in *tea-* and an unmarked present and an irrealis in *ap-*. In addition there is a form used in subordinate sentences, *n-* or *m-*.

The typical structure of a verb is as follows:

> Tense/Aspect/Mood – Agreement1 – Stem – (Derivation) – Agreement2

In general, person agreement goes in the first agreement slot as a prefix and number agreement comes in the second agreement slot as a suffix (cf. Table 1). However this isnot always the case and for example the first person singular prefix can sometimes appear after the verb stem (Herrera Castro, 2010).

Although a small subset of positional stems (e.g. the verbs *chet-* 'be seated', *lemb-* 'be stopped', *py-* 'be lying down', etc.) have the following structure:

> Stem – Tense/Aspect/Mood – Agreement1 – (Derivation) – Agreement2

There are restrictions on which morphemes in each slot can cooccur, where these restrictions are on either side of the stem, for example the suffix -*as* for first person singular can only appear with the past tense *t-*, these are implemented using flag diacritics (Beesley and Karttunen, 2003).

4.2.2 Nouns

Nouns in Huave inflect for possession using a set of possessive prefixes and suffixes. They may also take a plural suffix and an impersonal suffix.

There are four subcategories of prefixes and four subcategories of suffixes, which are assigned independently to nouns. The suffixes are assigned based on the stem vowel, while the prefixes are lexically determined. In (2), the words *pix* 'clothes' and *kwal* 'son, daughter' take different forms of the 3rd person singular possessive prefix.

(2) *apix* *mikwal* *María*
a-pix mi-kwal María
POSS.SG3-clothes POSS.SG3-son María
'María's son's clothes'

The vast majority of nouns do not take a plural suffix, instead indicating plurality either with a modifying numeral, quantifier or demonstrative or with agreement on the verb.

4.2.3 Adjectives

There are two categories of words that can be considered adjectival in Huave. The first category is small and contains property words such as *nine* 'small', *rran* 'white', and *jayats* 'new'. These are not marked for attribution, but may be marked for non-present when they appear as predicates (Herrera Castro, 2010). Compare the word *rran* 'white' in (3) and (4). In (3) it is used predicatively but does not receive any marking in the present tense, whereas in (4) it appears predicatively, but with irrealis morphology, the prefix *ap-*. Note that the word *nakants* glossed as 'red' is classified as a stative verb and not an adjective and so receives the *na-* prefix any tense.

(3) *Mikamix* *a* *naxey* *rran* *wüx* *angal.*
mi-kamix a naxey rran wüx a-ngal.
POSS.SG3-shirt the man white when SG3-buy
'The man's shirt was white when he bought it.'

(4) *Aaga müx kyaj nakants, oxep*
aaga müx kyaj na-kants, oxep
DET kayak DEM STAT-red, tomorrow
aprran ombas nej
ap-rran ombas nej
IRR-white POSS.SG3-body SG3
'This kayak is red, tomorrow it will be white.'

Another category are stative verbs which require a stative prefix *na-* to be used both attributively and predicatively (5).

(5) *Teon tangal nawaak tixem.*
Teon t-a-ngal na-waak tixem.
Antonio PAST-SG3-buy STAT-be.dry prawn
'Antonio bought dry prawns.'

These are handled with two different stem categories in the lexicon.

4.2.4 Other categories

There are two prepositions in the language *tiül* 'in', which can be contracted to the following noun (6) and *wüx* 'on'.

(6) a. *tiül mikambajaats*
tiül mi-kambaj-aats
in POSS.SG3-village-PL.INCL
'in our village'

b. *timikambajaats*
ti-mi-kambaj-aats
in-POSS.SG3-village-PL.INCL
'in our village'

There are a set of personal pronouns, following the same person–number schema as the possessives and verbal morphology. These appear in both neutral and emphatic forms, *ikoots* 'we', *ikootsa* 'we-EMPH'. In addition there are several determiners, the most widely used being *aaga* 'the' and the set of demonstratives *kam*, *küy* 'this', *kyaj* 'that' *kyün* 'yon'.

4.3 Morphophonology

We used morphographemic rules in the *twol* formalism to model the phonological alternations. This formalism was first proposed by Koskenniemi (1983) and consists of finite-state constraints over possible input–output string pairs. In HFST (Lindén et al., 2011), constraints are applied in parallel via the composition operator and the output of each of the constraints is intersected. There are currently a total of 8 constraints, covering palatalisation, vowel reduction, assimilation, devoicing and aspiration. Figure 2 gives an example of three of the constraints

```
"Long vowel without suffix"
%{:%}:Vx <=> Vx _ ;
     except
        Vow _ Cns+ %>: [ .#. | %>: %{A%}: ] ;
     where Vx in ( a e i o ü ) ;

"Aspiration after shortened vowels"
%{:%}:j <=> Vow _ Cns+ %>: [ .#. | %>: %{A%}:
] ;

"Desonorisation of occlusive sonorant"
Cx:Cy <=> Vow %{:%}: _ %>: [ .#. | %>: %{A%}:
] ;
     where Cx in ( b d g )
           Cy in ( p t k )
     matched ;
```

Figure 2: Three phonological constraints to implement the forms *andüüb* /a-ndüüb/ 'She follows' and *tandüjpiw* /t-a-ndüjp-iw/ 'They followed' from the stem *ndüüb* /ndüːb/ 'follow'. When adding a suffix of one syllable, the long vowel in the stem is shortened /üü/ → /üj/ and aspirated and as a result of the vowel no longer being long, the final stop appears as /p/ (/b/ appears after long vowels).

covering the process that happens when a single-syllable suffix is added to a stem with a long vowel.

5 Results

The output in Figure 3 is the result of running a sentence from Herrera Castro (2010) through the morphological analyser. The remainder of this section describes the evaluation procedure.

5.1 Corpora

There are few published texts that are available online in text format. The largest available text is *Jayats nanderac wüx miteatiüüts Jesucristo* (Wycliffe Bible Translators, 2009), the translation of the New Testament. This consists of over 230k tokens and was produced over a number of years. It was used in the development of the analyser for checking forms and for determining which stems to add to the lexicon.

To evaluate the text on unseen data, we obtained some other texts from a range of domains, but none consisting of more than 20,000 tokens. The texts we used were two texts from the domain of education: (1) a book for teaching adult literacy, *Sateow at sarang nawiig wüx ximbeay* (INEA, 2014).[3] and (2) a Licenciate thesis on education (Buenavista, 2012). The second two texts were smaller and more literary, a collection of stories in Huave collected by the Summer Institute of Linguistics (Stairs and

[3]The title translates into English as "I read and write in my language".

```
^Pe/pero<cnjcoo>$
^tasaj/<past><sg3>saj<v><tv>$
^mikwal/<px2sg>kwal<n>/<px3sg>kwal<n>$
^nej/nej<prn><pers><sg3>$
^natangüy/<rel>tang<v><iv><refl>$
^nüx/nüx<n>$
^este/este<part>$
^marang/<subj><sg3>rang<v><tv>$
^che/che<evid>$
^najngow/najngow<n>$
^./.<sent>$
```

Figure 3: Example output from the analyser for the sentence *Pe tasaj mikwal nej natangüy nüx este marang che najngow.* "But he told his older daughter to make soup." (lit. But he said to his grown daughter that she make soup.). Each line is a token, the part before the / is the surface form and following that is a list of potential analyses, each separated by a slash. There is one ambiguous token, the word *mikwal* $<$ *kwal* 'child of someone' which with the *mi-* prefix could be analysed as either second person singular (POSS.2SG) or third person singular (POSS.3SG). The word could be disambiguated in a subsequent step by the following third person pronoun, *nej*.

Stairs, 2006) and a collection of poetry by Raúl Rangel González entitled *Andeak xemeaats* (Rangel González, 2020).[4]

5.2 Naïve coverage

Our first method of evaluation was to calculate the naïve coverage and mean ambiguity on freely available corpora. Naïve coverage refers to the percentage of surface forms in a given corpora that receive at least one morphological analysis. Note that forms counted by this measure may have other analyses which are not delivered by the transducer. The mean ambiguity measure was calculated as the average number of analyses returned per token in the corpus. The results can be found in Table 2. Each corpus was first split into 10 equal-sized parts and then the coverage was calculated and the mean and standard deviation obtained.

5.3 Precision and recall

We tested the precision and recall by using a test corpus created from the glossed example sentences in Herrera Castro (2010). We made a unique wordlist from these sentences and selected 100 words at random. We then passed these through out analyser and edited the output to include all the analyses found in the glosses — that is, if there was a gloss in the text for which the corresponding analysis was not present, we added the analysis. This gave a list of words where each word had all of its possible analyses according to the glossed texts (we call this the gold standard).

We define true positives, tp, as those analyses which were in both the transducer's output and in the gold standard list of analyses. We define false positives, fp, as those analyses that were in the transducer output but not in the gold standard list of analyses. And we define false negatives, fn as those analyses which were in the gold standard list, but not in the transducer output. Incorrect analyses by the transducer are counted as false positives as we consider them to be incorrect hypotheses generated by our transducer about a form in the language and to distinguish them from false negatives. False negatives are typically caused by something missing in the implementation or lexicon, while false positives are typically caused by incorrect implementation or incorrect lexicon or category assignment.

Tokens which received no analyses were counted as false positives. We defined precision, P (1), recall, R (2) and F_1-score (3).

$$P = \frac{\mathrm{tp}}{(\mathrm{tp} + \mathrm{fp})} \quad (1)$$

$$R = \frac{\mathrm{tp}}{(\mathrm{tp} + \mathrm{fn})} \quad (2)$$

$$F_1 = 2\frac{PR}{P + R} \quad (3)$$

Intuitively, precision is the likelihood of an analysis presented by the transducer being an analysis found in the gold standard, while recall is the likelihood of an analysis found in the gold standard being in the transducer. Table 3 presents the results of the evaluation.

Note that this method is only an approximation of the precision and recall of the analyser as the corpus may not contain all valid analyses for a given token.

6 Future work

In its current state, the analyser handles most of the inflectional processes of the language and some derivation. The lexicon is still very small and we would like to expand it, to include at least all the stems in the two dictionaries we have available.

There are two processes which are not well supported currently, the first is infixation of *-ra-* for forming the passive with some transitive

[4]The title translates into English as "The voice of my spirit".

Corpus	Genre	Tokens	Coverage (%)
Jayats nanderac wüx miteatiüüts Jesucristo	Religion	235,267	92.74 ± 0.16
Sateow at sarang nawiig wüx ximbeay	Education	18,490	82.49 ± 1.82
Licenciate thesis (Buenavista, 2012)	Education	18,343	82.05 ± 0.44
Cuentos Huaves II	Fiction	5,793	91.63 ± 1.00
Andeak xemeaats	Poetry	2,235	82.54 ± 2.75
Total:		280,307	91.26 ± 0.16

Table 2: The naïve coverage of the analyser over the available text corpora. The coverage is calculated over ten equal size splits and standard deviation is given. It is clear that the coverage is greatest and the estimate most reliable on the New Testament, which is also our largest text. However it is also noteworthy that the coverage over the fiction texts is also over 90%.

	Precision	Recall	F_1-score
All	70.1	64.7	67.3
Known	90.4	81.5	85.7

Table 3: Precision, recall and F-score for the test set. The metrics are substantially higher for the set of words that are known as they are ones where both a stem exists in the lexicon and the morphotactics are implemented as these are generally cases of missing alternative stems, for example a noun stem is present in the lexicon for a given surface form, but not a verb stem which generates the same surface form.

verbs, it is not clear from the literature what morpho/phonotactic restrictions there are. The one example that we found (7) is functional, but the solution has yet to be extended to other stems.

(7) a. *Aaga pet atsamb a miüs.*
aaga pet a-tsamb a miüs
DET dog SG3-bite the cat
'The dog bites the cat.'

b. *Tatsaramb a miüs*
t-a-tsa⟨ra⟩mb the cat
PAST-SG3-bite⟨PASS⟩bite the cat
'The cat is bitten.'

Another process is reduplication, examples of this have so far been lexicalised, but other solutions exist. It remains to be seen how productive the process is in texts (from our 100-token test set there was one word exhibiting reduplication).

Object agreement (as found in other languages of Mesoamerica such as Nahuatl or the Mayan languages) is also found in Huave but it is very reduced compared to other languages, only appearing in clauses where there is a singular subject and plural object, for example in (8) from Herrera Castro (2010).

(8) *Tanajawüw a pet*
ta-na-jaw-üw a pet
PAST-S.SG1-see-O.PL3 the dog
'I saw the dogs.'

This last phenomenon has yet to be implemented, but we anticipate it being straightforward.

7 Concluding remarks

We have presented the first morphological analyser for San Mateo Huave, a language isolate spoken in the state of Oaxaca in the south of Mexico. The analyser comprises a finite-state transducer based on the Helsinki Finite-State Tools. It covers a reasonable percentage — 80–93% of tokens in running text over a number of freely available corpora of San Mateo Huave. The analyser is available as free/open-source software under the GNU General Public Licence.[5]

Acknowledgements

We would like to thank the anonymous reviewers for their helpful comments.

References

Kenneth R. Beesley and Lauri Karttunen. 2003. *Finite State Morphology*. CSLI Studies in Computational Linguistics. CSLI Publications, Stanford, California.

Francisco Belmar. 1901. *Estudio del huave*. Instituto Nacional de Antropología e Historia, Oaxaca.

Hugo Alberto Hidalgo Buenavista. 2012. Makiaacheranüw wüx namix mongich ikoots matajküw majneaj andeaküw ombeay mol tiül noik nendüy najiüt meawan, monjüy amb anayiw neat akiaacheyej niüng monkiajchay nenüt Moisés Sáenz najlüy tikambaj,

[5] https://github.com/apertium/apertium-huv/

kiaj kawak okwiaj latiük, tiül miiüt pajtiam. Master's thesis, Escuela Normal Bilingüe e Intercultural de Oaxaca.

Emily Chen and Lane Schwartz. 2018. A morphological analyzer for St. Lawrence Island / Central Siberian Yupik. In *Proceedings of the 11th Language Resources and Evaluation Conference (LREC 2018)*, Miyazaki, Japan. European Languages Resources Association (ELRA).

Samuel Herrera Castro. 2010. Alineamiento y frase verbal en Huave de San Mateo Del Mar, Oaxaca. Master's thesis, Escuela Nacional de Antropología e Historia, México, D.F.

Samuel Herrera Castro. 2016. *Sintaxis y semántica de la frase nominal en Huave de San Mateo Del Mar, Oaxaca*. Ph.D. thesis, Colegio de México, México, D.F.

INALI. 2016. Atlas de las lenguas indígenas de México. Https://atlas.inali.gob.mx/.

INEA. 2014. *Sateow at sarang nawiig wüx ximbeay. Ombeayiüts*.

INEGI. 2020. Censo de población y vivienda 2020. Technical report, Instituto Nacional de Estadística y Geografía. https://www.inegi.org.mx/programas/ccpv/2020/.

Adriano M. Ingunza, John E. Miller, Arturo Oncevay, and Roberto Zariquiey. 2021. Representation of Yine (Arawak) morphologyby finite state transducer formalism. In *Proceedings of the First Workshop on Natural Language Processing for Indigenous Languages of the Americas*, page 102–112. Association for Computational Linguistics.

Lauri Karttunen. 1993. Finite-state constraints. In John Goldsmith, editor, *The Last Phonological Rule: Reflections on constraints and derivations*. University of Chicago Press.

Kimmo Koskenniemi. 1983. *Two-level Morphology: A General Computational Model for Word-Form Recognition and Production*. Ph.D. thesis, Helsingin yliopisto.

Krister Lindén, Erik Axelson, Sam Hardwick, Tommi Pirinen, and Miikka Silfverberg. 2011. HFST—framework for compiling and applying morphologies. *Communications in Computer and Information Science*, 100:67–85.

P. H. Matthews. 1972. Huave verb morphology: Some comments from a non-tagmemic viewpoint. *International Journal of American Linguistics*, 38(2):96–118.

Sarah Moeller, Ghazaleh Kazeminejad, Andrew Cowell, and Mans Hulden. 2018. A neural morphological analyzer for arapaho verbs learned from a finite state transducer. In *Proceedings of Workshop on Polysynthetic Languages*, pages 12–20.

Rolf Noyer. 1993. Mobile affixes in huave: Optimality and morphological well-formedness. In *Proceedings of the twelfth west coast conference on formal linguistics*, pages 67–82, Stanford. CSLI.

Rolf Noyer. 2012. Diccionario etimológico y comparativo de las lenguas huaves. https://www.ling.upenn.edu/~rnoyer/DECH_August2012.pdf.

Rolf Noyer. 2013. Generative phonology of san mateo huave. *International Journal of American Linguistics*, 79(1):1–60.

Marjorie Pak. 2014. Phonological evidence for the syntax of VOS and SVO in Huave. In *Proceedings of the Workshop on the Sound Systems of Mexico and Central America*.

Robert Pugh, Francis Tyers, and Marivel Huerta Mendez. 2021. Towards an open source finite-state morphological analyzer for zacatlán-ahuacatlán-tepetzintla nahuatl. In *Proceedings of the 4th Workshop on the Use of Computational Methods in the Study of Endangered Languages Volume 1 (Papers)*, pages 80–85.

Raúl Rangel González. 2020. *Andeak xemeaats*. La voz de mi espíritu.

Ivy Richardson and Francis M. Tyers. 2021. A morphological analyser for K'iche'. *Procesamiento de Lenguaje Natural*, 66:99–109.

Emily Stairs and Barbara Hollenbach. 1969. Huave verb morphology. *International Journal of American Linguistics*, 35(1):38–53.

Emily Stairs and Elena Hollenbach. 1981. *Diccionario huave de San Mateo del mar*, chapter Gramática huave. Instituto Lingüístico de Verano, México, D.F.

Glen Stairs and Emily Stairs. 1981. *Diccionario huave de San Mateo del Mar*. Instituto Lingüístico de Verano, México, D.F.

Glen Stairs and Emily Stairs. 1983. Huave de San Mateo Del Mar, Oaxaca. Technical report, Centro de Investigación para la Integración Social, México, D.F.

Glen Stairs and Emily Stairs. 2006. *Cuentos Huaves II*. Instituto Lingüístico de Verano, México, D.F.

Jonathan Washington, Ilnar Salimzyanov, and Francis Tyers. 2014. Finite-state morphological transducers for three Kypchak languages. In *Proceedings of the Ninth International Conference on Language Resources and Evaluation (LREC-2014)*, pages 3378–3385, Reykjavik, Iceland. European Languages Resources Association (ELRA).

Wycliffe Bible Translators. 2009. *Jayats nanderac wüx miteatiiüts Jesucristo*. Wycliffe Bible Translators.

A Survey of Computational Infrastructure to Help Preserve and Revitalize Bodwéwadmimwen

Robert E. Lewis Jr.
Bodwéwadmimwen Ėthë ték, Inc.
(The Center for Potawatomi Language)
robert.bodwe@gmail.com

Abstract

This paper surveys the previous language initiatives that Potawatomi language communities have undertaken with technology to help them preserve and revitalize Bodwéwadmimwen (the Potawatomi language) and provides a menu of newer computational tools that could supplement previous initiatives or create new ones. The most immediate steps that could be taken are to establish unicode numbers for several characters, compile a usable corpus of language materials, and build a morphological parser that could be implemented on top of an online dictionary. The creation of automatic speech recognition and language models would have to wait for a usable language corpus to be created. Additionally, the utility of automatic speech recognition is largely contingent on whether language community workers perceive it as a crutch or something more. While the focus of this paper is on archival materials, a necessary step to improve any of these computational tools is to continue to learn and document Bodwéwadmimwen.

1 Introduction

Computational linguistics allows one to create useful tools for interacting with technology to preserve and revitalize Bodwéwadmimwen (the Potawatomi language). Several Potawatomi communities sought out these tools relatively early on; however, they have not taken full advantage of the tools computational linguistics has to offer. To do computational linguistics on Bodwéwadmimwen, one needs to know how to program, needs to know about the linguistic principles of Bodwéwadmimwen, and needs linguistic data to do computational linguistics on. This paper has two goals. The first goal is to survey the previous language initiatives that Potawatomi communities have undertaken with technology to help them preserve and revitalize Bodwéwadmimwen. The second goal is to provide a menu of newer computational tools that could supplement previous initiatives as well as describe how new initiatives could be undertaken with new computational tools to preserve and revitalize Bodwéwadmimwen.

2 Bodwéwadmimwen and Technology

Potawatomi is called Bodwéwadmimwen by its speakers. Bodwéwadmimwen was historically spoken around the Great Lakes; but due to United States, Canadian, and Mexican treaties, Potawatomi communities have been split up and removed from the Great Lakes. There are now seven federally recognized Potawatomi Nations in the United States spread from Michigan and Wisconsin to Kansas and Oklahoma. In addition, there are Potawatomi communities and people of Potawatomi heritage in Canada and Mexico. Bodwéwadmimwen is a critically endangered language. It is classified as stage 8a (Moribund) on the Expanded Graded Intergenerational Disruption Scale (EGIDS) (Lewis and Simons, 2010) as there are only five first language speakers who are all elders. There is also a small dedicated group of adult second language learners in every Potawatomi community.

Bodwéwadmimwen is a polysynthetic language, highly inflective, with agglutinative morphology. It is an Algonquian language closely related to Ojibwe; however, Bodwéwadmimwen has had a substantial amount of borrowing from the Fox Branch languages (Sauk, Meskwaki, and Kickapoo). There are six writing systems that have been used by Potawatomi people: the Dot system, the Traditional writing system, the Wisconsin Native American Language Program (WNALP) writing system, the BWAKA nonprofit writing system, the Prairie Band Potawatomi Nation (PBPN) writing system, and the Learners writing system. Of these, the Traditional,

WNALP, PBPN, and Learners writing systems are regularly used by language communities. There are several additional writing systems used my missionaries in religious texts.

Bodwéwadmimwen is an extremely low resource language. Language documentation consists of a mix of texts, recordings, and videos. Excluding dictionaries and word lists, documentation includes several religious texts and a grammar from the 1800s (Lykins, 1844; Hoecken, 1844, 1846a,b; Gailland, 1868a,b), linguistic field notes transcribed by Charles F. Hockett in the 1930s and 1940s, Hockett's dissertation and a series of articles in the *International Journal of American Linguistics* (Hockett, 1939, 1948a,b,c,d), and more recently community documentation held by Potawatomi Language and Culture Departments arising out of their own documentation efforts, e.g. texts in the appendix of Lockwood (2017). Some of this documentation is not transcribed and/or translated.

The fact that Bodwéwadmimwen is a low-resource language and the current state of a text and audio corpus will dictate the type of computational tools that can be built for it in the short term.

3 Previous initiatives

3.1 Font maintenance

The Traditional and WNALP writing systems are supported on most platforms. All of the letters and symbols to write in the Traditional writing system are on the standard QWERTY keyboard. Additionally, Languagegeek makes available a keyboard download for the WNALP's writing system that works for Windows and Mac computers: `https://www.languagegeek.com/`. The only character that the WNALP writing system uses that is not on the QWERTY keyboard is *é*. Note that these are only two of the six writing systems, and at least four of the writing systems are regularly used by community members (i.e. Traditional, WNALP, PBPN, and Learners).

3.2 Online dictionaries

Bodwéwadmimwen was one of the first endangered languages to make use of an online dictionary as chronicled in (Buszard-Welcher, 2001). The website and the Bodwéwadmimwen nonprofit BWAKA were created by Prairie Band Potawatomi member Smokey McKinney to document the Potawatomi of his father and other Potawatomi people. The online dictionary contains more than 1,200 words and is hosted by the Kansas Heritage Group: `http://www.kansasheritage.org/PBP/homepage.html`. Since this first website, other publicly available online dictionaries have been created. The Citizen Potawatomi Nation (CPN) has an online dictionary with around 10k words: `https://www.potawatomiheritage.com/language/`. The Pokagon Band of Potawatomi also has an online dictionary with 741 words: `https://wiwkwebthegen.com/dictionary`. All three of these dictionaries use different writing systems. Smokey McKinney's dictionary uses the BWAKA writing system, the CPN uses the WNALP writing system, and the Pokagon Band use the Learners writing system.

4 Where to go from here?

4.1 Font maintenance

Not all systems support the PBPN and Learners writing systems. The characters *ė*, *ś*, *t̄*, and *ťt* in the PBPN writing system and the characters *ė* and *ê* in the Learners writing system are difficult for community members to write and not supported by many fonts. Since the PBPN and Learners writing systems are also regularly used in speech communities, a necessary step would be to have the special characters given their own unicode numbers.

4.2 Automatic speech recognition

Language documentation that only exists in audio or video format needs to be transcribed. A text transcript allows one to quickly identify what is in video and audio files. Manual transcription, however, is a time consuming process. Just a few minutes of audio can take up to an hour or more to transcribe. With lots of recordings and little staff this could lead to a transcription bottleneck (Seifart et al., 2018; Himmelmann, 2018).

Automatic speech recognition (ASR) software could be used to speed up the creation of text files for the video and audio that do not have transcripts. This technology could exist with a fairly small Bodwéwadmimwen text and audio corpus. Coto-Solano et al. (2022) use a transcript of 5,033 sentences and 3 hrs 57 mins of audio to do automatic speech recognition on Cook Island Māori, and find Kaldi (Povey et al., 2011) and XLSR (Conneau et al., 2020) the most effective models. Even with a relatively small corpus size, it may be difficult to compile about four hours of audio only in Bodwéwadmimwen for training the software on. To the best of my knowledge, outside of community documentation initiatives, there exists few monolingual Bodwéwadmimwen recordings. Most recordings, such as classroom recordings, contain large amounts of code switching.

Additionally, automatic speech recognition would likely only be able to provide a rough transcription. Coto-Solano et al. (2022) finds a word error rate (WER) of 18±2 and a character error rate (CER) of 7.5±0.8 for Kaldi and a WER of 23±2 and a CER of 6.1±0.6 for XLSR after training. The error rates increase when tested on heldout speakers to a WER of 46.4±15.6 and a CER of 14.9±7.2 averaged across the speakers. Thus, automatic speech recognition may be good for a first pass transcription to speed up the work of manual transcription, but it certainly would still be necessary to go back and hand verify the transcript.

Moreover, Cook Island Māori is not as complex as Bodwéwadmimwen in terms of phonotactics and morphology. It follows that these models have less phonotactic and morphological variation to learn for Cook Island Māori than they would for Bodwéwadmimwen. It may be that Bodwéwadmimwen's linguistic complexities would increase the WER and CER for Bodwéwadmimwen. In fact, this is what is found for the Iroquoian language Seneca which is closer to Bodwéwadmimwen in terms of morphological complexity. Prud'hommeaux et al. (2021) finds an average WER of 50.7 and CER of 31 when using Kaldi ASR on Seneca with 270 minutes of audio and 1843 utterances (3498 unique words).

In sum, using ASR technology would increase the size of Bodwéwadmimwen textual documentation while reducing the time to do so, but it would likely require pooling audio from across Potawatomi communities to make it work.

4.3 Corpus

A corpus of Bodwéwadmimwen language material must be created. One cannot do computational linguistics without a corpus of language data.

The workings of a usable corpus already exist based on current documentation of Bodwéwadmimwen. Several narratives have been published from Hockett's field notes (Buszard-Welcher, 2003; Lewis, 2020) and a community based project (Lockwood, 2017).

Additionally, I have begun the work of creating a larger corpus. I have copies of religious texts from the 1800s and Hockett's field notes from the 1930s and 1940s. These documents are handwritten. So far I have typed up Hockett's field notes as text files, but I need to go back through and hand verify the corpus. The text of Hockett's field notes consists of seventy-four narratives and is of roughly 4,913 word types. This number will likely fluctuate as the corpus is edited for accuracy.

Based on my experience with Hockett's field notes and the size of the current documentation of Bodwéwadmimwen, it would take a substantial financial and personnel commitment to make it possible to convert all existing data to a useable corpus. For example, it took me about ten years to type up and edit Hockett's field notes. I had to acquire a substantial amount of knowledge to be able to accurately transcribe and edit Bodwéwadmimwen. If a sizable commitment was made though, it would likely take less than a decade to do the work for the remaining current documentation.

The next step is to process the religious texts. The religious texts are in several different writing systems. They, as well as any other textual materials added to the corpus, would have to be converted into a phonemic writing system. One foreseeable problem is whether a copy of these materials can be found that is sufficiently legible to scan or even transcribe. Smokey McKinney, who has already typed up several books of the Bible on his website, notes that the copy of Gailland's Gospel According to Matthew is illegible in a number of places (`http://www.kansasheritage.org/PBP/books/home.html`).

The harder, and more time consuming, task is to transcribe documentation that only exists in audio and video format. Unless automatic speech recognition software is leveraged, and works, transcription is likely to be the most time consuming and expensive process of converting existing data to a usable corpus. It is worth noting here that community language workers sometimes prefer to transcribe audio from scratch rather than being assisted by ASR (Prud'hommeaux et al., 2021). To echo Prud'hommeaux et al. (2021)'s findings, there is value in using ASR to speed up transcription, but there is also value in engaging in tasks that will help language learners improve their language knowledge.

Finally, there are gaps in the documentation and description of Bodwéwadmimwen that need to be closed soon before a number of tech tools can be implemented. For example, there is little conversation based documentation as pointed out by Buszard-Welcher (2015). This is likely to skew any language models of Bodwéwadmimwen. While we are a long way off from getting a computer to find an answer to a question in Bodwéwadmimwen, we want to make sure we document these types of language in order to one day create such a computational tool.

4.4 Online dictionaries

There are gaps in the documentation and description of Bodwéwadmimwen at the dictionary level. The Pokagon Band dictionary contains 741 words. Smokey McKinney's online Kansas Potawatomi dictionary contains more than 1,200 words. The Forest County Potawatomi Community's print dictionary contains about 5k words (Forest County Potawatomi Community, 2014), and the CPN online dictionary contains about 10k words. The size of these lexicons are still considerably small compare to the mental lexicon of first language speakers. Materials from Hockett's field notes, religious texts, and untranscribed audio and video files are likely to increase these numbers.

Moreover, Smokey McKinney's online Kansas Potawatomi dictionary is woefully out of date. The late Smokey McKinney pointed this out to me. While the online dictionaries for the CPN and the Pokagon Band of Potawatomi are periodically updated, one cannot search in their dictionary with an inflected Potawatomi word. Technically, this has to do with the website's structure and information retrieval and not the dictionary. A morphological parser is needed on the back-end. That is, to make any online dictionary's website able to search for a definition with an inflected word (e.g. finding the same lexical entry for the inflected verbs *gi-zgebwé* 's/he bite' and *ngi-zgebwé* 'I bite'), stemming and lemmatization needs to be done.

Beyond stemming and lemmatization, dictionaries only provide so much information to learners. They do not provide a breakdown of the verb. This is relevant for Potawatomi because most verbs are made up of three lexical components (an initial, medial, and final). The internal structure of stems could also be added to an online dictionary's website. Loftis and Lewis (2021) is an aid in this process that simply needs to be embedded in the appropriate data structure. The data structure use for the online Ojibwe People's Dictionary is a good example.

Additionally, to the extent that a dictionary is meant to be accessible to language learners from various Potawatomi communities, it would be possible to write a programming script that moves from one writing system to another. A feature that the late Smokey McKinney had shared his desire for with me before he passed on. Recall that not every Potawatomi writing system is phonemic. Therefore, documentation only written in a phonemic writing system would need to be rendered into a phonetic one for certain communities' use. It may be possible to write sound rules that take a phonemic writing system to a phonetic one, but it is up for debate whether the same sound rules are at play for each dialect. There are also other dialect differences that would need to be addressed to make a single dictionary accessible to all communities (e.g. differences in vowel raising/lowering, vowel diphthongization/monothongization, and consonant lenition). Most of these dialect differences hold across the board but some are sure to be optional, exceptional, and perhaps even idiosyncratic.

4.5 Morphological parser

There is not currently a stand alone morphological parser for Bodwéwadmimwen. Fortunately, there has been work done on other Algonquian languages that may speed up the creation of a parser for Bodwéwadmimwen (Meskwaki (Luka, 1996), Plains Cree (Harrigan et al., 2017; Schmirler et al., 2018), Odawa (Bowers et al., 2017), and Michif (Davis et al., 2021)).

Bodwéwadmimwen makes frequent use of vowel syncope (and to a lesser extent palatalization) which can be difficult to write a parser for. Again fortunately, Odawa does too. Perhaps, Bowers et al. (2017) could be easily adapted and implemented for the Bodwéwadmimwen data since Bodwéwadmimwen is closest morphologically and phonologically to Odawa of the Algonquian languages. Additionally, Luka (1996)'s parser could be useful for accounting for the Fox Branch morphology in Bodwéwadmimwen (e.g.

the negative *bwa-*).

Of course, in addition to these two parsers, Potawatomi specific rules would need to be created to fully implement a morphological parser for Bodwéwadmimwen, but the future looks promising. In fact, most of the inflectional paradigms have been documented (Hockett, 1939; Lockwood, 2017), so implementation is only a time consuming matter of creating a corpus and lexical database, writing the code, and testing with a corpus. The inflectional paradigms do need to be separated out into dialect groups though, which heretofore has not been done.

Moreover, it is important to think about how much vocabulary does Potawatomi share with Ojibwe or with the Fox Branch languages when building a morphological parser. Loftis and Lewis (2021) begin to address this question by providing a par-wise comparison of Potawatomi verbal components to those in Ojibwe and the Fox Branch languages (mainly the Meskwaki language). They find initials to be the most different of the three core components of a verb (i.e. initials, medials, and finals) between Potawatomi and Ojibwe. This has important theoretical import as it may result in a Bodwéwadmimwen morphological parser that looks different from an Ojibwe (Odawa) one for handling initials of a verb stem.

To complicate this picture, Ojibwe too has had a substantial amount of borrowing from Cree, so it is not always clear whether Potawatomi or Ojibwe was the one to borrow a word. A comparison of Ojibwe, Cree, and Bodwéwadmimwen morphological parsers may shed light on this question of borrowing.

4.6 Language models

Language models statistically model a well-formed sentence. They can be used for things like spell-check and auto complete on phones and computers. Language models are not out of the question for Bodwéwadmimwen, but they remain off the table unless a sizable corpus is made available. This is because language models require a large amount of data to build a statistical model of a sentence. In other words, a language model must be trained on data. The more data a model is trained on, the better the model is likely to be. The state-of-the-art language models are neural models. Neural models require a large amount of text which Bodwéwadmimwen does not have. Therefore, rule based applications are the way to go in the short term.

It, however, depends on the task one needs the language model for. A relatively small corpus could suffice in some cases. Flor et al. (2019) shows that 5% of a dataset of (20-500K words) is robust enough to build a spell-check tool. The change from 5% of a dataset to 75% only increased the accuracy by 1%. Therefore, if a Bodwéwadmimwen corpus can be built to at least meet that threshold, then tools like a spell-checker are viable.

5 Conclusion

This paper surveyed the previous language initiatives that Potawatomi language communities have undertaken with technology to help them preserve and revitalize the Potawatomi language. The paper also provided a menu of newer computational tools that could supplement previous initiatives as well as described how new initiatives could be undertaken with new computational tools to preserve and revitalize the Potawatomi language.

The lowest hanging fruit would be to explore unicode numbers for difficult characters, continue to compile a usable corpus of language materials, and build a morphological parser that could be implemented on top of an online dictionary. While ASR offers to speed up the work of transcription, it may be spurred by community language workers if it is viewed as a crutch. Additionally, only after all archival materials are put into a usable Bodwéwadmimwen corpus, will it become clear whether there is a sufficient amount data to effectively train language models.

Meanwhile, a necessary step is to continue to learn and document Bodwéwadmimwen, especially conversational language.

References

Dustin Bowers, Antti Arppe, Jordan Lachler, Sjur Moshagen, and Trond Trosterud. 2017. A Morphological Parser for Odawa. In *Proceedings of the 2nd Workshop on the Use of Computational Methods in the Study of Endangered Languages*, pages 1–9, Honolulu. Association for Computational Linguistics.

Laura Buszard-Welcher. 2001. Can the web help save my language? In Leanne Hinton and Ken Hale, editors, *The Green Book of Language Revitalization in Practice*, pages 331–348. Academic Press, San Diego, California.

Laura A. Buszard-Welcher. 2003. *Constructional Polysemy and Mental Spaces in Potawatomi Discourse*. Ph.D. thesis, University of California, Berkeley, Berkeley, California.

Laura A. Buszard-Welcher. 2015. Challenges of Editing and Presenting the Corpus of Potawatomi Stories Told by Jim and Alice Spear to Charles Hockett. In David J. Costa, editor, *New Voices for Old Words: Algonquian Oral Literatures*, pages 454–489. University of Nebraska Press.

Alexis Conneau, Alexei Baevski, Ronan Collobert, Abdelrahman Mohamed, and Michael Auli. 2020. Unsupervised cross-lingual representation learning for speech recognition. *CoRR*, abs/2006.13979.

Rolando Coto-Solano, Sally Akevai Nicholas, Samiha Datta, Victoria Quint, Piripi Wills, Emma Ngakuravaru Powell, Liam Koka'ua, Syed Tanveer, and Isaac Feldman. 2022. Development of automatic speech recognition for the documentation of Cook Islands Māori. In *Proceedings of the Thirteenth Language Resources and Evaluation Conference*, pages 3872–3882, Marseille, France. European Language Resources Association.

Fineen Davis, Eddie Antonio Santos, and Heather Souter. 2021. On the computational modelling of Michif verbal morphology. In *Proceedings of the 16th Conference of the European Chapter of the Association for Computational Linguistics: Main Volume*, pages 2631–2636, Online. Association for Computational Linguistics.

Michael Flor, Michael Fried, and Alla Rozovskaya. 2019. A benchmark corpus of English misspellings and a minimally-supervised model for spelling correction. In *Proceedings of the Fourteenth Workshop on Innovative Use of NLP for Building Educational Applications*, pages 76–86, Florence, Italy. Association for Computational Linguistics.

Forest County Potawatomi Community. 2014. *Ézhebmadzimgek gdebodwéwadmi-zheshmomenan: Potawatomi Dictionary*. Forest County Potawatomi Community, Crandon, Wisconsin.

Maurince Gailland, S.J. 1868a. Grammaire de la langue potêvatémie. In *Laura Buszard-Welcher Papers on the Potawatomi language*. Survey of California and Other Indian Languages, University of California, Berkeley.

Maurince Gailland, S.J. 1868b. *Neměmiseniükin ipi Neměnigamowinin*. Wrightson & Co., Cincinnati, Ohio.

Atticus G. Harrigan, Katherine Schmirler, Antti Arppe, Lene Antonsen, Trond Trosterud, and Arok Wolvengrey. 2017. Learning from the computational modelling of Plains Cree verbs. *Morphology*, 27(4):565–598.

Nikolaus P. Himmelmann. 2018. Meeting the transcription challenge. *Language Documentation & Conservation*, 15:33–40.

Charles F. Hockett. 1939. *The Potawatomi Language*. Ph.D. thesis, Yale University, New Haven, Connecticut.

Charles F. Hockett. 1948a. Potawatomi I: Phonemics, Morphophonemics, and Morphological Survey. *International Journal of American Linguistics*, 14(1):1–10.

Charles F. Hockett. 1948b. Potawatomi II: Derivation, Personal Prefixes, and Nouns. *International Journal of American Linguistics*, 14(2):63–73.

Charles F. Hockett. 1948c. Potawatomi III: The Verb Complex. *International Journal of American Linguistics*, 14(3):139–149.

Charles F. Hockett. 1948d. Potawatomi IV: Particles and Sample Texts. *International Journal of American Linguistics*, 14(4):213–225.

Christian Hoecken. 1844. *Potewatemi nememissinoikan*. W.J. Mullin, Saint Louis, Missouri.

Christian Hoecken. 1846a. Pewani ipi Potewatemi missinoikan, eyowat nemadjik, catholiqus endjik. In *Laura Buszard-Welcher Papers on the Potawatomi language*. Survey of California and Other Indian Languages, University of California, Berkeley.

Christian Hoecken. 1846b. Potewatemi nememissinoikan ewiyowat nemadjik catholiques endjik. In *Early Publications in American Indian Languages Collection*. Smithsonian Libraries and Archives, Washington DC.

M Paul Lewis and Gary F Simons. 2010. Assessing endangerment: expanding Fishman's GIDS. *Revue roumaine de linguistique (RRL)*, 55(2):103–120.

Robert E. Lewis, Jr. 2020. *Potawatomi Discourse Markers*. Ph.D. thesis, The University of Chicago, Chicago, Illinois.

Hunter T. Lockwood. 2017. *How the Potawatomi Language Lives: A Grammar of Potawatomi*. Ph.D. thesis, University of Wisconsin-Madison, Madison, Wisconsin.

Thomas Loftis and Robert E. Lewis, Jr. 2021. *Building Potawatomi Verbs*. Self-published.

Barbara Luka. 1996. PC-Kimmo for Fox: A Computational Tool for the Morphological Parsing of Fox Texts. In *Papers of the Twenty-Seventh Algonquian Conference*, pages 180–194, Winnipeg. University of Manitoba.

Johnston Lykins. 1844. *The Gospel According to Matthew and the Acts of the Apostles — Oti ere Mnoahemowun kaonuperuk Mrto*. W. C. Buck, Louisville, Kentucky.

Daniel Povey, Arnab Ghoshal, Gilles Boulianne, Lukáš Burget, Ondřej Glembek, Nagendra Goel, Mirko Hannemann, Petr Motlíček, Yanmin Qian, Petr Schwarz, and et al. 2011. The Kaldi Speech Recognition Toolkit. In *IEEE 2011 workshop on automatic speech recognition and understanding*. IEEE Signal Processing Society.

Emily Prud'hommeaux, Robbie Jimerson, Richard Hatcher, and Karin Michelson. 2021. Automatic speech recognition for supporting endangered language documentation. *Language Documentation & Conservation*, 15:491–513.

Katherine Schmirler, Antti Arppe, Trond Trosterud, and Lene Antonsen. 2018. Building a constraint grammar parser for Plains Cree verbs and arguments. In *Proceedings of the Eleventh International Conference on Language Resources and Evaluation (LREC 2018)*, Miyazaki, Japan. European Language Resources Association (ELRA).

Frank Seifart, Nicholas Evans, Harald Hammarström, and Stephen C. Levinson. 2018. Language documentation 25 years on. *Language*, 94:e324–e345.

Morphological Data Generation from FLEx

Shengyu Liao
University of Florida

Beth Bryson
SIL International

Sarah Moeller
University of Florida

Abstract

Bootstrapping a neural morphological analyzer from artificial data is not often feasible for linguists who do not have specialized training. We show that grammatical information in FLEx, a software tool familiar to many linguists, can be used to generate word forms and their morphosyntactic descriptors. The results of a pilot experiment with Lezgi [lez] indicates that the grammatical information must be structured in FLEx with data generation in mind to generate usable training data. Adjustments with this goal in mind improved a neural morphological analyzer trained on the generated data, from .49 to .60 weighted average F_1-score on the morphological descriptor labels.

1 Introduction

Significant data is needed to train a machine learning natural language processing (NLP) model but that training data is difficult to obtain for low-resource languages. Therefore, training data is sometimes synthesized from hand-crafted resources such as a finite state transducer (FST), using published grammatical descriptions. The additional synthetic data allows NLP models to generalize better to any data in the language.

Creating resources from which synthetic data can be generated usually requires special training. Linguists, who are most familiar with the grammar, may not possess the necessary skills. FSTs, for example, necessitate a rare combination of computer programming and linguistic knowledge. NLP training data for low-resource languages might be generated more equitably if such barriers were reduced. Ideally, linguists could provide the necessary grammatical information in a format that is both machine- and human-readable and they could enter the information in a familiar interface.

This paper describes a proof-of-concept for reducing barriers for non-computationally trained linguists. It will allow artificial training data to be generated for low-resource languages with a tool already familiar to many linguists. As such, this paper asks two questions: 1) Can grammatical information already entered in *Fieldworks Language Explorer* (FLEx), a popular software for linguistic analysis and annotation, as part of a linguist's workflow be used "as is" to generate training data for a morphological machine learning model? 2) Is the quality of data generated with the limited mechanisms of FLEx sufficient for training a usable morphological analyzer?

We show it is possible to synthesize inflected word forms and their morphosyntactic labels using the grammatical information provided in the *Grammar* and *Lexicon* tools of FLEx. We also show that to produce quality training data, the grammatical information must be entered with data generation in mind. Adjustments to a linguist's approach to using FLEx can improve the quality of generated data.

2 Related Work

Morphology comprises word-building properties and accompanying morphosyntactic phenomena. Both NLP and general linguistics benefit from morphological analysis (Cotterell et al., 2015). Morphological analysis is foundational to deeper grammatical analysis and description. Parsing morphologically complex languages is important to NLP because the high number of inflected and compound words in morphologically complex languages compound the out-of-vocabulary (OOV) problem (Hammarström and Borin, 2011; Goldsmith et al., 2017). Addressing this problem affects downstream applications such as machine translation, voice recognition, and development of language learning apps.

When naturally occurring annotated language data is limited, generating synthesized or semi-synthesized word forms for training data has improved performance for tasks such as learning morphology (Silfverberg et al., 2017) or word embeddings (Silva and Amarathunga, 2019). The data can be used by itself to train morphological analyzers (Moeller et al., 2018) or as an augmentation of natural data. For example, synthetic data augmentation has been used successfully in nearly all SIGMORPHON shared tasks (cf. Cotterell et al., 2016).

Synthesized data for morphology usually results in nonce words that have correctly inflected wordforms and accompanying morphosyntactic descriptive labels (e.g. affixes glosses). Synthesized morphological data can be generated from resources that incorporate the language's morphological rules and grammatical information, such as found in spell checkers, dictionaries, Wiktionary tables, or Unimorph (Ahlberg et al., 2014; Bergmanis and Goldwater, 2019; Cotterell et al., 2015; Durrett and DeNero, 2013). FST-generated synthetic data has been used to train or augment neural morphological analyzers (Hämäläinen et al., 2021; Lane and Bird, 2019; Moeller et al., 2019; Schwartz et al., 2019; Silfverberg and Tyers, 2019). However, developing a robust FST model for a given language is time-consuming and requires in-depth knowledge of both the language and of finite state modeling tools (Maxwell, 2015a,b).

3 Morphology in FLEx Software

Field linguists use specially designed software to analyze data, annotate texts, build lexicons, and deduce the structure of a language. One such software is *Fieldworks Language Explorer* (FLEx)[1].

Users can specify morphological and lexical information in FLEx. The mechanisms in FLEx for describing the morphological patterns of a language include elements in the *Lexicon* area of its interface:

- Entries that specify the underlying form of a morpheme (roots/stems or affixes) (called *Lexeme Form*)
- Lists of each morpheme's allomorphs
- Environments (either phonological or lexical) for allomorphs
- Morphological process rules (e.g., infixes, reduplication, metathesis)

[1]`https://software.sil.org/fieldworks/`

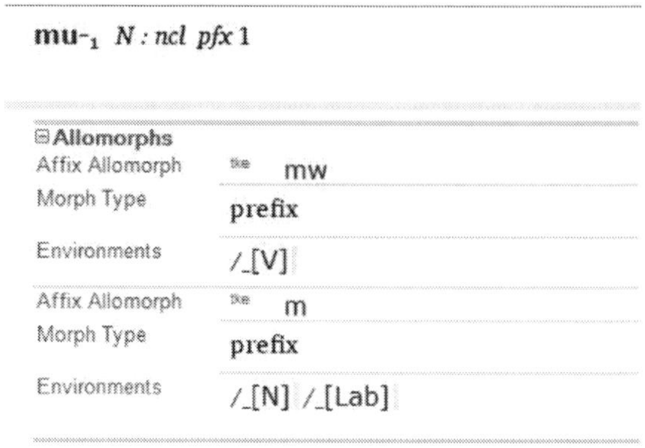

Figure 1: A FLEx *Lexicon* entry showing the morpheme, its gloss, and its allomorphs with the phonological environments that constrain their realization.

- Specification of lexical category information for roots/stems and affixes

as well as items in the *Grammar*:

- Lists of phonemes, natural classes, inflection features, and environments
- Morphology position class charts specifying the relative position and complementary distribution of inflectional affixes

An example of a lexical entry with information about allomorphs and their environments in the FLEx *Lexicon* is shown in Figure 1. An example of a morphological template is shown in Figure 2.

Also, users can add morphological annotation to texts in the *Texts & Words* interface of FLEx. As shown in Figure 3, users may label words with their lexical category (part of speech or POS), segment words into morphemes, gloss the morphemes, and link those morphemes and glosses to the *Lexicon*.

3.1 Morphological Parser

In FLEx, a user may set up a rule- and lexicon-based morphological parser[2]. The parser provides automated assistance by presenting all possible parses (segmentations and glosses) for words in texts based on the grammatical information specified in the *Lexicon* and *Grammar*. The parser cannot "learn" to parse unspecified morphological patterns, but can only process novel forms if all the word's morphemes have an entry in the *Lexicon* and all relevant constraints are specified. The linguist can refine the lexical categories of morphemes and

[2]There are two automatic parsers in FLEx. For this experiment, the XAMPLE parser was used.

STEM	-(NUMBER)	-Oblique-erg	-SemCase	-(enclitic)
	-ар PL	-ди$_1$ OBL	-з$_1$ DAT -н GEN	-ни and;FOCUS

Figure 2: An example FLEx morphological template for Lezgi [lez] nouns. The chart shows the type of affixes, their complementary distribution, and position in relation to the stem.

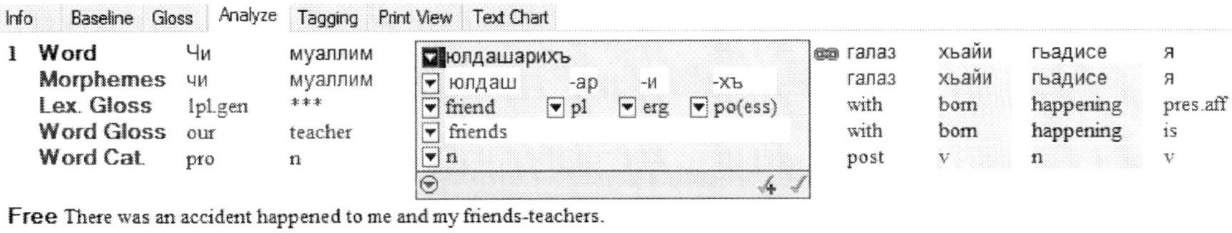

Figure 3: Interlinearized glossed texts for Lezgi [lez] in FLEx. Morpheme segment annotations are on the second line, morpheme glosses on the third, and word glosses on the fourth. POS tags are below the word glosses.

specify allomorph environments in the *Lexicon* or edit the position class morphology templates in the *Grammar*. These adjustments can constrain the parser to only offer valid suggestions.

3.2 Tools for Data Generation

With the help of a few additional tools, the grammatical information provided in FLEx to set up the morphological parser can also be used to generate synthetic morphological data. Currently, these tools produce synthesized word forms and their inflectional parses.

The additional tools needed for data generation are FlexTools, our custom Python modules, and STAMP (Weber et al., 1990). FLExTools[3] is a software workbench that runs Python scripts that can directly read and manipulate the FLEx data store, thus achieving capability not built into FLEx itself. We enhanced some existing FlexTools modules[4] to generate inflectional parses, using the information in FLEx. STAMP is a tool that can synthesize surface word forms from information produced by the parser in FLEx. Our package containing FlexTools, our custom modules, and STAMP is downloadable.[5]

4 Generating Synthetic Data from FLEx

The two modules we created for FlexTools are called *Generate all parses* and *Run STAMP*[6]. In FlexTools, the *Generate all parses* module accesses the FLEx data store and generates morphosyntactic parses for all combinations of affixes that the *Grammar* allows for all specified root morphemes in the *Lexicon*. These parses include the gloss of every affix taken from their lexical entries and the POS tag of the root morpheme:

[baby]<N>{PL}{OBL}{DAT}

In a later step, this parse output could be customized to include the information needed for various experiments. Our model is intended to analyze inflectional information, so the *Generate all parses* module was customized to also output a version with only the POS tag and affix glosses but no stem glosses, resulting in: *N;PL;OBL;DAT*.

The *Run STAMP* FLExTools module then builds the necessary input for synthesis, using the morphological information in FLEx and the morphosyntactic parses created by the *Generate all parses* module. It runs the background program STAMP (Weber et al., 1990) on these files, to generate inflected word forms. For instance, from *[baby]<N>{PL}{OBL}{DAT}*, STAMP generates the Lezgi word form: "балайриз" which corresponds to our customized inflectional tags: *N;PL;OBL;DAT*.

Currently, the files that are produced with the inflected words and morphosyntactic parses require additional processing.[7] Several issues must be taken into consideration. First, obvious "ungram-

[3]`https://github.com/cdfarrow/flextools`

[4]We started with modules from the FLExTrans (Lockwood, 2015) package and customized them for our purposes.

[5]`https://github.com/shengyu-liao/Morphological-Data-Generation-from-FLEx`

[6]The *Run STAMP* module is based on one of the core modules of the FLExTrans package. It was modified only slightly for this experiment. The *Generate all parses* module is also based on a module written by Lockwood that is not part of the FLExTrans package.

[7]Our post-processing code can be obtained in our GitHub repository linked in footnote 5.

Issue	Consequence	Solution
Template slot has no affixes	Generation script halted	Correct the template
Space in affix gloss	Gloss appears in word	Remove space in *Lexicon*
Stem/affix has no POS	Skipped in generation	Add POS in *Lexicon*
Space in POS *Abbreviation*	Gloss appears in word form	Remove space
Multiple morphemes in *Lexicon*	Both appear in word	Create separate entries in *Lexeme Form* field

Table 1: Issues that may be encountered when generating inflected word forms and parses from FLEx grammatical information, along with suggested solutions.

matical" words should be removed. These words are usually indicated by non-alphabetic characters. For example, when a synthetic surface word form fails some constraints in the synthesis process, the STAMP program inserts a "%" at the beginning of the generated string. When the stem has no gloss in the *Lexicon*, a "1.1" is added in the string. Other examples of non-alphabetic characters generated during the process and which should be eliminated include "," (i.e. a comma was used in the *Lexicon* gloss) and "{" and "}" (i.e. the stem morpheme is missing a gloss in the *Lexicon*).

A second issue is that word forms must be "cleaned" by removing generated symbols that represent null affixes. This step cannot be generalized with a single Python script in the online package because the symbols may be specific to each database. For example, the symbol "*0" indicates null affixes in the Lezgi FLEx database. Others might use "∅" or "ø" (Unicode codepoint U+2205 and U+00F8, respectively).

A third issue that must be considered during the generation process and post-processing stage is whether uninflected words should be included. If all the affix slots in a template in the *Grammar* are optional, then the bare root will be generated as the word form but its parse will include only a POS tag. If these bare roots are not desired, the templates must be constructed so that at least one affix column is non-optional.

Finally, any FLEx database is likely to contain issues that need to be corrected or eliminated before the information can serve as quality training data. Some issues that we encountered, along with ideal solutions, are described in Table 1. Most can be avoided if users follow consistent conventions when entering information in the *Lexicon* and *Grammar*. For example, when multiple English words or grammatical tags are used to gloss a single morpheme, separating them by a period "." instead of a space (e.g. '1SG.PAST' rather than '1SG PAST') resolves the issue on the second line of the table.

5 Case Study: Lezgi

The Lezgi FLEx database that was used in our pilot experiment contained one morphological grammar template for nouns, a lexicon of root morphemes, and ten oral texts.[8] The FLEx database was compiled and partially annotated as a basis for a master's thesis in Linguistics.

Access to this data comes from linguists who gathered the data with informed consent for research purposes by the speaker community. One co-author (Moeller) acted as a consultant for Lezgi community members during a dictionary workshop and also trained a non-linguist native speaker to use FLEx and do some initial morphological segmentation and glossing.

The texts are transcribed in the language's Cyrillic orthography. We adjusted the lexicon and grammar templates with data generation in mind. We also extracted word forms and glosses from the texts to serve as a test dataset for the neural morphological analyzer.

5.1 Lezgi Noun Morphology

Lezgi (Lezgian; ISO 639-3 code: lez; Glottolog code: lezg1247) is a Nakh-Daghestanian (Northeast Caucasian) language spoken by over 600,000 speakers in Russia and Azerbaijan (Eberhard et al., 2022). The FLEx data is from the endangered Qusar dialect of Azerbaijan which differs from standard written Lezgi in a few notable ways. It borrowed a locative case morpheme from Azerbaijani which is used alongside the native inessive case morpheme with the same meaning. Also, an unusual stacking of the dative and directive cases

[8]The FLEx database will be deposited at SIL Language and Culture Archives.

occurs occasionally in the texts to indicate movement towards something.

Lezgi is a highly agglutinative language with overwhelmingly suffixing morphology. Fourteen noun cases are formed by case-stacking which is a unique characteristic of Nakh-Daghestanian languages. Instead of a unique morpheme for each case, case-stacking composes various case inflections by "stacking" sequences of case suffixes one after each other.

itim	SG.ABS 'man'
itim-ar	PL.ABS 'men'
itim-ar-di	PL-ERG 'men'
itim-di-k	OBL-AD.ESS 'near a man'
itim-di-k-di	OBL-AD-DIR 'toward a man'
itim-ar-di-k-ay	PL-OBL-AD-EL 'from men'

Table 2: A simplified example of Lezgi case-stacking on the noun root *itim* 'man'.

A simplified example of Lezgi case-stacking is shown in Table 2. Absolutive (ABS) and essive (ESS) cases and singular number (SG) are marked by null morphemes. The plural suffix (PL) attaches directly to the noun stem. The ergative (ERG) and the oblique (OBL) suffixes attach after the number. The adessive case (AD.ESS) attaches to the oblique suffix. The elative (EL) and directive (DIR) cases are added in the fourth slot after the root. In the longest possible sequences (e.g. adelative and addirective cases), the final suffixes indicate directed-motion meaning. In the second-to-longest sequences (e.g. adessive case), locative meaning is indicated by one suffix after the oblique affix. The oblique affix is identical in form with the ergative morpheme but serves a purely grammatical function of forming the oblique stem onto which other cases may be "stacked".

5.2 Test Data

To create a set of grammatically correct word forms and morphological descriptive labels for testing, 100 root morphemes were randomly chosen from the 541 noun roots in the *Lexicon*. The 441 roots were set aside to generate synthesized data. Using the FLEx concordance, words in the texts that were formed from these 100 roots were included in the test set. Any derived nouns in the texts that were not formed from either the 100 test noun roots or the 441 training noun roots were also included in the test set. See Table 3 for the final training and test set sizes.

5.3 Modifying the *Grammar* and *Lexicon*

The original training data was generated from the grammatical information that had been entered by the linguist during their routine analysis and annotation work. Generating data from this "as-is" version produced over 300k training instances but presented two issues. First, allomorph environments had not been specified, resulting in a large proportion of invalid strings where root morphemes were combined with the first allomorph rather than the correct allomorph, as constrained by morphophonological rules. Second, the grammar template had been constructed as a comprehensive picture of Lezgi noun morphology and this resulted in many invalid morpheme co-occurrences.

In the *Lexicon*, constraints had to be added that specified the phonological environments of each allomorph listed in the lexical entries. Lexically determined allomorphs could sometimes be specified by creating a new lexical entry and ad hoc allomorphy rules. There are mechanisms in FLEx for constraining lexically determined allomorphy but the generation code we used did not yet implement those constraints[9]. During generation, allomorphs are tested in order, selecting the first one where the constraints are met. The "head" Lexeme Form functions as the "elsewhere" or default allomorph. Therefore, the allomorphs needed to be re-ordered to reflect a decreasing scope of specificity for the environments that trigger them.

The original morphology template lacked co-occurrence constraints needed to prevent overgenerated morpheme combinations. The linguist had rapidly set up the template for recognition of forms found in the text, not with the rigor needed to describe all and only the valid forms. The original single, comprehensive template was converted into multiple smaller templates that allow all possible morpheme combinations but no invalid combinations. For example, the original template had a column for the ergative and the oblique cases, followed by an optional column that included the adessive case. This generates an ungrammatical word form with both the ergative case and the adessive case. To correctly depict the correct forms in Table 2, two templates were needed. One template allows the ergative suffix but no additional

[9]This feature has now been implemented and is included in the modules available for download.

suffixes, and a second template has a non-optional column for the oblique affix followed by a non-optional column for the adessive case.

After adjusting the Lezgi *Lexicon* and *Grammar* with data generation in mind, the number of generated pairs of word forms and glosses was greatly reduced, as shown in Table 3, while the overall grammaticality of the data was increased. The adjusted dataset contains (a) a higher percentage of word forms that are phonologically valid and (b) fewer instances that have invalid co-occurrences of affixes.

6 Experiment

We tested the quality of data generation from FLEx by training two neural morphological analyzers using only the word forms and morphosyntactic labels synthesized from the grammatical information specified in the FLEx interfaces.

The morphological analysis task is treated as a problem of converting an input sequence of characters $\vec{x} = (x_1, \ldots, x_n)$ to an output sequence of labels $\vec{y} = (y_1, \ldots, y_n)$. The output sequence of labels are morphosyntactic descriptors indicating part-of-speech and inflectional information (i.e. affix glosses). An example input-output instance is shown below. We selected the Transformer (Vaswani et al., 2017), a stateless encoder-decoder model that uses additional attention layers to boost speed and performance, and implemented the *fairseq* (Ott et al., 2019) version with modifications that have been shown to be successful in low-resource character-level morphological tasks (Wu et al., 2021).[10]

INPUT (word): б а л а й р и з

OUTPUT (parse): N PL OBL DAT

We trained two models in order to compare the efficacy of adding morphophonological constraints to the *Lexicon* and adjusting the morphology templates in the FLEx *Grammar*. One model is trained on the "as-is" grammatical information originally provided by the linguist. The second model is trained on the adjusted grammatical information. A 9/1 split of the generated data was used for training and development. The test data for both models is the same. The models were tested on naturally occurring tokens that had been manually annotated with the morphosyntactic glosses/labels.

[10] 4 encoder-decoder layers, 4 self-attention heads, 256 embedding size, 1024 hidden size of feed-forward layer, layer normalization before self-attention, decoding left-to-right in a greedy fashion.

Version	Training	Test
original	216,000	2,125
adjusted	38,784	

Table 3: Total number of Lezgi training and test instances. Training data is generated data. Test data are naturally occurring words formed from roots that were not used to generate training data. The two rows show the training data generated before and after the information in the *Lexicon* and *Grammar* areas was adjusted with data generation in mind.

	Original	Adjusted
word acc.	6%	29%
weighted P	0.57	0.63
weighted R	0.49	0.63
weighted F_1	0.49	0.60
macro P	0.13	0.34
macro R	0.11	0.46
macro F_1	0.10	0.36

Table 4: Results comparing models trained only on original grammatical information and grammatical information adjusted for data generation. The accuracy reports the percentage of test words for which all glosses/labels were correctly predicted. The micro P(recision), R(ecall), and F_1 scores are the average scores weighted by the distribution of labels. Macro scores are unweighted.

The performance of the two models is shown in Table 4. Performance is compared on two measures: per token and per label. The adjusted approach to preparing grammatical information in FLEx improved all the results. The accuracy of per word analyses is a little less than 30%. The highest average F_1 score of .6 is weighted by the distribution of the gloss labels and indicates that the adjusted model did reasonably well recognizing inflectional affixes. The greatest improvement is seen in the macro scores which are not weighted by the number of instances of each label. The increase from .10 to .36 F_1 indicates that the biggest effect made by the adjustments and additional constraints in the *Grammar* and *Lexicon* was an improvement in recognizing the less common inflectional forms.

7 Discussion

The first question this paper put forth was whether grammatical information entered in FLEx as part of a linguist's workflow could be used "as is" to generate synthetic training data for a morphological model. By any measure, the quality of our originally generated data is not sufficient to train a high performing neural morphological analyzer. However, the original grammatical information was provided by a linguist with no idea of applying NLP, but rather with the goal of implementing a morphological parser within FLEx while expecting the parser to be constrained by forms found in naturally occurring data. In order to generate new wordforms, adjustments had to be made in the *Lexicon* and *Grammar* mechanisms that would constrain overgeneration. These adjustments improved the quality of the artificial data.

We found that building the morphology templates in the *Grammar* is not difficult for someone who is familiar with FLEx, but it is important to understand, as the grammar and lexicon are built, how and why overgeneration should be constrained. We did discover, however, that knowing how and where to specify complicated allomorphy rules and lexically-determined constraints may require assistance even for linguists who use FLEx on a regular basis. The FLEx website has a long playlist of training videos but videos related to the parser setup are minimal. The parser is the main mechanism for generating synthetic training data.

The second question this paper put forth regards the quality of the generated data as measured by the performance level of the trained model. Once the information was adjusted, the resulting model has a weighted average F_1 score of .6. This is comparable to a threshold that "pre-annotation" by a morphological NLP model has been shown to improve human annotation (Felt, 2012). By that measure, FLEx-generated data may be useful to train an NLP model useful for human assistance. For example, if a large amount of words need to be morphologically analyzed, it may save time and increase accuracy to pre-annotate the data with a model trained on FLEx-generated data and then have humans correct the labels. This situation assumes that a small lexicon and a decent grammar sketch are available.

The main aim of this pilot experiment is to reduce barriers that discourage "paper-and-pen" linguists from being involved in NLP for low-resource languages. Specifying grammatical information in a familiar tool is one way linguists can help build resources needed to train NLP models. The results of this pilot project in FLEx are promising but additional work is needed. Further work is needed to develop the data generation mechanisms. We did quite a bit of programming to make any data synthesis possible, including modifying and enhancing existing FlexTools modules. There is a potential for independent programmers to contribute modules and improve the quality of the FLEx-generated synthetic data.

Finally, there is an additional direct benefit to a linguist who attempts to generate synthetic data from FLEx. The steps to create and improve FLEx-generated training data also improve the software's morphological parser. Even if the quality of the generated data for a given language is too poor to train a usable neural analyzer, users can benefit from an improved automatic parser that annotates new data in *Texts & Words*. The drawback to the rule-based parsers in FLEx is that, unlike a machine learning model, they cannot "guess" the inflectional information of new forms. If a word's root (or affix) morphemes are not already entered in the *Lexicon* by the user, the parser cannot do anything with that word form. The benefit of generating training data to improve a probabilistic model such as the one we tested, is that these models can provide reasonable guesses at inflectional analyses for word forms with previously unseen morphemes. Even these automated hypotheses may be beneficial when an annotator is faced with large numbers of new words.

8 Conclusion

Generating artificial training data based on knowledge of a language's structure is one way to address the low-resource language challenge. In previous work, this has required special training for either NLP researchers or language experts. We have shown that it is possible to generate artificial data using FLEx, a tool linguists are already familiar with. This means an NLP expert does not need to be a language domain expert and the linguist does not need specialized training. However, the quality of the synthetic data and, therefore, the usefulness of the trained model depends on how well the goal of data generation is understood by the FLEx user. In the future, we would like to work more closely with the linguist or a native speaker to understand the patterns of errors in the generated data and determine what mechanisms either in FLEx or the FlexTools modules could reduce them. Future work should expand the type of generated data to include morpheme boundaries and train models that perform morpheme segmentation as well as labeling of inflectional information. Training morphological NLP models holds promise for language documentation and description to automate the interlinearization process and provide resources for developing language technology that could benefit the community such as language learning apps and machine translation.

Acknowledgements

We are grateful to the Lezgi linguist and speakers for sharing the Lezgi FLEx database, providing additional Lezgi annotations, and answering questions about the language. We are also grateful to other linguists who offered or shared databases in other languages: Aaron Broadwell, the Sena linguists, and especially Jeff Shrum. Thank you to Ron Lockwood for sharing FLExTrans modules and assisting with advice and testing. We would also like to thank the anonymous reviewers for their helpful comments and suggestions. The usual disclaimers apply.

References

Malin Ahlberg, Markus Forsberg, and Mans Hulden. 2014. Semi-supervised learning of morphological paradigms and lexicons. In *Proceedings of 14th Conference of the European Chapter of the Association for Computational Linguistics*, pages 569–578, Gothenburg, Sweden. Association for Computational Linguistics.

Toms Bergmanis and Sharon Goldwater. 2019. Data augmentation for context-sensitive neural lemmatization using inflection tables and raw text. In *Proceedings of the 2019 Conference of the North American Chapter of the Association for Computational Linguistics: Human Language Technologies, Volume 1 (Long and Short Papers)*, pages 4119–4128, Minneapolis, MN. Association for Computational Linguistics.

Ryan Cotterell, Christo Kirov, John Sylak-Glassman, David Yarowsky, Jason Eisner, and Mans Hulden. 2016. The SIGMORPHON 2016 shared task—Morphological reinflection. In *Proceedings of the 14th SIGMORPHON Workshop on Computational Research in Phonetics, Phonology, and Morphology*, pages 10–22, Berlin, Germany. Association for Computational Linguistics.

Ryan Cotterell, Thomas Müller, Alexander Fraser, and Hinrich Schütze. 2015. Labeled morphological segmentation with semi-Markov models. In *Proceedings of the Nineteenth Conference on Computational Natural Language Learning*, pages 164–174, Beijing, China. Association for Computational Linguistics.

Greg Durrett and John DeNero. 2013. Supervised learning of complete morphological paradigms. In *Proceedings of the 2013 Conference of the North American Chapter of the Association for Computational Linguistics: Human Language Technologies*, pages 1185–1195, Atlanta, GA. Association for Computational Linguistics.

David M. Eberhard, Gary F. Simons, and Charles D. Fennig, editors. 2022. *Ethnologue: Languages of the world*, 25 edition. SIL International, Dallas, TX.

Paul Felt. 2012. Improving the effectiveness of machine-assisted annotation. Master's thesis, Brigham Young University, Provo, UT.

John A. Goldsmith, Jackson L. Lee, and Aris Xanthos. 2017. Computational learning of morphology. *Annual Review of Linguistics*, 3(1):85–106.

Mika Hämäläinen, Niko Partanen, Jack Rueter, and Khalid Alnajjar. 2021. Neural morphology dataset and models for multiple languages, from the large to the endangered. In *Proceedings of the 23rd Nordic Conference on Computational Linguistics (NoDaLiDa)*, pages 166–177, Reykjavik, Iceland (Online). Linköping University Electronic Press, Linköping, Sweden.

Harald Hammarström and Lars Borin. 2011. Unsupervised learning of morphology. *Computational Linguistics*, 37(2):309–350.

William Lane and Steven Bird. 2019. Towards a robust morphological analyzer for Kunwinjku. In *Proceedings of the 17th Annual Workshop of the Australasian Language Technology Association*, pages 1–9, Sydney, Australia. Australasian Language Technology Association.

Ronald M. Lockwood. 2015. A linguist-friendly machine translation system for low-resource languages. Master's thesis, University of Washington, Seattle, WA.

Michael Maxwell. 2015a. Accounting for allomorphy in finite-state transducers. In *Proceedings of the 12th International Conference on Finite-State Methods and Natural Language Processing 2015 (FSMNLP 2015 Düsseldorf)*. Association for Computational Linguistics.

Michael Maxwell. 2015b. Grammar debugging. In Cerstin Mahlow and Michael Piotrowski, editors, *Systems and frameworks for computational morphology. SFCM 2015.*, number 537 in Communications in Computer and Information Science, pages 166–183. Springer, Cham, Germany.

Sarah Moeller, Ghazaleh Kazeminejad, Andrew Cowell, and Mans Hulden. 2018. A neural morphological analyzer for Arapaho verbs learned from a finite state transducer. In *Proceedings of the Workshop on Computational Modeling of Polysynthetic Languages*, pages 12–20, Santa Fe, NM. Association for Computational Linguistics.

Sarah Moeller, Ghazaleh Kazeminejad, Andrew Cowell, and Mans Hulden. 2019. Improving low-resource morphological learning with intermediate forms from finite state transducers. In *Proceedings of the 3rd Workshop on the Use of Computational Methods in the Study of Endangered Languages Volume 1 (Papers)*, pages 81–86, Honolulu, HI. Association for Computational Linguistics.

Myle Ott, Sergey Edunov, Alexei Baevski, Angela Fan, Sam Gross, Nathan Ng, David Grangier, and Michael Auli. 2019. fairseq: A fast, extensible toolkit for sequence modeling. In *Proceedings of the 2019 Conference of the North American Chapter of the Association for Computational Linguistics (Demonstrations)*, pages 48–53, Minneapolis, MN. Association for Computational Linguistics.

Lane Schwartz, Emily Chen, Benjamin Hunt, and Sylvia L.R. Schreiner. 2019. Bootstrapping a neural morphological analyzer for St. Lawrence Island Yupik from a finite-state transducer. In *Proceedings of the 3rd Workshop on the Use of Computational Methods in the Study of Endangered Languages Volume 1 (Papers)*, pages 87–96, Honolulu, HI. Association for Computational Linguistics.

Miikka Silfverberg and Francis Tyers. 2019. Data-driven morphological analysis for Uralic languages. In *Proceedings of the Fifth International Workshop on Computational Linguistics for Uralic Languages*, pages 1–14, Tartu, Estonia. Association for Computational Linguistics.

Miikka Silfverberg, Adam Wiemerslage, Ling Liu, and Lingshuang Jack Mao. 2017. Data augmentation for morphological reinflection. In *Proceedings of the CoNLL SIGMORPHON 2017 Shared Task: Universal Morphological Reinflection*, pages 90–99, Vancouver, Canada. Association for Computational Linguistics.

Amila Silva and Chathurika Amarathunga. 2019. On learning word embeddings from linguistically augmented text corpora. In *Proceedings of the 13th International Conference on Computational Semantics - Short Papers*, pages 52–58, Gothenburg, Sweden. Association for Computational Linguistics.

Ashish Vaswani, Noam Shazeer, Niki Parmar, Jakob Uszkoreit, Llion Jones, Aidan N. Gomez, Łukasz Kaiser, and Illia Polosukhin. 2017. Attention is all you need. In *Proceedings of the 31st International Conference on Neural Information Processing Systems (NIPS 2017)*, pages 5998–6008, Long Beach, CA. Curran Associates Inc., Red Hook, NY.

David J. Weber, H. Andrew Black, Stephen R. McConnel, and Alan Buseman. 1990. *STAMP: A tool for dialect adaptation*. Number 15 in Occasional Publications in Academic Computing (OPAC). Summer Institute of Linguistics, Dallas, TX.

Shijie Wu, Ryan Cotterell, and Mans Hulden. 2021. Applying the transformer to character-level transduction. In *Proceedings of the 16th Conference of the European Chapter of the Association for Computational Linguistics: Main Volume*, pages 1901–1907, Online. Association for Computational Linguistics.

A text-to-speech synthesis system for Border Lakes Ojibwe

Christopher Hammerly, Sonja Fougère
Department of Linguistics
University of British Columbia
Vancouver, Canada
chris.hammerly@ubc.ca
sonjaf16@student.ubc.ca

Giancarlo Sierra, Scott Parkhill
Harrison Porteous, Chad Quinn
CultureFoundry
Victoria, Canada
giancarlosierra, scottparkhill
harrison, chadquinn
@culturefoundrystudios.com

Abstract

This paper describes the development of a text-to-speech synthesis system for Border Lakes Ojibwe, which is being deployed within a web-based language learning platform. We discuss our approach to community engagement, recording and editing transcribed sets of utterances for model training, the technical implementation of the speech synthesis model itself, how the system is being used by teachers and learners within the web-based platform, strategies for future extensions of this type of work to other Indigenous voices, dialects and languages, and possibilities for applications in additional educational contexts and beyond.

1 Introduction

Ojibwe (known by speakers as Anishinaabemowin) is an Indigenous language of the Algonquian family consisting of a diverse set of mutually intelligible varieties spoken throughout large swaths of what is colonially known as Canada (through much of Ontario and westward to Manitoba) and the United States (from Michigan to outlying communities in Montana). In part as a consequence of the colonial policies of the United States and Canada such as the residential school system, which explicitly aimed to decrease the use of Indigenous languages and disrupt the passing of cultural knowledge, many Ojibwe speaking communities have seen a decline in the number of fluent speakers and in children learning the language from a young age.

Despite this difficult context, there are an estimated 28,130 speakers of the Ojibwe language within Canada (O'Donnell and Anderson, 2016), and robust revitalization efforts all across Ojibwe country. We present one component of our team's ongoing work to build technologies that can be used as tools for language revitalization: a text-to-speech (TTS) synthesis system, which is being deployed through a web-based platform for language learning that currently has over 3,000 active users. We describe an initial project that has built these tools for use by language instructors and learners in school and community settings within the Treaty #3 lands of Northwestern Ontario, where the Border Lakes variety of the Southwestern Ojibwe dialect group is spoken (Valentine, 1994). We especially focus on our process for creating training data for Indigenous speech synthesis systems.

2 Background

2.1 Positionality and community engagement

The project was initiated by the Seven Generations Education Institute in Fort Frances, Ontario as part of their *Anishinaabemodaa* "Waking up Ojibwe" language initiative, and has been conducted in collaboration with a team of researchers at the University of British Columbia, the Halifax-based language revitalization organization SayItFirst, and the Victoria-based educational start-up CultureFoundry. We include positionality statements from each member of the team who has worked directly on the technical side of the TTS:

- Hammerly is of mixed Anishinaabe and Norwegian-American descent and a member of the White Earth Nation in Minnesota, who currently works as a professor of linguistics.
- Frazier is of Acadian descent, hailing from rural Nova Scotia, and works as a graduate student in linguistics.
- Sierra is an Ecuadorian mestizo with Indigenous Latin American and European ancestry who now resides in British Columbia and works as a software engineer.
- Parkhill is a white Canadian and works as a software developer.
- Porteous is of European-Canadian descent with multidisciplinary interests, working in

programming and software development for language revitalization efforts.

- Quinn is of European-Canadian descent with a background in computational intelligence, and is currently leading CultureFoundry.

This work emerged in early 2020 from long-standing collaborations between members of our team and individuals and organizations within Treaty #3 lands. The Seven Generations Education Institute, whose leadership has continually guided this project, is an Indigenous owned and controlled community post-secondary institution operated by a board that represents ten First Nations in the Rainy River area. They initially approached their long-time partner in educational resource creation SayItFirst about building an online educational platform for Ojibwe. These organizations then partnered with CultureFoundry to create the platform and related tools, including the TTS system presented here. In August 2020, CultureFoundry approached Hammerly to work on the project. Hammerly has worked with elders and language teachers in the Rainy River region since 2016 in his capacity as a PhD Student in linguistics, as a professor of linguistics, and as a program assistant at an adult language immersion camp in Northern Minnesota. While he is part of the wider Ojibwe community, he has no known direct family connections to Treaty #3 communities.

During the summer of 2020 before work on the project began, members of SayItFirst approached community elders on behalf of our team in the traditional way with an offering of *asemaa* (tobacco) and a gift, and asked for guidance regarding whether such a project should be undertaken. After positive feedback during this consultation, we started work on the project, and have continued to consult with these elders on an ongoing basis as they record sentences for model training. For example, one concern that has been raised as we have presented this work in academic settings (including by a reviewer of this paper) is whether we have placed restrictions on the generation of obscene or inappropriate speech. Based on our consultations, we have not placed any restrictions on what can be generated. The idea conveyed to us is that all parts of the language have their place and should be able to be represented, and that there is trust and respect within the community that will guide how these tools are used. We also note that ownership of all recordings associated with this project are retained by the individuals who are contributing their voices, participants are paid for the time they spend creating recordings, and the participants have the right to pull out of the project (e.g. to stop making recordings or have existing recordings used within the project) at any time.

2.2 Related work on speech synthesis

While there is a rich history of research and development on speech synthesis for Western and other so-called majority languages (e.g. Taylor, 2009), speech synthesis for Indigenous languages, including text-to-speech systems, is still a significantly under-developed area of research. One of the most significant challenges is many Indigenous languages are also "low resource", in the sense that there are no existing data sets such as transcribed corpora of speech that can be leveraged for training, and many active speakers are aging and face significant time pressures to engage with a wide range of cultural and linguistic revitalization efforts.

We are aware of a number of recent efforts to develop speech synthesis for Indigenous languages of North America: Pine et al. (2022), who developed such systems for Kanien'kéha (also known as Mohawk; Iroquoian), Gitksan (Tsimshianic), and SENĆOŦEN (Coast Salish) with data sets ranging from 25 minutes to 3.5 hours, comparing Tacotron2 (Shen et al., 2018) and FastSpeech2 (Ren et al., 2021) models; Harrigan et al. (2019), who present a speech synthesizer for Plains Cree (Central Algonquian) based on 2.5 hours of speech and the Simple4All system (Simple4All, 2011–2014); Lütkebohle (2020) who describes a TTS system with Tacotron2 for Cherokee (exact number of hours unclear, but less than 3); Duddington and Dunn (2007) for Mohawk using eSpeak; and Whitman et al. (1997) for Navajo (details unknown).

3 Building utterance data sets

We recorded new sets of utterances to form the training data for our model. We chose this path for a number of reasons. First, to our knowledge, there are no existing large-scale data sets of high-quality transcribed audio for any dialect of Ojibwe. Second, a major priority set out by our community partners is to create a speech synthesis system that reflect the particular way that members of Border Lakes communities speak, including capturing micro-variation that exists between speakers and

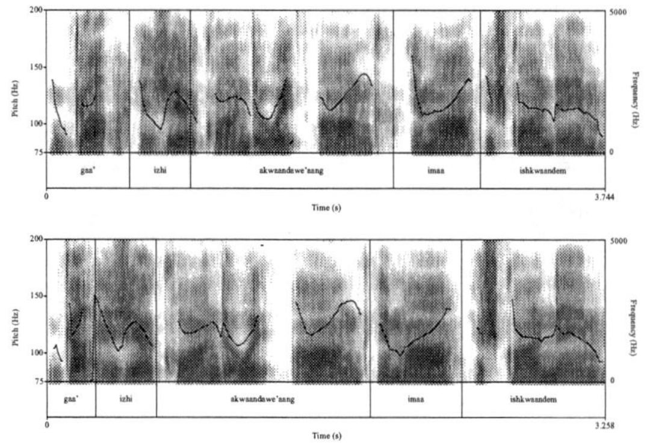

Figure 1: Spectrogram and pitch-track comparison of a speaker audio (top) versus synthesized audio (bottom) of the same string of text.

sub-varieties within Treaty #3 lands. Finally, this gives greater control over the quality of the TTS output, with the input being tailored to its specific application for educational contexts.

We are currently working with three speakers of Border Lakes Ojibwe—one highly fluent heritage speaker who primarily learned Ojibwe as an adult, but received significant exposure as a child, and two elders who learned Ojibwe from birth, one male and one female, each from a different community within the region. This will ultimately result in three distinct speech synthesis systems for the Border Lakes variety. The overall plan is to record a large set of training utterances with the heritage speaker (20,000 utterances) and a smaller set of utterances with the two elders (5,000 utterances) in order to minimize the strain on time for the elders. We then plan to use the heritage speaker model as a base, using the two elder data sets to fine-tune new voices. At present, we are still in the early stages of utterance recording with the two elders who are contributing their voices, therefore we focus here on the process for the heritage speaker model, where we have recorded over 15,000 utterances.

3.1 Utterance corpus

We entertained two possible approaches to creating a set of utterances: (i) source text from existing stories and books in Ojibwe for speakers to record, or (ii) record new stories and sentences and transcribe them into text. Given the high labor demands associated with transcription, and the current absence of automated speech recognition software for Ojibwe, which could streamline the transcription process, we pursued the former option: to record existing texts to build our training data set.

We first sourced all books we could find in Ojibwe, restricting our set to those identified with the broader Southwestern Ojibwe dialect group. All books were written using the "double vowel" orthography system based in the latin alphabet (originally devised by Charles Fiero), which is the standard system used across the Southwestern group and thus an important component of model training within this context.

We then digitized the collected books and used optical character recognition (OCR) software. We then converted the Ojibwe portions of each volume to plain text, and used a combination of regular expression-based automation and by-hand checking by an RA familiar with the Ojibwe language to ensure that all OCR errors were corrected in the plain text versions (e.g. 'm' being parsed as 'ln'). Finally, we created "split" versions of the texts that consisted of a single utterance per line. Splitting was done automatically as a first pass using sentence-final characters (i.e. '.', '?', and '!'). Since longer sentences are harder for speakers to fluently record and potentially decrease the quality of training due to increased issues at the forced-alignment stage, we isolated sentences that were longer than 170 characters and split them by hand, ensuring that breaks were made at natural points such as commas or other major clausal boundaries.

3.2 Utterance recording

For our recording hardware, we used a Rode NT-1 KIT cardioid condenser microphone with a Focusrite Scarlett 2i2 USB audio interface and a Microsoft Surface laptop. We additionally included a set of portable acoustic panels to improve isolation. The biggest challenge for the recording process was to create high-quality audio outside of a studio environment. Use of a studio was not possible for a number of reasons, with the primary issue being that the nearest studio was at least a 90 minute drive from our speakers. We therefore opted for an at-home and portable recording set-up that struck a balance between accessibility, comfort, and quality. We further instructed speakers to find a quiet room away from appliances or environmental noise.

We used SpeechRecorder (Draxler and Jänsch, 2004) as our recording software, which provides a user-friendly interface for prompting and recording a single high-quality audio file for each individual utterance. We split our utterance set into

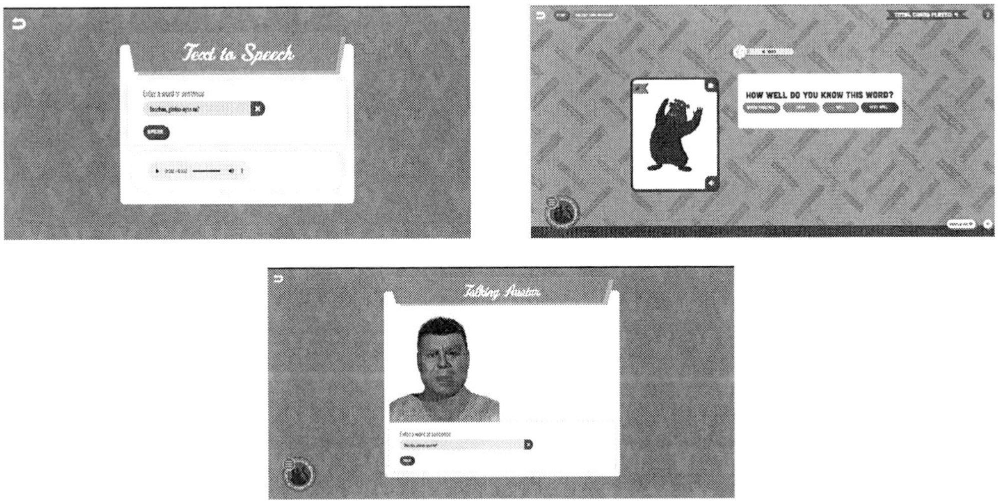

Figure 2: Integration of text-to-speech system as standalone component (upper left), in the flashcard activity (upper right), and with talking avatar (bottom).

projects of 300-500 utterances, and speakers were instructed to talk as if they were speaking to a learner of Ojibwe, and to re-record any utterances with pauses, disfluencies, or missing words. Furthermore, our speakers could edit text within the application if they noticed a typo, wanted to change a word to better fit their dialect, or change spelling to better match the conventions of the community. This was a critical feature, as the texts represented a range of sub-varieties within the Southwestern group. These corrected and adapted versions were used as the transcriptions for the model training. To ensure all portions of the audio were captured, we built-in a pre-recording delay of 1,000 ms and a post-recording delay of 500 ms. All audio was recorded as a .wav file on a single channel at a rate of 44,100 Hz and a 16 bit depth.

3.3 Utterance editing

There were two main facets of the raw recordings that required editing prior to use for model training: (i) all utterances were preceded and followed by silence (see previous section for reasoning), and (ii) despite much care being taken by our speakers, there was occasional background noise from fans and other home appliances. We created a python-based pipeline using the packages *librosa* (McFee et al., 2015), *numpy* (Harris et al., 2020), and *noisereduce* to automate the editing of these recordings to trim silences from the beginning and end of each utterance (leaving all pauses and silences that occurred during an utterance), to reduce noise via spectral gating and with a low-pass filter, normalize loudness across utterances from different sessions, and re-sample to a rate of 22,050 Hz, the rate recommended for training our model.

4 Speech synthesis model

For the text-to-speech, we adopted VITS (Kim et al., 2021), a parallel end-to-end model, trained using the Coqui AI TTS library (Gölge, 2021). Our current data training set includes 11,265 unique utterances recorded by our heritage speaker collaborator, which was comprised of 54,866 words and 556,455 characters. The utterances had a mean length of 4.87 words (SD = 2.56, Range = [1, 22]) and 49.39 characters (SD = 25.06, Range = [3, 170]). All utterances include the edited audio file and associated transcription in the double vowel orthography. After editing, the utterance set used to train the model had a total duration of 696.93 minutes or 11.62 hours. The mean duration of each utterance was 3.87 seconds (SD = 2.04 , Range = [.279, 16.02]). We trained the model from scratch on an array of GPUs consisting of 4x NVIDIA RTX A6000s, 400GB of RAM, 48GB of VRAM per GPU, with 56 virtual CPUs. Total training time was 92.6 hours with a batch size of 64 for 80k steps with otherwise standard model parameters.

As discussed in more detail in §6, we have not yet systematically evaluated the results produced by our model. However, we present a side-by-side comparison of a test utterance recorded by our speaker, but not used to train the TTS, and the same string produced synthetically with the resulting TTS system in Figure 1. We have also demonstrated the feature to numerous community groups, teachers, and elders, and this informal feedback has been uniformly positive, usually including a sense of disbelief and surprise that the voice has been generated synthetically rather than from real recordings based on the tone and accuracy of the pronunciations.

5 Deployment in web-based application

The TTS system is being deployed in various ways within the *Anishinaabemodaa* web-based language learning platform produced in collaboration with teams at the Seven Generations Education Institute, SayItFirst, CultureFoundry, and the University of British Columbia.

There are three primary ways that the TTS system is being deployed or planned to be deployed (Figure 2). First, there is a "text-to-speech" page in the application where users can input any word or sentence in Ojibwe and generate an audio file of synthesized speech. This audio can be sped up and slowed down within the application and downloaded for offline use.

Second, the model for the platform allows teachers to input and generate their own materials, including lists of vocabulary that students should learn. These can then be integrated into games, including a flashcard activity. When a new word is added, audio files of synthesized speech are automatically generated, which can then be accessed by learners by clicking on the audio icon on the flashcard. This allows teachers maximum flexibility to have instant multi-modal media for each new word added to their lessons.

Finally, we have integrated the TTS system into a beta version of an animated talking avatar, providing a multi-modal tool where learners can input a string of text and see and hear how that text is pronounced. The current version is based off a lip-syncing technology developed by Speech Graphics, but has the limitation of being tuned to an English library. Our team is currently undertaking development of a Unity-based 3D model that can be customised to the articulatory properties of Ojibwe.

6 Outlook and extensions

So far, our TTS model of Ojibwe based on the voice of a single heritage speaker has been applied for pedagogical purposes. Moving forward, we envision the developed system as a tool for increasing the accessibility of written materials in the Ojibwe language. For example, those who may have limited literacy in the language, or Ojibwe language users with visual impairments, can use the TTS system to generate audio for a given text to be able to engage with listening rather than reading.

Second, we are currently in the process of recording data sets with two elders who are L1 speakers of Border Lakes Ojibwe. With this, we have had success with the same pipeline based in Speech Recorder, which provides flexibility and independence for our collaborators. Data from these multiple speakers will be combined to jointly train a multi-speaker TTS model.

Finally, we are making plans for systematic evaluation of our model on a variety of dimensions. So far, we have collected informal and anecdotal feedback from our partners about the quality of synthesized speech being produced, which has been uniformly positive. We plan to use a mixture of objective measures such as Mel cepstral distortion (Weiss et al., 2021), subjective measures such as ABX testing (Choi et al., 2021), and objective measures such as eye tracking (Govender and King, 2018). In all cases, we will engage in a user-centered research program that focuses on evaluation relative to the context of use and the needs of the community (Wagner et al., 2019).

References

Hyeong-Seok Choi, Juheon Lee, Wansoo Kim, Jie Lee, Hoon Heo, and Kyogu Lee. 2021. Neural analysis and synthesis: Reconstructing speech from self-supervised representations. *Advances in Neural Information Processing Systems*, 34:16251–16265.

Christoph Draxler and Klaus Jänsch. 2004. Speechrecorder: A universal platform independent multi-channel audio recording software. In *LREC*.

Jonathan Duddington and Reece Dunn. 2007. eSpeak: Speech Synthesizer. `https://espeak.sourceforge.net/`.

Eren Gölge. 2021. Coqui TTS. `https://www.coqui.ai`.

Avashna Govender and Simon King. 2018. Using pupillometry to measure the cognitive load of synthetic speech. *System*, 50(100):2018–1174.

Atticus Harrigan, Timothy Mills, and Antti Arppe. 2019. A preliminary Plains Cree speech synthesizer. In *Proceedings of the Workshop on Computational Methods for Endangered Languages*, volume 1.

Charles R. Harris, K. Jarrod Millman, Stéfan J. van der Walt, Ralf Gommers, Pauli Virtanen, David Cournapeau, Eric Wieser, Julian Taylor, Sebastian Berg, Nathaniel J. Smith, Robert Kern, Matti Picus, Stephan Hoyer, Marten H. van Kerkwijk, Matthew Brett, Allan Haldane, Jaime Fernández del Río, Mark Wiebe, Pearu Peterson, Pierre Gérard-Marchant, Kevin Sheppard, Tyler Reddy, Warren Weckesser, Hameer Abbasi, Christoph Gohlke, and Travis E. Oliphant. 2020. Array programming with NumPy. *Nature*, 585(7825):357–362.

Jaehyeon Kim, Jungil Kong, and Juhee Son. 2021. Conditional variational autoencoder with adversarial learning for end-to-end text-to-speech. In *International Conference on Machine Learning*, pages 5530–5540. PMLR.

Ingo Lütkebohle. 2020. Tacotron2 and Cherokee TTS. `https://www.cherokeelessons.com/content/tacotron2-and-cherokee-tts/`.

Brian McFee, Colin Raffel, Dawen Liang, Daniel P Ellis, Matt McVicar, Eric Battenberg, and Oriol Nieto. 2015. librosa: Audio and music signal analysis in Python. In *Proceedings of the 14th python in science conference*, volume 8, pages 18–25.

Vivian O'Donnell and Thomas Anderson. 2016. The Aboriginal languages of First Nations people, Métis and Inuit. Technical report, Statistics Canada.

Aidan Pine, Dan Wells, Nathan Brinklow, Patrick Littell, and Korin Richmond. 2022. Requirements and motivations of low-resource speech synthesis for language revitalization. In *Proceedings of the 60th Annual Meeting of the Association for Computational Linguistics (Volume 1: Long Papers)*, pages 7346–7359.

Yi Ren, Chenxu Hu, Xu Tan, Tao Qin, Sheng Zhao, Zhou Zhao, and Tie-Yan Liu. 2021. Fastspeech 2: Fast and high-quality end-to-end text to speech. In *International Conference on Learning Representations*.

Jonathan Shen, Ruoming Pang, Ron J Weiss, Mike Schuster, Navdeep Jaitly, Zongheng Yang, Zhifeng Chen, Yu Zhang, Yuxuan Wang, Rj Skerrv-Ryan, et al. 2018. Natural TTS synthesis by conditioning wavenet on mel spectrogram predictions. In *2018 IEEE international conference on acoustics, speech and signal processing (ICASSP)*, pages 4779–4783. IEEE.

Simple4All. 2011–2014. Simple4all: developing automatic speech synthesis technology. `https://simple4all.org/`.

Paul Taylor. 2009. *Text-to-speech synthesis*. Cambridge university press.

Jerry Randolph Valentine. 1994. *Ojibwe dialect relationships*. The University of Texas at Austin.

Petra Wagner, Jonas Beskow, Simon Betz, Jens Edlund, Joakim Gustafson, Gustav Eje Henter, Sébastien Le Maguer, Zofia Malisz, Eva Szekely, Christina Tånnander, et al. 2019. Speech synthesis evaluation—state-of-the-art assessment and suggestion for a novel research program. In *Proceedings of the 10th Speech Synthesis Workshop (SSW10)*.

Ron J Weiss, RJ Skerry-Ryan, Eric Battenberg, Soroosh Mariooryad, and Diederik P Kingma. 2021. Wavetacotron: Spectrogram-free end-to-end text-to-speech synthesis. In *ICASSP 2021-2021 IEEE International Conference on Acoustics, Speech and Signal Processing (ICASSP)*, pages 5679–5683. IEEE.

Robert Whitman, Richard Sproat, and Chilin Shih. 1997. A Navajo Language Text-To-Speech Synthesizer. AT&T Bell Laboratories.

From Raw Data to Acoustic Analysis: A Roadmap based on Acquaviva Collecroce

Simon Gonzalez
The Australian National University
simon.gonzalez@anu.edu.au

Abstract

This paper presents a workflow framework of computational tools to be used in the process of forced alignment and analysis for endangered languages. We introduce a roadmap which uses established methodologies in the area of data processing and analysis, with a strong focus on socio-phonetic studies. The tools are organized into practical stages that can be followed systematically by researchers of under-resourced languages. We have implemented these tools in Acquaviva Collecroce, an endangered language from southern Italy and spoken by approximately 600 speakers. Alongside the tools, we also give suggestions based on our experience, which can contribute to the preservation and revitalization of endangered languages.

1 Introduction

The use of computational tools in endangered languages has proven critical for the revitalization and preservation of languages. There is an increase interest in using latest technologies to strengthen our understanding and processing of minority languages (Adams et al., 2018; Adams et al., 2020; Michaud et al., 2018; Levow, 2019; Levow et al., 2021), including speech to text (Foley et al., 2019; Michaud et al., 2018; Mitra, 2016), speech recognition (Amith et al., 2021; Foley et al., 2018; Hjortnaes et al., 2020; Matsuura et al., 2020; Shi et al., 2021; Thai et al., 2020), phonemic transcription (Adams et al., 2017; Amith and Castillo García, 2020), and forced alignment (Cavar et al., 2016; Coto-Solano, 2017; Gonzalez et al., 2018). The field of Automatic Speech Recognition (ASR) has strongly influenced this endeavor (Prud'hommeaux et al., 2021; Jimerson and Prud'hommeaux, 2018; Jimerson et al., 2018). One of the greatest contributions is that advanced technologies, which had traditionally been available only to major languages, can now be accessed by less resourced languages.

The implementation of computational techniques in language documentation has established a toolkit of skills that need to be met to access these technologies, which shows that the tasks carried out in these processes are complex in nature. These tasks are generally done by computational linguists with the required expertise, who can decide on what tools and techniques are used in any given project. In deciding what to choose, there are many options to select from, and the decision on the workflow depends on the resources available. Since there is no ultimate or perfect process, the decisions must be based on what works best, as long as the goal of language documentation is achieved. Also, given the increasing effectiveness of current algorithms developed, the documentation of endangered languages is in a crucial moment where the work done by computational linguistics can be maximized to its best potential. However, there is still more work needed to efficiently link long-established linguistic analysis traditions and advances in data processing.

Once the data is processed through computational techniques, the task is then to identify what are the best approaches for endangered languages to make the leap towards systematic analysis of the data available. One area that is a suitable test ground for this transition between computational outputs and linguistic analysis is the field of sociolinguistics. The relevance of sociolinguistics for endangered languages is that languages are better analyzed in their social context and not just as isolated entities. Sociolinguistics then helps interpret language patterns related to factors such as gender, age, ethnicity, for example. Therefore, an important contribution from computational linguists to endangered languages is to develop technologies that take computational outputs and allow researchers to analyze linguistic patterns following robust methodologies standard in the respective fields, all this, in relatively short periods of time. In this paper, we focus on technologies that are pertinent to the analysis of speech data, with a focus on socio-phonetics.

1.1 Speech Technologies and Data Size

One of the main challenges faced by languages with small amounts of speech data, is that the technologies available tend to require a minimum threshold of speech. This threshold is generally way more than what the vast majority of world languages cann afford to have. The reasoning behind this is that the more data available, the more robust the acoustic models are to accurately identify speech boundaries based on the phonetic features extracted. It does not mean that under-resourced languages cannot be processed, but rather that the results are not as reliable as those having more data available for training and testing their models. However, we argue that even smaller languages can be maximized by using all available material, and the results are still of great value for language researchers.

In this sense, computational tools used in under-resourced languages are not the means on their own, but rather they are the facilitators for quantifying speech data and identifying language patterns not available otherwise. It will then be the role of the linguist to use all the outputs and look at areas of interest, such as vowel spaces, allophonic variation, morpheme sequence occurrence, intonation, for example. In this sense, it is important to make the difference between what a computational linguist wants and what the field researcher needs. A clear example is about error accuracy. (Semi-) automatic computational models evaluate their performance based on their accuracy (or error rate). Higher accuracy is always desired, but even lower accuracy models can make a big difference in a researcher working with an under-resourced language.

1.2 Phonetic Analysis and Endangered Languages

Among the areas of linguistic interest is the acoustic/phonetic study of under-resourced languages, and forced alignment has played a crucial role in the way (and amount of data) phoneticians analyze smaller languages. The forced alignment process (See more details in Section 4) takes audio files and their corresponding time-stamped transcriptions, generally at the sentence level, and segments the data into the corresponding individual phonological segment (e.g. vowels and consonants). This tool has sped up processes that would otherwise take more time, by exponential differences. This is especially meaningful when language researchers are working against the clock in languages that unfortunately do not have much time to be analysed. Forced alignment has allowed smaller languages to be fully analyzed as it has been done in major languages. The way it works by current workflows is by taking the automatically aligned segments and extracting the relevant acoustic features, such as duration, formants, centre of gravity, to name a few. Sociophonetic research has exploited this by extracting acoustic features and finding correlations with social and geographic factors, especially in the area of vowel spaces.

2 Aim of Paper

In this paper, we combine these overlapping fields and develop an efficient roadmap that can be implemented in endangered languages with at least time-stamped orthographic transcriptions. The nature of the paper is then a hybrid one. On the one hand, it proposes a methodological approach brings together different techniques, and on the other hand, it provides resource materials that can be freely used under open-source frameworks. This roadmap includes the testing and implementation of a socio-phonetic computational workflow, from data processing to data analysis. All this is developed following best practices in the field of sociolinguistics and creates a single toolkit that can be adapted to any language.

The algorithms and instructions are placed on a GitHub repository for public use. The final output is an ordered set of code files and instructions. It is our intention to bring more systematicity and data normalization that combines the power of computational tools and linguistic analysis traditions. We believe that the implications can be many-fold. First, tools like these can shed more light into language patterns never observed before. Second, it makes data from under-resourced languages comparable with other languages, including major ones. Finally, it equips a language community to have the starting tools for more advanced technologies, such as ASR and other (semi)-automated processes. All this will contribute to the ultimate goal of this type of work: language documentation, conservation, and revitalization.

3 Methodology

3.1 Forced Alignment and Endangered Languages

Forced alignment is strongly used in endangered languages. In initial approaches, when aligning a new language, researchers ran pre-existing acoustic models from a similar language for the new language (Coto-Solano, 2017). Though effective to some extent, the main flaw of this approach is that there are always features in a language that are not accurately captured by another language acoustic model. One of the main motivations for this approach was that new languages did not have the same amount of data, thus having less accurate alignments. In this sense, data size was a limitation in the forced alignment task. Then, with the emergence of more powerful data processing techniques such as neural network and deep learning, newer approaches became more robust and more efficient at dealing with lower amount of data (McAuliffe et al., 2017), to a point, that a threshold was reached, in which the adding more data would not significantly improve the acoustic model (Fromont and Watson, 2016). This opened the door to training and aligning new languages without the need for huge amounts of data. As expected, minority and endangered languages greatly benefited from these advances (Gonzalez et al., 2018; Gupta and Boulianne, 2020; Hildebrandt, 2017).

Across time, the processes became more streamlined to such a point that forced aligning a new language from scratch is more efficient and accurate than using a pre-trained language model. If compared to ten years ago, the process is simpler but without compromising accuracy. Despite these advances, there are still many stages to simplify the process of forced alignment and its practical applications. In this paper, we propose a more succinct yet efficient workflow of data alignment and analysis. Since the paper has a methodological approach, which can be followed step by step, we present the tools and solutions in sections.

3.2 Data Selection

The first task is to identify the language to be forced aligned. A good source available for use is Pangloss (Michailovsky et al., 2014), which is an open archive created to help in the preservation of world languages, with a strong focus on endangered and minority languages. Currently, it hosts over 170 languages with more than 700 hours of recordings. An approximate of half of the audiovisual material (video and audio) has annotated files. We then chose to work with Na-Našu (Molise Slavic) (Breu, 2020), which is a micro-language with three dialects, including *Acquaviva Collecroce*. The material available for this dialect comes from a village called *Kruč*, within the province of Campobasso, in the Molise region of southern Italy (See Figure 1 for reference). The dialect has been documented by Adamou and Breu (2013) and Breu (2017).

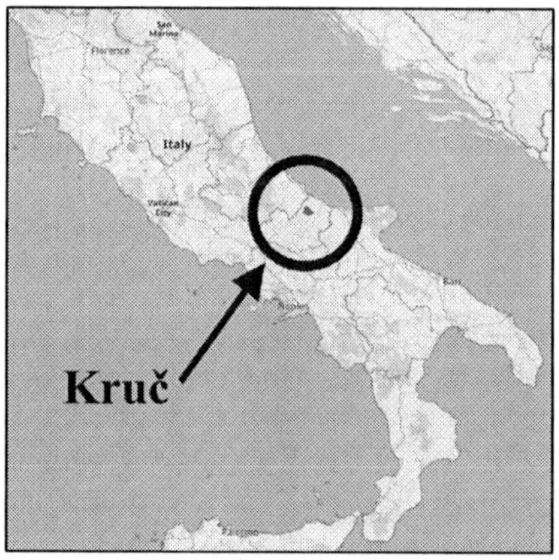

Figure 1: Location of Kruč, where the Acquaviva Collecroce is found.

The language material available on the website was a compilation of 27 audio recordings with their corresponding transcription files. The data was recorded in 2010 by Walter Breu, and the transcriptions have three main layers of information. The first one is a time-stamped transcription at the utterance level (described in the original documentation as orthographic, representing a broad phonological transcription). This time-stamp information is the one that is relevant for the current study, because it is used to create the TextGrids explained in section **4.2**.

The second layer was a phonetic transcription of all the words, which is not used in the current study. The motivation is to use the broad phonological transcription, which forms the basis for the forced-alignment process, as explained below. The third layer available includes morphemic breakdowns. Even though these are not used in the forced-alignment process, this information is relevant for the analysis of vowels, which can help identify whether there are morpho-syntactic effects of vowel formants, for example, running a model that measures whether there are differences between vowels that appear in stems or vowels that appear in affixes. This is a good example on how forced-alignment tools can help contribute to understand phonetic/phonological features and their relationship with other features in the language. The final annotation layer included translation into Italian and German. For the purposes of this study, they were not included in any stage of the process.

3.3 Speakers

The Acquaviva Collecroce dialect is estimated to have just over 600 speakers as for 2019, according to the Italian National Institute of Statistics (ISTAT). There were over 2200 speakers at the beginning of 1950s, with sharp decreases since then due to migration. The speakers in the corpus were two females and four males, born between 1932 and 1960 (See Table 1).

Speaker	Gender	Recordings Duration (Min)	Speech Duration (Min)
GN	Male	16.3	15.6
GR	Male	10.2	9.5
PG	Female	0.7	0.5
PG	Male	3.5	2.9
PL	Male	9.9	9.6
SN	Female	13.2	11.7

Table 1: Speakers in the corpus with their corresponding durations.

Since this is a first analysis on this dataset, we have focused on Gender to identify socio-phonetic differences. Age is another relevant factor that can be analysed to understand phonetic differences. This can be done in further stages of the research.

Speakers were recorded narrating stories, which is a good source of naturalistic data. This is a relevant characteristic in this study, since it is the type of data that is generally available for endangered languages and much suitable for socio-phonetic analyses, as compared to more controlled data such as wordlists and isolated tokens (e.g. Hay and Foulkes, 2016; Grama et al., 2020; Catherine E. Travis and Ghina, 2021).

3.4 Data format

The structure of the transcription files varies according to the format given by corpus developers. In the current case, the transcription format is available as XML files (See Figure 2 for reference). In the original recordings there were at least two speakers per file: one interviewer and a speaker, but the transcriptions provided included the transcription for the speakers only.

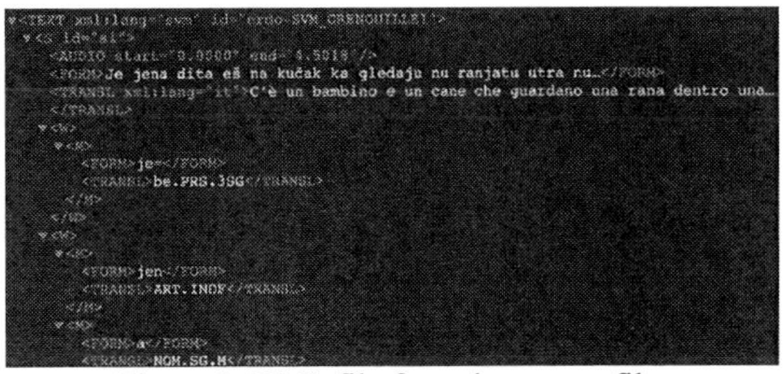

Figure 2: XML file from the source file.

The transcription files were processed in R, using a script developed by the main author. The script first identifies the sentence ID (`<S id="s1">` in Figure 2), under which three dependent sections are extracted: the start time, end time (`<AUDIO start="0.0000" end="4.5018"/>`), and the transcribed sentence (`<FORM>Je jena dita eš na kučak ka gledaju nu ranjatu utra nu...</FORM>`). The audio files were available in MP3 format, sampled with 44.1 kHz. They had different durations, with the shortest file being 38 seconds and the largest 7.5 minutes, and the mean duration being 2 minutes in length.

4 Forced-Alignment Process

The forced-alignment process involves four main stages, presented in Figure 3. Each stage is expanded in the section below. One important observation for these stages is that investing time in the pre-processing of the files would ensure better outputs and dealing with less bugs in future stages. We present some recommendations in each section.

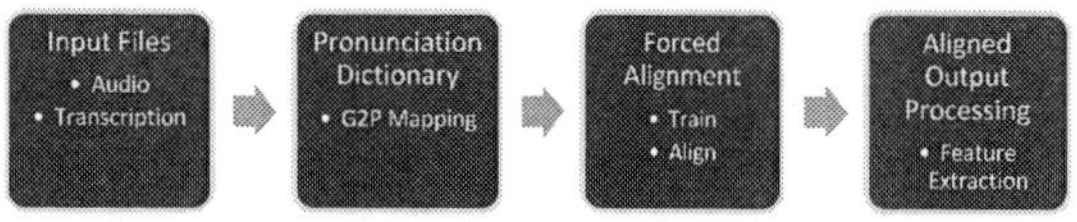

Figure 3: Main stages in the forced alignment process.

4.1 Pronunciation Dictionary from Input Files

First, a pronunciation dictionary must be created. In some approaches, these dictionaries are created from a lexicon file available for the language. However, for languages without curated lexicon files, pronunciation dictionaries can be created from the orthographic transcriptions. In this study, we took the available raw transcription of the data and then tokenized the transcriptions to have unique individual words.

These are then used to create the g2p (grapheme to phoneme) mapping. The amount of processing for creating this dictionary varies from language to language. For example, in Spanish there is a closer letter to phoneme mapping, where there is an almost full mapping between orthographic letters and phonemes, except for silent 'h' and digraphs ('ll', 'ch') (Gonzalez, 2022). This is different from English, where the mapping cannot always follow the orthographic spelling. As an example, the orthographic letter 'a' can have different phonemic representations, e.g. /eɪ/, /ə/, /aː/. The latter case would present a more challenging task for the mapping. For the case of Acquaviva Collecroce, the transcriptions done by the original creators was a broad phonological representation. This facilitated the g2p task and we decided to split words into individual letters, which are then considered the phonemes for each entry, as shown in Figure 4 below.

```
baliže   b a l i ž e
balun    b a l u n
balunič  b a l u n i č
baluniča     b a l u n i č a
bane     b a n e
banu     b a n u
baratol  b a r a t o l
baštunam     b a š t u n a m
baštunič     b a š t u n i č
```

Figure 4: Sample entries for the pronunciation dictionary.

In this case, the g2p mapping had a one-to-one correspondence. However, this is not always that case. In cases where no such correspondence exists in the transcription file, as in the Spanish example, the recommendation is to assign a phonemic symbol that does not overlap with other symbols. This must be done a priori before creating the dictionary so in the final product each grapheme or grapheme sequence is accounted for.

4.2 Transcriptions in TextGrid Format

The first processing of the text involves text normalization, which includes identifying spelling mistakes, non-speech annotations (e.g. notes from the transcribers, alternative pronunciations, etc.). This ensures that all entries can be mapped to the same word and not having multiple forms for the same entry. Another step here is to identify whether there are special characters that should not be included in the text, such as parenthesis, brackets, and slashes. Once the text has been normalized, the next step is to convert the text into a time-stamped file, since available forced aligners read transcriptions with time-stamped formats.

An R script was developed to create transcription files in TextGrid files, a format used in Praat (Boersma and Weenink, 2022). This format is widely used in linguistics, with strong emphasis for acoustic phonetic analysis. TextGrids are files containing time-stamped texts. The content is divided into tiers, where the text can be split into smaller sections with their respective boundaries. This is very useful when researchers need to break the content into different categories, such as identifying different speakers or annotating different linguistic layers, such as words, segments, features, for example. A sample TextGrid file from our data is shown in Figure 5, together with its corresponding audio file represented in the waveform above.

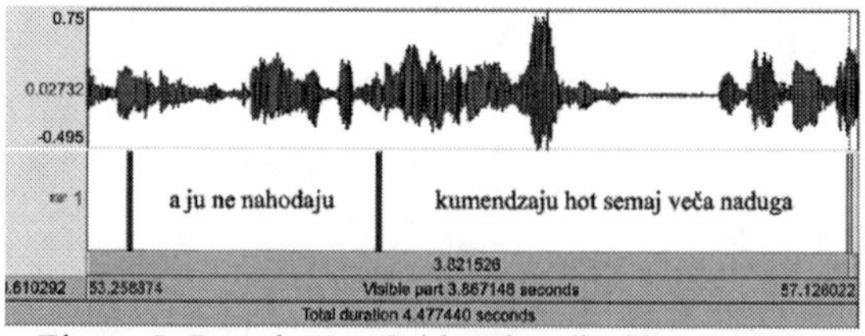

Figure 5: Sample TextGrid and audio files, with the transcription tier.

The figure shows the transcription for one speaker. The blue lines represent the time boundaries which correlate with the time information from the audio file. Based on our experience, we have identified that the size of the intervals has an impact on the output of the forced aligned file.

Since aligners analyze the acoustic signal as linear in time, if there are alignment errors at the beginning of an interval, they will likely roll the error over the following segment boundaries in the same interval. For example, if the aligner marks the beginning of a stop sound earlier than the actual start (e.g., due to a spike in the acoustic signal caused by a cough or a mouse click), then this will also influence where the boundaries of the following segments are placed. If the error is at the start of a long interval, then it will most likely render the full interval inaccurate. However, if the error takes place at the beginning of a shorter interval, less data will be compromised, because the acoustic mapping restarts at the beginning of each interval. Thus, we recommend the intervals are closely mapped with natural pauses and speech boundaries. This will also facilitate the mapping of words into natural speech units.

4.3 Running the Forced Alignment

Once we have prepared the pronunciation dictionary and transcription files with the corresponding audio files, the next step is to run the forced aligner. Previous studies have shown that the Montreal Forced Aligner (MFA) (McAuliffe et al., 2017), based on Kaldi (Povey et al., 2011), is one of the most accurate aligners currently available, especially used in sociophonetic studies (Gonzalez et al., 2020). We used the MFA following the instructions from the source website https://montreal-forced-aligner.readthedocs.io/en/latest/. The main challenge here is to have the correct setup to ensure that the aligner runs though the data without any bugs. For this, it is recommended to have all audio files in the same format, including, bit rate, sampling rate, and following good labelling practice for the files (which is mainly relevant for feature extraction in future stages).

4.4 Forced alignment outputs

MFA provides the aligned outputs as TextGrid files with two tiers, one for the forced-aligned words and another for the forced-aligned phonemic segments. We have found it efficient to recombine this output with the original input in the same TextGrid to include the utterance-level transcription. This is especially important when examining features such as intonation and prosodic patterns, where whole utterances would be relevant for analysis and not just words and segments on their own. The output would then be as shown in Figure 6 below.

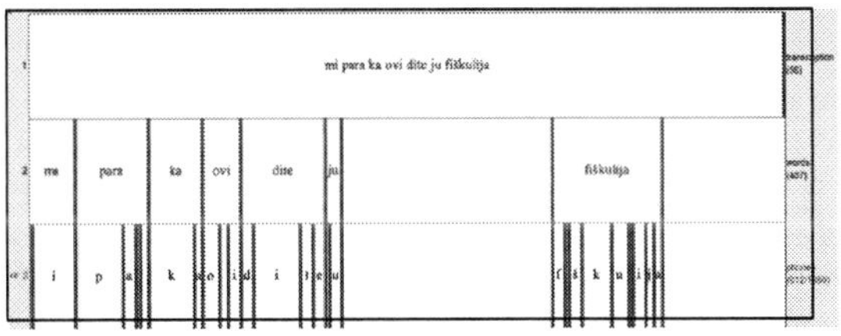

Figure 6: TextGrid with combined tiers: original transcription (Tier 1), and aligned words (Tier 2) and phonemes (Tier 3).

As with any automatic process, a sanity check is always important to assess the accuracy of the outputs. Previous studies have identified that the errors can be systematic, with some phonological contexts being more susceptible for more inaccuracies (Gonzalez et al., 2020). In this case, we propose an initial assessment where duration can be used to look at errors. This is based on durational differences, where outliers, too long or too short, can be considered errors in the alignment. It is also common practice in cases where there are enough resources to manually check a proportion of the outputs by trained phoneticians.

5 Data Wrangling (Data Processing)

In this stage, we gather all the data from the TextGrids, which also prepares them for the extraction of acoustic and phonetic features. This process is done in R (R Core Team, 2022), using a combination of libraries such as rPraat (Boril and Skarnitzl, 2016), dplyr (Wickham et al., 2022), tidyr (Wickham and Girlich, 2022), for example. The main frequency counts from the forced aligned outputs are shown in Table 2.

Speaker	Gender	Consonants	Vowels	Words
GN	Male	4298	3573	2012
GR	Male	3175	2588	1487
PG	Female	204	159	103
PG	Male	491	389	252
PL	Male	3569	2920	1668
SN	Female	2866	2449	1483
Total		**14603**	**12078**	**7005**

Table 2: Main frequency Counts from forced aligned outputs.

We extract all the information from the three tiers: utterance, word, and phoneme. This process takes phoneme labels, start and end time information, and phonological contexts (previous and following segments). Then, the same type of information is extracted for words and utterances. The final product is a full description of each phoneme with its environments, phonetic, phonemic, and lexical, as shown in Figure 7 below.

Speaker	Gender	Previous	Segment	Following	Duration	PrevWord	Word	FollWord	WordDur
GN	M	l	e	d	0.12	ka	gledaju	nu	0.52
GN	M	r	a	n	0.17	nu	ranjatu	utra	0.6
GR	M	r	i	v	0.09	je	riva	prije	0.17
GR	M	t	u	c	0.04	je	tuculala	di	0.44
PG	F	v	i	d	0.08	bi	vidila	ka	0.32
PG	F	d	i	p	0.1	nonda	di	parket	0.18

Figure 7: Sample output after data wrangling.

5.1 Acoustic Features

Acoustic features are a crucial component in socio-phonetic studies. There is a wide range of acoustic features that can be used, and here we focus on three, namely, Intensity (used in prosody), Pitch (prosody and tonality), and Formants (vowels and sonorant consonants). These features cover a wide range of areas of interest. We use Praat as the main program for extracting the acoustic values, taking as input the time-specified data wrangled in the previous stage.

For the acoustic information to be extracted, the first step is to convert each audio file into a formant file in Praat. From this file, we can then extract information from the F1 and F2 for vowel analysis. Based on some experimentation, we have identified that combining R and Praat can streamline the process more efficiently, by using each program to their best capacity. For example, R is very efficient at data wrangling and analysis, but Praat cannot efficiently dealt with the level of wrangling and dataset processing as in R, especially when dealing with multiple file formats. On the other hand, Praat is much more efficient at acoustic processing and querying phonetic features as compared to R. This is why we do the data wrangling in R and the feature extraction in Praat. We then do the data analysis in R again once all the necessary information has been collected from the audio, formant, and TextGrid files.

5.2 Populating Data from Praat

Once this step is finished, we have a fully annotated dataset with individual features and their corresponding acoustic features. This functions as the main data hub from which various analyses can be carried out from the dataset. In the following stages, we present the steps for processing vowels and prepare them for acoustic analysis (See Figure 8).

Segment	Speaker	Time	formant_1	pitchValue	intensityValue	mfcc_5
e	GN_M_1	0.324	435.644779	143.2858523	72.95193861	146.0820365
a	GN_M_1	0.678	540.9370843	128.096409	74.44932052	155.946977
i	GN_M_1	1.11	335.1292519	153.6110352	71.98936304	170.2450033
a	GR_M_1	52.1712	486.1003805	139.0686298	80.94875149	124.2078462
e	GR_M_1	52.2932	486.8311409	132.6412425	80.45326531	95.35667664
o	GR_M_1	52.3532	397.4000227	141.6490183	84.11465582	102.6605409
u	PG_M_1	10.0255	337.7970078	159.3213093	76.3552603	-100.4482523
i	PG_M_1	10.8055	639.8518027	136.3856407	68.11278488	-107.7933192
u	PG_M_1	10.8355	385.7087415	133.8610273	74.54216515	-118.1969266

Figure 8: Sample output after feature extraction.

5.3 Vowel Analysis and Visualization

Identifying Vowels in the Dataset: The analysis of vowels must account for important differences in each speaker's vocal tract. To have interpretable and robust comparisons, there must be a process of normalization techniques that give more credibility to analysis. In this study, we apply vowel normalization based on the Lobanov (Lobanov, 1971) technique. This allows the analysis of both static and dynamic measurements to be compared across speakers. Again, this gives researchers of endangered languages quick access to the vocalic spaces in the data. In this process, we use the vowel package (Kendall and Thomas, 2018) for vowel normalization and ggplot2 (Wickham, 2016) for data visualization.

Visualization and Analysis: The visualization gives importance access to vowel behaviors in the data, and this can be split into the sociolinguistic factors available, in this case, Gender. Figure 9 shows the vowel duration of a selection of five landmark vowels and their differences based on Gender. The data indicates that there is an increasing mean duration starting from /a/, then /e/, /i/ and /u/, ending in /o/, which is the longest vowel. The mean durations are similar for both Genders, but with more distinctions for /o/ and /u/. Further statistical differences can reveal whether ther are significant differences based on phonological contexts.

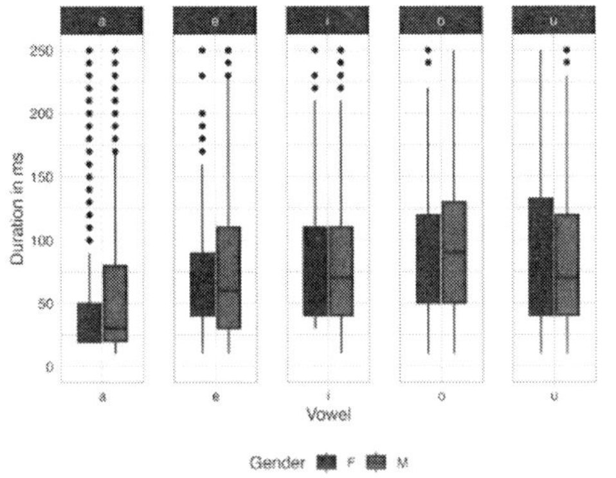

Figure 9: Vowel durations and Gender Differences.

Different from duration analysis, vocalic space analysis reveals important differences for Genders in Figure 10. First, the selection of the five vowels shows a different picture from the location of /u/, as compared to other languages such as French, English and Spanish, where the /u/ is higher and more retracted. In terms of the spread, it shows that Males are producing more compressed vowels than Females, especially for the Front non-Low vowels /i/ and /e/. Mean durations, represented by point size, shows that the main durational differences are observed for /a/. This is an indication that if there is a first potential area to examine socio-phonetic differences would be the formant and duration differences between Males and Females.

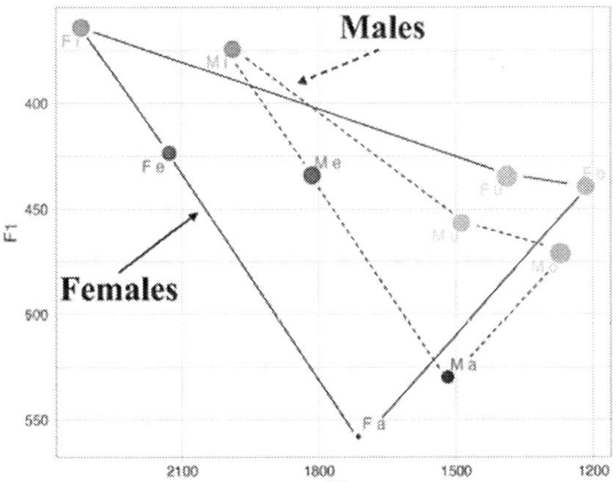

Figure 10: Vowel space for Males and Females from normalized formant values. Vowel size represents mean durations.

5.4 Assessing Consonantal Analysis

For the consonant analysis, we look at duration differences for the Coronal fricatives /s, z/ (alveolar) and /š, ž/ (Post-Alveolar), split by Gender. Two main observations can be drawn from Figure 11 below. First, durations are similar, but with Post-Alveolars having wider spread than Alveolars. Second, Females are producing mean larger durations than Males, except for /ž/. This indicates that the differences for these consonants are likely more based on Gender differences rather than phonological factors, a question than can be further studied with in-depth analysis.

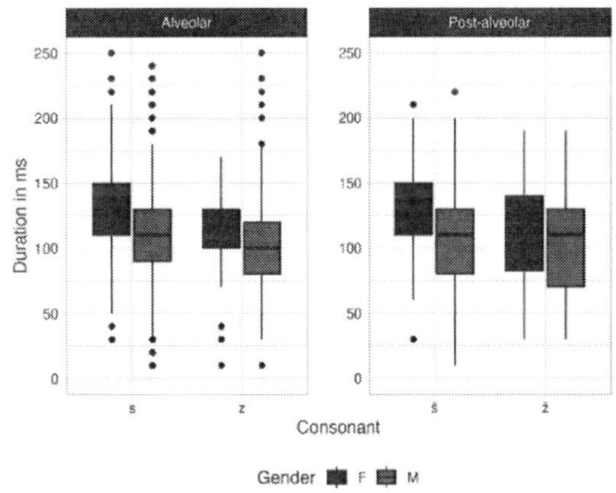

Figure 11: Coronal Fricative Duration Differences across Place of Articulation and Gender.

5.5 Assessing Prosodic Features

Finally, we look at pith as a suprasegmental feature. Figure 12 shows the pitch tracks for a section of the recording of speaker GN Male. There are six main utterances with their intonations shown in the blue lines. The arrows in each number represent the trajectory of the intonation, with all having a falling pattern, except from 5 having a slight rising pattern. These intonation patterns can further be examined with the output and prepared data.

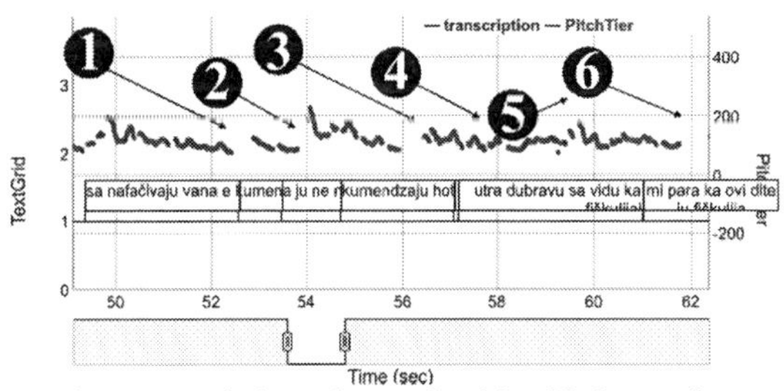

Figure 12: Pitch tracks used to identify intonation patterns in the language.

6 Discussion

This paper presents a roadmap of tools, from data processing to socio-phonetic analysis. We have taken Acquaviva Collecroce, an endangered language and whose data can be freely accessible.

This work has put together a range of computational tools and packages that can facilitate data processing and analysis in a simple, yet efficient way. Table 3 shows a summary of the tools. It is not our intention to present an ultimate workflow, but rather a practical toolkit that allows users to implement it in endangered language studies. The resource materials are open source and can be adapted an expanded to the required needs of the users.

Oder	Stage	Program	Description
1	Pre-Processing	R	Data gathering
2	Pre-Processing	Praat	TextGrid creation
3	Alignment	Python	Running the forced alignment
4	Post-Processing	R	Wrangling outputs
5	Acoustic Features	Praat	Extracting phonetic features
6	Analysis	R	Data visualization and main analyses

Table 3: Main stages of the workflow, with the corresponding program languages.

7 Conclusions

The field of computational linguistics is making invaluable contributions to the perseveration and revitalization of endangered languages. In this paper, we have a presented a set of relevant computational tools developed to help researchers from forced alignment to acoustic phonetic studies, including segmental and suprasegmental analysis. We have developed the tools for an endangered language, Acquaviva Collecroce, which is a practical example of the power and applicability of the tools presented here.

8 Future Work

Our future work will include an online application where these steps are streamlined and automated from user inputs to visualizing results and carrying out linguistic analysis. This is work in progress and we hope this contributes to the technologies developed to help endangered languages globally.

References

Oliver Adams, Trevor Cohn, Graham Neubig, & Alexis Michaud. 2017. Phonemic transcription of low-resource tonal languages. In *Proceedings of the Australasian Language Technology Association Workshop*, Brisbane, 6–8 December, 53–60. (https://www.aclweb.org/anthology/U17-1006/)

Oliver Adams, Trevor Cohn, Graham Neubig, Hilaria Cruz, Steven Bird, and Alexis Michaud. 2018. Evaluating phonemic transcription of low-resource tonal languages for language documentation. In *LREC 2018 (Language Resources and Evaluation Conference)*, pages 3356–3365.

Oliver Adams, Benjamin Galliot, Guillaume Wisniewski, Nicholas Lambourne, Ben Foley, Rahasya Sanders-Dwyer, Janet Wiles, Alexis Michaud, Séverine Guillaume, Laurent Besacier, et al. 2020. User-friendly automatic transcription of lowresource languages: Plugging ESPnet into Elpis. In *ComputEL-4: Fourth Workshop on the Use of Computational Methods in the Study of Endangered Languages*, pages 51–62.

Jonathan D. Amith, Jiatong Shi and Rey Castillo García. 2021. End-to-End Automatic Speech Recognition: Its Impact on the Workflow for Documenting Yoloxóchitl Mixtec. In *Proceedings of the First Workshop on Natural Language Processing for Indigenous Languages of the Americas*, pages 64–80 June 11, 2021. ©2021 Association for Computational Linguistics

Jonathan D. Amith and Rey Castillo García. 2020. *Audio corpus of Yoloxóchitl Mixtec with accompanying time-coded transcriptons in ELAN.* http://www.openslr.org/89/. Accessed: 2021-03-05.

Evangelia Adamou and Walter Breu. 2013. Présentation du programme EUROSLAV 2010. Base de données électronique de variétés slaves menacées dans des pays européens non slavophones. In: S. Kempgen, M. Wingender, N. Franz, M. Jakiša (eds.), Deutsche Beiträge zum 15. *Internationalen Slavistenkongress Minsk* 2013. München, 13–23.

Paul Boersma and David Weenink. 2022. *Praat: doing phonetics by computer* [Computer program]. Version 6.3, retrieved 15 November 2022 from http://www.praat.org/.

Tomas Boril and Radek Skarnitzl. 2016. Tools rPraat and mPraat. In Sojka P, Horák A, Kopeček I, Pala K (eds.), *Text, Speech, and Dialogue: 19th International Conference, TSD* 2016, Brno, Czech Republic, September 12-16, 2016, Proceedings, 367–374. ISBN 978-3-319-45510-5, doi:10.1007/978-3-319-45510-5_42, http://dx.doi.org/10.1007/978-3-319-45510-5_42.

Walter Breu. 2020, online 1. "Molise Slavic", in: *Encyclopedia of Slavic Languages and Linguistics Online*, Editor-in-Chief Marc L. Greenberg. Consulted online on 20 August 2020. First published online: 2020 http://dx.doi.org/10.1163/2589-6229_ESLO_COM_034736

Walter Breu. 2017. Slavische Mikrosprachen im absoluten Sprachkontakt. Band I. Moliseslavische Texte aus Acquaviva Collecroce, Montemitro und San Felice del Molise. *Glossierte und interpretierte Sprachaufnahmen aus Italien, Deutschland, Österreich und Griechenland.* Wiesbaden.

Malgorzata Cavar, Damir ´ Cavar, and Hilaria Cruz. 2016. Endangered language documentation: Bootstrapping a Chatino speech corpus, forced aligner, ASR. In *Proceedings of the Tenth International Conference on Language Resources and Evaluation (LREC'16)*, pages 4004–4011.

Rolando Coto-Solano and Sofía Flores Solórzano. 2017. Comparison of two forced alignment systems for aligning Bribri speech. *CLEI Electronic Journal* 20(1). 2:1–2:13.

Ben Foley, Josh Arnold, Rolando Coto-Solano, Gautier Durantin, E Mark, Daan van Esch, Scott Heath, Frantisek Kratochvil, Zara Maxwell-Smith, David Nash, et al. 2018. Building speech recognition systems for language documentation: The CoEDL Endangered Language Pipeline and Inference System (ELPIS). *The 6th Intl. Workshop on Spoken Language Technologies for Under-Resourced Languages.*

Ben Foley, Alina Rakhi, Nicholas Lambourne, Nicholas Buckeridge, and Janet Wiles. 2019. ELPIS: An accessible speech-to-text tool. *Proc. Interspeech 2019*, pages 4624–4625.

Robert Fromont and Kevin Watson. 2016. Factors influencing automatic segmental alignment of sociophonetic corpora. Corpora 11(3). 401–431.

Simon Gonzalez, Catherine Travis, James Grama, Danielle Barth, and Sunkulp Ananthanarayan. 2018. Recursive forced alignment: A test on a minority language. 145-148. In *17th Australasian International Conference on Speech Science and Technology.*

Simon Gonzalez, James Grama, and Catherine E. Travis. 2020. Comparing the performance of forced aligners used in sociophonetic research. *Linguistics Vanguard*, vol. 6, no. 1, 2020, pp. 20190058. https://doi.org/10.1515/lingvan-2019-0058

Simon Gonzalez. 2022. The Development of a Comprehensive Spanish Dictionary for Phonetic and Lexical Tagging in Socio-phonetic Research (ESPADA). In *Proceedings of the 16th Linguistic Annotation Workshop (LAW-XVI) @LREC 2022*, pages 8–14, Marseille, 24 June 2022

James Grama, Catherine E. Travis, and Simon Gonzalez. 2020. Ethnolectal and community change ov(er) time: Word-final (er) in Australian English. *Australian Journal of Linguistics*, vol 40, no. 3, pp. 346-368. https://doi.org/10.1080/07268602.2020.1823818

Vishwa Gupta and Gilles Boulianne. 2020. Speech transcription challenges for resource constrained indigenous language Cree. In *Proceedings of the 1st Joint Workshop on Spoken Language Technologies for Under-resourced languages (SLTU) and Collaboration and Computing for Under-Resourced Languages (CCURL)*, pages 362–367.

Jen Hay and Paul Foulkes. 2016. The evolution of medial /t/ over real and remembered time. *Language* 92(2): 298-330. http://dx.doi.org/10.1353/lan.2016.0036.

Kristine A. Hildebrandt, Carmen Jany, and Wilson Silva. 2017. Documenting variation in endangered languages. *Language Documentation & Conservation Special Publication 14.* University of Hawai'i Press.

Nils Hjortnaes, Niko Partanen, Michael Rießler, and Francis M Tyers. 2020. Towards a speech recognizer for Komi: An endangered and low-resource Uralic language. In *Proceedings of the Sixth International Workshop on Computational Linguistics of Uralic Languages*, pages 31–37.

Robbie Jimerson and Emily Prud'hommeaux. 2018. ASR for documenting acutely under-resourced indigenous languages. In *Proceedings of the Eleventh International Conference on Language Resources and Evaluation (LREC 2018).*

Robert Jimerson, Kruthika Simha, Ray Ptucha, and Emily Prud'hommeaux. 2018. Improving ASR output for endangered language documentation. In *The 6th Intl. Workshop on Spoken Language Technologies for Under-Resourced Languages.*

Tyler Kendall and Erik R. Thomas. 2018. *vowels: Vowel Manipulation, Normalization, and Plotting.* http://blogs.uoregon.edu/vowels/.

B. M. Lobanov. 1971. Classification of Russian vowels spoken by different listeners. *Journal of the Acoustical Society of America* 49:606-08.

Gina-Anne Levow. 2019. Promoting Language Technology for Endangered Languages with Shared Tasks. In *Proceedings of the Language Technologies for All (LT4All)*, pages 116–119, Paris, UNESCO Headquarters, 5-6 December, 2019.

Gina-Anne Levow, Emily P. Ahn, Emily M. Bender. 2021. Developing a Shared Task for Speech Processing on Endangered Languages. In

Proceedings of the 4th Workshop on the Use of Computational Methods in the Study of Endangered Languages, 1:96–106, Online, March 2–3, 2021.

Kohei Matsuura, Sei Ueno, Masato Mimura, Shinsuke Sakai, and Tatsuya Kawahara. 2020. Speech corpus of Ainu folklore and end-to-end speech recognition for Ainu language. In *Proceedings of The 12th Language Resources and Evaluation Conference*, pages 2622–2628.

Michael McAuliffe, Michaela Socolof, Sarah Mihuc, Michael Wagner, and Morgan Sonderegger. 2017. Montreal Forced Aligner: Trainable text-speech alignment using Kaldi. *INTERSPEECH-2017*, Stockholm Sweden, 498–502.

Boyd Michailovsky, Martine Mazaudon, Alexis Michaud, Séverine Guillaume, Alexandre François, and Evangelia Adamou. 2014. Documenting and researching endangered languages: the Pangloss Collection. *Language Documentation & Conservation*, 8:119–135.

Alexis Michaud, Oliver Adams, Trevor Anthony Cohn, Graham Neubig, and Séverine Guillaume. 2018. Integrating automatic transcription into the language documentation workflow: Experiments with Na data and the Persephone toolkit. *Language Documentation & Conservation*, 12.

Vikramjit Mitra, Andreas Kathol, Jonathan D Amith, and Rey Castillo García. 2016. Automatic speech transcription for low-resource languages: The case of Yoloxóchitl Mixtec (Mexico). In *Proc. Interspeech 2016*, pages 3076–3080.

Daniel Povey, Arnab Ghoshal, Gilles Boulianne, Lukas Burget, Ondrej Glembek, Nagendra Goel, Mirko Hannemann, Petr Motlicek, Yanmin Qian, Petr Schwarz, et al. 2011. The kaldi speech recognition toolkit. In *IEEE 2011 workshop on Automatic Speech Recognition and Understanding, CONF*, pages 1–4. IEEE Signal Processing Society

Emily Prud'hommeaux, Robbie Jimerson, Richard Hatcher, and Karin Michelson. 2021. Automatic Speech Recognition for Supporting Endangered Language Documentation. *Language Documentation & Conservation,* 15:491-513

R Core Team. 2022. *R: A language and environment for statistical computing.* R Foundation for Statistical Computing, Vienna, Austria. URL https://www.R-project.org/.

Jiatong Shi, Jonathan D. Amith, Rey Castillo García, Esteban Guadalupe Sierra, Kevin Duh, and Shinji Watanabe. 2021. Leveraging end-to-end ASR for endangered language documentation: An empirical study on Yoloxóchitl Mixtec. *arXiv* preprint arXiv:2101.10877.

Bao Thai, Robert Jimerson, Raymond Ptucha, and Emily Prud'hommeaux. 2020. Fully convolutional ASR for less-resourced endangered languages. In *Proceedings of the 1st Joint Workshop on Spoken Language Technologies for Under-resourced languages (SLTU) and Collaboration and Computing for Under-Resourced Languages (CCURL)*, pages 126–130.

Catherine E. Travis and Inas Ghina. 2021. Gender, mobility and contact: Stability and change in an Acehnese dialect. *Asia-Pacific Language Variation.* 7(2): 142-167. https://doi.org/10.1075/aplv.20007.tra

Hadley Wickham. 2016. *ggplot2: Elegant Graphics for Data Analysis.* Springer-Verlag New York. ISBN 978-3-319-24277-4, https://ggplot2.tidyverse.org.

Hadley Wickham and Maximilian Girlich. 2022. *tidyr: Tidy Messy Data.* https://tidyr.tidyverse.org, https://github.com/tidyverse/tidyr.

Hadley Wickham, Romain François, Lionel Henry, and Kirill Müller. 2022. *dplyr: A Grammar of Data Manipulation.* https://dplyr.tidyverse.org, https://github.com/tidyverse/dplyr.

Studying the impact of language model size for low-resource ASR

Zoey Liu
University of Florida
liu.ying@ufl.edu

Justin Spence
University of California, Davis
jspence@ucdavis.edu

Emily Prud'hommeaux
Boston College
prudhome@bc.edu

Abstract

This paper investigates the impact of language model (LM) size on low-resource ASR, using data from five widely-spoken low-resource languages and one endangered Native American language. Our findings demonstrate that having larger LMs does not necessarily result in lower WER; this is most evident for the endangered language, where larger LMs actually led to significantly worse performance than that observed in the widely-spoken low-resource languages. We conjecture that one of the potential driving forces behind this discrepancy is the domain mismatch between the transcripts of the audio data and the supplementary texts used to train the LM. We discuss the implications of our results in the context of creating ASR corpora for low-resource languages.

1 Motivation

The language model (LM) has long been noted as an important component for the decoding process of automatic speech recognition (ASR) (Bahl et al., 1989; Chelba et al., 2012; Sak et al., 2012; Arisoy et al., 2015; Park et al., 2019). The texts used for training LMs usually consist of transcripts of the audio training data along with additional texts from other sources, such as Web text, literature, or transcripts of previously recorded audio (see Section 3). When building an ASR corpus, researchers typically make efforts to gather large amounts of these supplementary texts in order to improve LM coverage and reduce out-of-vocabulary (OOV) rates.

For high-resource languages, considerable amounts of supplementary text are relatively easy to find and process. Acquiring additional data for low-resource languages can be more challenging. For some widely spoken low-resource languages, such as Swahili, which has millions of speakers and an established writing system, additional textual data can be acquired from websites and documents that have been digitized (Liu et al., 2022a). Thus, when building ASR corpora for widely spoken low-resource languages, researchers usually collect additional text data (Laleye et al., 2016; Juan et al., 2014; Gauthier et al., 2016).

The situation for endangered languages is much more complex. Collecting additional text for endangered languages often involves digitizing archival materials held by tribal authorities or archiving organizations. Processing these materials requires manual oversight and linguistic expertise, particularly when there are multiple conflicting orthographic traditions.

While obtaining additional texts for widely spoken low-resource languages may also be labor-intensive, it is more straightforward to ensure that the additional texts will belong to domains similar to that of the audio transcripts. In contrast, for endangered languages, particularly those of North America, the additional texts are often from restricted domains such as religious documents, grammar textbooks, or fieldwork materials from decades ago (Liu et al., 2022b). The subject matter and linguistic characteristics of these texts can be quite different from those of the recordings usually used for ASR acoustic training, which are typically recent recordings of elders telling stories or having conversations. These differences can lead to substantial *domain mismatch*.

These limitations on acquiring additional LM training text for low-resource languages raises the question: how important is additional text for improving low-resource ASR? Or put differently: is it necessary to take the time to acquire and process additional text to build a larger LM?

This study takes up these questions with data from five widely-spoken low-resource languages and one endangered language. We investigate to what extent and in what context LMs impact ASR performance. Given the different challenges for widely-spoken vs. truly low-resource languages, we expect the role of the LM to be different. It is

Language	Data sources		Audio			Additional written texts	
	Audio	Additional texts	Train	Test	N of words in audio training data	N of words	Proportion
Fongbe	daily living phrases	news; Bible	5h44m	1h26m	45,544	990,146	21.74
Wolof	read speech (Wikipedia/ Bible)	exactly same source as audio	15h11m	3h47m	121,220	601,639	4.96
Swahili	news	news; books	8h47m	2h11m	84,287	29,237,493	346.88
Iban	radio/television station	news	6h49m	1h42m	57,608	2,082,452	36.15
Bemba	literature; radio	religious magazines	19h40m	4h55m	106,657	4,614,319	43.26
Hupa (verified)	the elder's stories	grammar books	1h16m	19m	7,369	41,386	5.62
Hupa (coarse)	same as verified data	same as verified data	6h6m	1h31m	32,640		1.27

Table 1: Descriptive statistics for audio data and additional written texts used to train language models for each language in the experiments. Note that the numerical counts here were derived directly from the public repositories and may be different from those originally reported in the papers. **Proportion** refers to the relative ratio between N of words in additional texts and N of words in the transcripts of the audio training data.

possible that adding additional text to build larger LMs for an endangered language might not actually lower WER as much as one might expect, if at all.

2 Related Work

A number of studies have focused on providing ASR data sets and models for languages that have many speakers but limited existing ASR training resources (see Section 3), such as Fongbe (Laleye et al., 2016) and Iban (Juan et al., 2014). For languages that lack both resources and large numbers of speakers, there have also been efforts utilizing ASR technologies to support their documentation (Adams et al., 2018; Jimerson and Prud'hommeaux, 2018; Gupta and Boulianne, 2020b,a). For instance, Shi et al. (2021) built end-to-end models for the Oto-Manguean language, Yoloxóchitl Mixtec. Zahrer et al. (2020) studied phoneme recognition for the Muyu language from the Trans–New Guinea language family.

Another line of relevant work attends to investigating effective evaluation methods for low-resource ASR, in a way to strive for more generalizable model performance. Comparing three model architectures, including both neural and non-neural alternatives, across five languages, Morris et al. (2021) pointed out that no model architecture is a clear "winner"; rather the results for model rankings depend on the language. Liu et al. (forthcoming) explored how different data split methods influence WER scores for under-resourced scenarios using five languages as the test cases. Their findings demonstrated that the commonly-applied "held-out speakers" evaluation scheme for ASR falls short when there exists high speaker variability in the data set; in other words, the performance of ASR systems for low-resource languages, at least in the context that they investigated, is not *speaker-independent*.

3 Meet the data

We used ASR corpora for five widely-spoken low-resource languages, which are publicly available: Fongbe (Laleye et al., 2016), Wolof (Gauthier et al., 2016), Swahili (Gauthier et al., 2016), Iban (Juan et al., 2014), and Bemba (Sikasote and Anastasopoulos, 2022). We also included one data set developed for Hupa, a critically endangered language indigenous to North America. Details of the sources for the transcripts of the audio data and the additional texts gathered to train the LM are presented in Table 1. We present additional information for the Hupa language below.

The audio recordings for Hupa came from linguistic fieldwork which started in 2005 and is still ongoing. The recordings were produced by a single female elder speaker from the speech community, a scenario that is unfortunately common for critically endangered languages. Transcription of these recordings included several stages of manual correction, and ambiguous or unclear audio was confirmed with the elder before being considered as complete. Hence, some transcripts have been checked more thoroughly than others. Depending solely on the differences of transcription quality, the recordings and their transcripts were divided into two sets, which we will refer to as "verified" vs. "coarse" data respectively.

Looking across the data described here, it seems likely that there is less domain overlap between the audio data and the additional LM-training text for Hupa than for the other languages. For Fongbe, Swahili, Iban and Bemba, both the audio and the additional text are related to news or local radios; for Wolof, the audio data and the additional texts are from the exact same source. For Hupa, the grammar book data used for LM training are more formal in style and has little overlap in content with the contemporary fieldwork recordings.

4 Experiments

We probe whether the assumption that having a larger LM (i.e., an LM built on more words of training text) leads to lower WER will hold for low-resource languages. A recent study of ASR for Bemba (Sikasote and Anastasopoulos, 2022) compared the impact of two LMs on WER, one of which was 29 times larger than the other. The results showed that, surprisingly, the larger LM led to slightly worse performance than the smaller one. We sought to address whether the data of other languages demonstrates the same pattern. Specifically, we carried out different experimental settings (basic and simulated settings). In each setting we explored different configurations of the training texts for the LM in order to investigate the role of LM size on ASR performance.

4.1 Basic settings

For the data set(s) of each language, in the basic setting, we first created two different LMs, `LM_base` and `LM_large`: the former was built using *only* the transcripts of the audio training data, while training for the latter also included *all* the additional LM training text.

In addition to comparing ASR performance in a given language with and without supplementary LM training text, which can vary considerably in size, we also investigated the impact of the LM training corpus size relative to the size of the corpus of transcriptions. Note that for the coarse data set of Hupa, the size of the additional texts is only 1.27 times of that of the transcripts of the audio training data (Table 1). This is proportionally smaller by comparison to other languages as well as to the verified data set of Hupa. Therefore, for each of the other data sets, except for the coarse data of Hupa, we kept the audio training and test data the same, then randomly sampled (3 times) sentences from the additional texts such that the ratio between the size of these texts and that of the transcripts of the audio training data also approximates 1.27. These sampled sentences along with the transcripts of the audio training data were then combined to build what we refer to as a proportionally-sized LM, `LM_prop`.

4.2 Simulated settings

Given that the amount of audio training data is different for each language, it is possible that even when the LM size is the same proportionally, the WER results are dependent on the amount of audio. With that in mind, we also explored simulated settings to ensure that more fair conclusions could be drawn, especially when comparing widely-spoken vs. truly low-resource languages.

Here we focused on Fongbe, Iban, and Swahili (which have the smallest audio dataset sizes compared to Wolof and Bemba). Again, since Hupa has the least amount of either audio data (verified data set) or additional LM training text by proportion (coarse data set), our simulated settings involve data subsampling from each of the other three languages above in order to construct augmented data sets whose *audio training data size* is similar to that of the two data sets for Hupa. Hence, for each language, we created a verified and a coarse setting. (It would be ideal to create these two settings such that the audio data quality difference between the two mimic that between the verified and the coarse data sets of Hupa; however, it is not exactly clear how this can be achieved in a principled way, making it beyond the scope of this work.)

Take Iban as an example. Recall that each recording for every language has been manually segmented into utterances. For the verified setting, we first randomly sampled (3 times) a number of utterances such that the total duration of these utterances was similar to the total duration of audio of the verified data set for Hupa. We then created two different LMs, `LM_base` and `LM_prop` for the sampled audio data in the same way as we did for the basic settings described above. For the coarse setting, we carried out the same procedure except that the total duration of the sample audios was similar to that for the coarse data set of Hupa.

4.3 LMs and acoustic models

All LMs are trigram LMs trained with Witten-Bell discounting using the SRILM (Stolcke, 2002) toolkit. To build acoustic models, we used the open-source Kaldi toolkit (Povey et al., 2011). Specifically, we adopted a recipe of a fully connected deep neural network (DNN) from Kaldi with the default sequence training parameters; this model architecture has six hidden layers with 1024 hidden units in each. This architecture has been shown to outperform other statistical alternatives such as subspace Gaussian mixture models, as well as neural models such as the time delay neural networks (Morris et al., 2021; Morris, 2021).

For the data set of every language other than those for Swahili and Hupa, we conducted acoustic feature transformations for each individual speaker. For the data of Swahili, which lacks clear speaker identity information, and the two data sets of Hupa, which only contains recordings from one speaker, we carried out acoustic feature transformation for each recording date or recording session separately. Model training was carried out with state-level minimum Bayes risk criterion and a per-utterance Stochastic Gradient Descent weight update. For decoding, we used the Kaldi finite state transducer-based decoder.

4.4 Evaluation scheme

It is common to perform ASR evaluating using "held-out speaker(s)", namely holding out the data of one set of speakers as the test set and leaving the remaining data for training, without conducting cross-validation (i.e., using the data of different sets of speakers as the test set) (Gauthier et al., 2016; Zeyer et al., 2019). Nevertheless, Liu et al. (forthcoming) found this evaluation scheme to be problematic in that the performance of the acoustic models is *dependent on which speaker(s) were included in the test set*. Alternatively, they proposed using random splits, presenting strong evidence that the average WER across all held-out speakers is comparable not only to the average WER derived from multiple random splits of the full acoustic data, but also to the WER of *just one random split*.

Here we also adopted random splits for ASR evaluation. Specifically, the audio data of each language was randomly split into training/test sets (3 times) such that their respective total utterance duration approximates a ratio of 4:1.[1]

5 Results

We present the results from the basic settings in Table 2. Note that we are not trying to compare WER scores across languages, as they are evidently not comparable. Instead, our focus is to compare WER scores *derived from different LM sizes for each individual language*, then examine whether the effect of LM size is in the same direction across the data sets of the languages studied here. (While we attend to WER here, we also calculated character error rate (CER) as an additional evaluation metric; the patterns of CER largely follow those of WER). Table 2 suggests that having an LM built on a larger text data set does not always lead to lower WER. For widely-spoken low-resource languages, having larger LMs (both `LM_prop` and `LM_large`) resulted in lower WER for Iban, Bemba and Swahili. On the other hand, the WER scores became mildly worse for Fongbe and Wolof when the LM size was larger. Particularly for Hupa, the truly low-resource language studied here, larger LMs had a negative impact; this is most evident in the case of the coarse data set, where `LM_large` actually increased WER score by 37.73% compared to `LM_base`.

To further examine whether LM size potentially has a different effect on Hupa compared to other languages, and that the effects are not necessarily caused by other languages having more audio data, let us turn to the results from the simulated settings. As demonstrated in Table 3, in both the verified and coarse settings for most languages except for Fongbe, larger LM size resulted in lower WER

[1]Note that the ASR corpora of most languages here provide a lexicon file (required by Kaldi), possibly extracted from external dictionaries, for the decoding process of the acoustic models. Since we are interested in the size of LMs, we tried to control for additional factors as much as possible. Therefore every time a new model was to be trained, we generated a lexicon file directly from the corresponding LM.

Language	LM_base	LM_prop		LM_large	
	WER (CER)	WER (CER)	WER (CER) reduction	WER (CER)	WER (CER) reduction
Fongbe	59.81 (0.36)	60.44 (0.37)	-1.05 (-2.78)	61.7 (0.36)	-3.16 (0)
Wolof	28.75 (0.15)	29.11 (0.14)	-1.25 (6.67)	29.41 (0.14)	-2.3 (6.67)
Swahili	30.24 (0.13)	28.59 (0.13)	5.46 (0)	25.35 (0.11)	16.17 (15.38)
Iban	14.8 (0.06)	14.8 (0.06)	0 (0)	13.53 (0.05)	8.58 (16.67)
Bemba	46.09 (0.12)	44.38 (0.12)	3.71 (0)	42.82 (0.11)	7.09 (8.33)
Hupa (verified)	54.06 (0.31)	56.42 (0.29)	-4.37 (6.45)	54.83 (0.32)	-1.42 (-3.23)
Hupa (coarse)	43.68 (0.22)	-	-	60.16 (0.31)	-37.73 (-40.91)

Table 2: Evaluation results from basic settings; *reduction* (%) refers to WER (CER) reduction compared to the WER (CER) (%) when using `LM_base`.

Language	Setting	LM_base	LM_prop	
		WER/CER	WER/CER	reduction
Fongbe	verified	66.29 (0.42)	67.65 (0.46)	-2.05 (-9.52)
Fongbe	coarse	-	-	-
Swahili	verified	54.86 (0.28)	50.84 (0.26)	7.33 (7.14)
Swahili	coarse	30.42 (0.14)	28.26 (0.13)	7.1 (7.14)
Iban	verified	30.07 (0.13)	26.93 (0.12)	10.44 (7.69)
Iban	coarse	15.38 (0.06)	14.41 (0.06)	6.31 (0)

Table 3: Evaluation results from simulated settings; note that course setting does not apply to Fongbe given its audio data size; *verified* and *coarse* refer to the simulated settings following the setup of Hupa, and do not refer to the quality of the data; *reduction* (%) refers to WER (CER) reduction compared to the WER (CER) (%) when using `LM_base`.

instead, indicating better model performance.

These findings have two implications. First, they suggest that the influence of LM size on ASR performance varies between widely-spoken and truly low-resource languages, and that larger LMs are more likely to have negative effects for the latter, at least in the settings that we investigated. One possible explanation for this discrepancy is that described in Section 3, namely that there often exists a more substantial domain mismatch between the transcripts of the audio data and the additional LM texts for endangered languages, an important factor that was not mitigated by simply having more training texts for LMs. Second, comparing the results from Table 2 and Table 3, for widely-spoken low-resource languages in particular, it seems that the impact of LM size could also interact with the size of the audio data, in the sense that when the amount of audio data is small, having a larger LM tends to have more positive influence on ASR performance.

6 Discussion and Conclusion

With data from five widely-spoken low-resource languages and one endangered language of North America, we studied the impact of LM size on ASR performance. Our results demonstrate that, perhaps surprisingly, having larger LMs does not always result in lower WER. This observation is the most pronounced for the truly low-resource (endangered) language in contrast to the widely-spoken low-resource languages. In addition, our findings suggest that the effect of LM size is potentially modulated by the amount of audio data available; larger LMs more consistently lead to better model performance when the amount of audio data is relatively small.

The aforementioned observations indicate there would be value in collecting additional texts to build ASR corpora for widely-spoken low-resource languages. However, they raise questions about the utility of such endeavors for endangered languages, when the domain of these texts might be very different from that of the audio transcripts. For future work, it would be worthwhile to study a wider set of typologically diverse languages with varying sizes for the LMs, in order to assess how the languages' phonological and morphological properties might potentially affect ASR performance. Additionally, one should carry out experiments comparing the impact of LMs whose training texts are explicitly from different domains, which would help further confirm the influence of domain mismatch. Relevant findings could in turn inform the creation of ASR corpora for low-resource languages broadly.

Acknowledgements

We are grateful for the continued support from the Hupa indigenous community. We would like to especially thank Mrs. Verdena Parker for her generous and valuable input for the documentation work of Hupa throughout the years. In addition, we thank the anonymous reviewers for their helpful feedback. This material is based upon work supported by the National Science Foundation under Grant #2127309 to the Computing Research Association for the CIFellows Program, and Grant #1761562. Any opinions, findings, and conclusions or recommendations expressed in this material are those of the author(s) and do not necessarily reflect the views of the National Science Foundation nor the Computing Research Association.

References

Oliver Adams, Trevor Cohn, Graham Neubig, Hilaria Cruz, Steven Bird, and Alexis Michaud. 2018. Evaluation phonemic transcription of low-resource tonal languages for language documentation. In *Proceedings of the Eleventh International Conference on Language Resources and Evaluation (LREC 2018)*, Miyazaki, Japan. European Language Resources Association (ELRA).

Ebru Arisoy, Abhinav Sethy, Bhuvana Ramabhadran, and Stanley Chen. 2015. Bidirectional recurrent neural network language models for automatic speech recognition. In *2015 IEEE International Conference on Acoustics, Speech and Signal Processing (ICASSP)*, pages 5421–5425. IEEE.

Lalit R Bahl, Peter F Brown, Peter V de Souza, and Robert L Mercer. 1989. A tree-based statistical language model for natural language speech recognition. *IEEE Transactions on Acoustics, Speech, and Signal Processing*, 37(7):1001–1008.

Ciprian Chelba, Dan Bikel, Maria Shugrina, Patrick Nguyen, and Shankar Kumar. 2012. Large scale language modeling in automatic speech recognition. *arXiv preprint arXiv:1210.8440*.

Elodie Gauthier, Laurent Besacier, Sylvie Voisin, Michael Melese, and Uriel Pascal Elingui. 2016. Collecting resources in sub-Saharan African languages for automatic speech recognition: a case study of Wolof. In *Proceedings of the Tenth International Conference on Language Resources and Evaluation (LREC'16)*, pages 3863–3867, Portorož, Slovenia. European Language Resources Association (ELRA).

Vishwa Gupta and Gilles Boulianne. 2020a. Automatic transcription challenges for Inuktitut, a low-resource polysynthetic language. In *Proceedings of the Twelfth Language Resources and Evaluation Conference*, pages 2521–2527, Marseille, France. European Language Resources Association.

Vishwa Gupta and Gilles Boulianne. 2020b. Speech transcription challenges for resource constrained indigenous language Cree. In *Proceedings of the 1st Joint Workshop on Spoken Language Technologies for Under-resourced languages (SLTU) and Collaboration and Computing for Under-Resourced Languages (CCURL)*, pages 362–367, Marseille, France. European Language Resources association.

Robbie Jimerson and Emily Prud'hommeaux. 2018. ASR for documenting acutely under-resourced indigenous languages. In *Proceedings of the Eleventh International Conference on Language Resources and Evaluation (LREC 2018)*, Miyazaki, Japan. European Language Resources Association (ELRA).

Sarah Samson Juan, Laurent Besacier, and Solange Rossato. 2014. Semi-supervised G2P bootstrapping and its application to ASR for a very under-resourced language: Iban. In *Proceedings of Workshop for Spoken Language Technology for Under-resourced (SLTU)*.

Frejus A. A. Laleye, Laurent Besacier, Eugene C. Ezin, and Cina Motamed. 2016. First Automatic Fongbe Continuous Speech Recognition System: Development of Acoustic Models and Language Models. In *Federated Conference on Computer Science and Information Systems*.

Zoey Liu, Crystal Richardson, Richard Hatcher, and Emily Prud'hommeaux. 2022a. Not always about you: Prioritizing community needs when developing endangered language technology. In *Proceedings of the 60th Annual Meeting of the Association for Computational Linguistics (Volume 1: Long Papers)*, pages 3933–3944, Dublin, Ireland. Association for Computational Linguistics.

Zoey Liu, Justin Spence, and Emily Prud'hommeaux. forthcoming. Investigating data partitioning strategies for crosslinguistic low-resource ASR evaluation. In *Proceedings of the 17th Conference of the European Chapter of the Association for Computational Linguistics: Main Volume*.

Zoey Liu, Justin Spence, and Emily Tucker Prud'hommeaux. 2022b. Enhancing documentation of Hupa with automatic speech recognition. In *Proceedings of the Fifth Workshop on the Use of Computational Methods in the Study of Endangered Languages*, pages 187–192, Dublin, Ireland. Association for Computational Linguistics.

Ethan Morris. 2021. Automatic Speech Recognition for Low-Resource and Morphologically Complex Languages. Master's thesis, Rochester Institute of Technology.

Ethan Morris, Robert Jimerson, and Emily Prud'hommeaux. 2021. One size does not fit all in resource-constrained ASR. In *The Annual Conference of the International Speech Communication Association (Interspeech)*, pages 4354–4358.

Daniel S. Park, William Chan, Yu Zhang, Chung-Cheng Chiu, Barret Zoph, Ekin D. Cubuk, and Quoc V. Le. 2019. SpecAugment: A Simple Data Augmentation Method for Automatic Speech Recognition. In *Proc. Interspeech 2019*, pages 2613–2617.

Daniel Povey, Arnab Ghoshal, Gilles Boulianne, Lukas Burget, Ondrej Glembek, Nagendra Goel, Mirko Hannemann, Petr Motlicek, Yanmin Qian, Petr Schwarz, et al. 2011. The Kaldi speech recognition toolkit. In *IEEE 2011 workshop on automatic speech recognition and understanding*, CONF. IEEE Signal Processing Society.

Haşim Sak, Murat Saraçlar, and Tunga Gungor. 2012. Morpholexical and discriminative language models for Turkish automatic speech recognition. *IEEE transactions on audio, speech, and language processing*, 20(8):2341–2351.

Jiatong Shi, Jonathan D. Amith, Rey Castillo García, Esteban Guadalupe Sierra, Kevin Duh, and Shinji Watanabe. 2021. Leveraging end-to-end ASR for endangered language documentation: An empirical study on Yoloxóchitl Mixtec. In *Proceedings of the 16th Conference of the European Chapter of the Association for Computational Linguistics: Main Volume*, pages 1134–1145, Online. Association for Computational Linguistics.

Claytone Sikasote and Antonios Anastasopoulos. 2022. Bembaspeech: A speech recognition corpus for the bemba language. In *Proceedings of the Language Resources and Evaluation Conference*, pages 7277–7283, Marseille, France. European Language Resources Association.

Andreas Stolcke. 2002. SRILM-an extensible language modeling toolkit. In *Seventh international conference on spoken language processing*.

Alexander Zahrer, Andrej Zgank, and Barbara Schuppler. 2020. Towards building an automatic transcription system for language documentation: Experiences from Muyu. In *Proceedings of the 12th Language Resources and Evaluation Conference*, pages 2893–2900, Marseille, France. European Language Resources Association.

Albert Zeyer, Parnia Bahar, Kazuki Irie, Ralf Schlüter, and Hermann Ney. 2019. A comparison of Transformer and LSTM encoder decoder models for ASR. In *2019 IEEE Automatic Speech Recognition and Understanding Workshop (ASRU)*, pages 8–15. IEEE.

FileLingR: An R Script validation tool for depositors and users of digital language collections

Irene Yi
Stanford University
ireneyi@stanford.edu

Claire Bowern
Yale University
claire.bowern@yale.edu

Abstract

In this paper, we use findings from Babinski et al. (2022) to develop a new, user-friendly R script, FileLingR, as a collection validation script for both depositors and users of digital archival collections (i.e. a check for depositors before depositing collections in an archive and a way to keep track of collections in progress). Its multiple functions include listing each file and folder name as a way to keep track of a collection's full inventory, showing collection statistics by file extension type to flag missing files (e.g. unmatched file numbers in .eaf and corresponding audio/video), and extracting basic information about ELAN tiers.

1 Introduction

Digital language archives house countless collections of language material and documentation. Such material has always been crucial to language communities and academics for research, revitalization, and reclamation; these collections will only become more and more important with time (cf. Henke and Berez-Kroeker 2016). Reusability and long-term preservation of archival language collections have long been concerns in the field (cf. among others Nathan, 2010; Harris et al., 2015; Bird and Simons, 2003), yet collections still vary in their accessibility, usability, and completeness once they are deposited into archives.

Babinski et al. (2022) found that, in a review of randomly selected digital archival collections, there were a wide variety of issues in opening and using collection files for basic phonetic analysis. Such problems were related to file organization, version control, missing files, difficulty in matching files to metadata, missing metadata, inconsistent transcription tiers in .eaf (ELAN XML transcript files; Wittenburg et al. 2006), among others. Many of these problems arose from the manual compilation of documentation collections, and many could be avoided or improved upon with more consistent practices by individual depositors of collections. To this end, Babinski et al. (2022) provided a list of recommendations for depositors. These included clear file naming conventions, not leaving metadata compilation to the end of a project (a comment long made in fieldwork manuals; cf. Meakins et al. 2018; Bowern 2015), being explicit about the types of materials that must be archived, and not treating the archive as the end point in a documentation life cycle. However, ensuring the integrity and consistency of a documentation collection is difficult to achieve. Software such as LaMeta (Hatton et al., 2021) helps with language documentation projects that are usefully organized around the concept of a "session". But not all fieldwork projects are easily organized in that way.

Feedback from the documentation community indicates that a corpus curation tool will help both users accessing language collections, as well as depositors. In an LSA[1] webinar held in March 2022, Bowern et al. (2022) asked the nearly 60 audience members about difficulties they face in accessing archival materials. The percentages of participants who responded that they faced particular issues are presented in Table 1. All of these issues can lead to significant downstream problems in data processing. Problems with file formatting can lead to the inability of people trying to access archives to even open materials, let alone explore and modify them for any reclamation work they may wish to use them for. With missing or incorrect metadata, we run into issues of attribution, including potentially not limiting access rights appropriately. Another result is that language analysis (and subsequent decisions, such as what to include in language pedagogy) can be muddled when contextual information is unavailable or misleading.

In the process of accessing collections, being unable to find media files that correspond to transcripts due to inconsistent naming conventions can

[1]Linguistic Society of America

Problem	%
File formatting issues	52%
Missing or incorrect metadata	76%
Unable to match transcript files to corresponding audio or visual material	33%
Incomplete collections	71%

Table 1: Feedback from the LSA webinar about issues found in accessing archives

be a major roadblock, as it adds much labor to the load of the language worker trying to prepare the materials for their next stage of use, just trying to discern which files go with which. When someone is faced with an incomplete collection, language work is severely hindered, as the amount of information available is significantly reduced. While the nonexistence of files cannot be remedied, it's sometimes the case that a depositor missed something in the process of preparing a collection, and this simple slip-up leads to a reduction in the possibilities of downstream language work.

Given the importance and prevalence of these issues, the discussion leaders asked what kind of tools would be of practical use to the audience. 81% of the audience said that "a way to keep track of what is in a collection" would be beneficial, and 67% also said so for "a tool which identifies the likely problems in a collection".

`FileLingR`, the R script (R Core Team, 2017) described here, is a first attempt to meet these needs. We use the findings from Babinski et al. (2022) and Bowern et al. (2022) to develop `FileLingR`. This is a set of archival collection validation scripts for both depositors and users of digital archives. `FileLingR` collects and reports information about the contents and structure of a given collection. Crucially, this tool can be used as a check to identify unintentional errorsby depositors before collections end up in archives.

2 `FileLingR` architecture

`FileLingR` is an R Script that is accessed as an R Markdown Document (Rmd) through its GitHub repository.[2] Users specify the collection folder they would like to analyze. There are also a number of package dependencies that `FileLingR` requires, specified in the Rmd file. Users run the setup code block and load the relevant packages.[3]

`FileLingR` uses the following package dependencies:

- `devtools`: facilitates installation of R packages from GitHub. (Wickham et al., 2022)
- `github("dalejbarr/elan")`: parses ELAN files. (Barr, 2015)
- `plyr` : used for ELAN tier parsing functions (Wickham, 2011)
- `magrittr` : installation of the % % function, used in ELAN tier parsing functions (Bache and Wickham, 2022)
- `reticulate` : used in ELAN tier parsing functions (Ushey et al., 2023)
- `xfun` : used for manipulations of filenames: file_ext() to obtain a file extension, sans_ext() to remove a file extension, and with_ext() to change a file extension. (Xie, 2018)
- `yaml` : exports the results to .txt textfiles. (Garbett et al., 2023)

`FileLingR` parses a directory structure and recursively reads in the directory and file names as a text string. It then manipulates those strings to extract file extensions (e.g. .xml, .wav, etc.), creates a dataframe (akin to a spreadsheet) from the segmented text strings, and summarizes the counts of different strings.[4]

3 Functions

`FileLingR`'s functions include providing a way to keep track of a collection's full inventory by listing the entire directory structure with files and folders. This is helpful for `Users` when discovering what is available in a given collection and `Depositors` when validating their own collections to identify potential issues. `FileLingR` uses file extensions to provide collection statistics and flags likely missing files (e.g. unmatched file numbers in .eaf and corresponding audio/video). `FileLingR`'s functionality

[2]The repository link can be found at chirila/FileLingR.

[3]As an anonymous reviewer pointed out, some of the package dependencies that `FileLingR` currently uses have not been updated in more than 5 years. We have forked the repository as an interim solution.

[4]While `FileLingR` does not currently implement this function, it could be easily extended to match metadata strings to a file with additional information. For example, speaker initials could be matched to a lookup table that provides more information about the participants in the research.

also extends to extracting basic information about ELAN tiers to find information about participants in a recording event.

A more explicit set of features is listed below:[5]

- File Counts: lists the number of files of each filetype (by extension).
- ELAN Files: provides a list of EAF files with aligned audio/video transcripts.
- Missing Audio: provides a list of the ELAN transcript files (EAFs) which do not have an associated audio or video file (checks for .wav or .mp4 format).
- Settings Files: provides a list of which ELAN files are missing .pfs/.pfsx files (not usually necessary for loading a project).
- Missing Transcripts: provides a list of the audio files that are missing corresponding .eaf files (and which .eaf files are missing .txt exports).
- Export: exports results to a set of plaintext files, which provide the following:
  - 'Sitemap' – a full list of directories and files.
  - Missing Files – files which are missing matches (audio or transcripts).
  - Matched Files – files which have associated metadata.
  - Filetype Summary – the types of file extensions present in the collection, and the count of each filetype.

4 Further discussion and conclusions

This is Version 1.0 of `FileLingR` and several extensions are currently planned. Extended support of file formats is a high priority. While `FileLingR` lists all file formats in the collection, it only works in detail with .wav and .mp4 files, since these are the most common audio and video filetypes that field linguists use. However, `FileLingR` can be easily extended to include a larger array of audio filetypes.

We plan to implement further information about the contents of ELAN files, such as a list of unique characters used in each tier (useful for identifying misplaced information, questionable transcripts, or orthography type). This can be especially helpful in identifying encoding issues –identifying the use of characters in the Unicode Private Use Area, for example, can help depositors be aware that their transcriptions may not be visible to anyone working on an interface without a font that will render those characters appropriately (cf. SILPUA. We envision a use case where transcripts containing placeholders such as 'XXX' or '???' are identified.

We also plan further extensions that mitigate additional issues identified in Yi et al. (2022) and Babinski et al. (2022); for example, collections that are archived as "working" collections but are missing crucial files, where users make use of non-transferable features. Such cases include using file offsets for ELAN transcripts, which work in the ELAN browser but make other uses of the files impossible (or which don't transfer to other instances of the files).

Further expansions include checking for empty directories (plausibly present for work in progress, but can serve as a more explicit signal to flag problems for projects in final stages before archiving) and conflicts between filenames or minimally differing filenames (such as files with underscores vs. hyphens, files that have suffixes of the form `-final`, `-rev`, `-temp`, and the like). Note that `FileLingR` currently will not search a user's entire hard drive for materials. That is, it assumes that all materials for a documentation project are located in a single, specified directory tree (for the same reason, it will not browse across multiple drives).

Through its functionalities, this script complements tools such as LaMeta (Hatton et al., 2021) in identifying missing or inconsistent information in existing collections. As mentioned earlier, LaMeta makes an assumption about the nature of data in the form of hoping users organize their data around a notion of "sessions." While the LaMeta allows for very broad interpretations of that notion, there are cases in which it is not always appropriate as an organizing principle (e.g. [SOMETHING]). `FileLingR` massages the problem of having to fit into that model by simply looking for file cor-

[5]A reviewer suggested that the sitemap would be more usefully displayed as a tree, and that such a tree can be 'easily' compiled using shell scripts. This is a possible extension, though we question whether such a function would make `FileLingR` more user friendly to audiences who are not very familiar with shell scripts and manipulating code. The current list of files can easily be imported into a spreadsheet, for example, whereas an ascii-drawn file tree is not so straightforwardly manipulated. Some users of `FileLingR` are no doubt familiar with shell scripts, while others are not.

respondences, being ambivalent about specifics regarding directory setup. This at least allows users to perform checks before moving onto further stages, regardless of how the next steps will involve restructuring–users know what all is there, at the very least, and they can find out what might be missing. We plan further integration with LaMeta, by providing support for .meta XML files. In the future we will also give users the option to specify a metadata file with filenames. `FileLingR` would then return (i) a list of files found in the directory that are missing in the metadata file, and (ii) a list of items in the metadata file that are not found in the directory.

We welcome further feature requests from members of the user community, to be submitted on the GitHub site for the project.

An anonymous reviewer suggested that `FileLingR` could be redesigned to be an interface for archives to validate content, as well as for collectors to validate and submit metadata to particular archives. As Sullivant (2020) has noted, linguistic metadata comes in at least five different types. There is *descriptive metadata*, which makes it possible for users to find objects in the collection by describing what is in a file (e.g. the speakers or signers who contributed to its recording, the content of the recording, and the like). *Technical metadata* provides information about the files in the collection, such as their length and format. *Structural metadata* contains the information which links items in collections to one another (that is, providing the information which gives relationships between items), while *preservation metadata* is about the item's status in the collection and its long-term storage and durability. Finally, *rights metadata* gives access information, copyright status, and ownership details.

Within descriptive metadata, there can be information about the participants, the language, the recording context, and other material immediately relevant to the recording event. Metadata itself may contain information that is subject to access rights. For example, it may not be appropriate to release personal information about contributors to a collection. Some types of metadata can be automatically compiled, while others cannot. `FileLingR` can provide technical metadata summaries and can facilitate some types of structural and preservation metadata, but it cannot (and probably should not) attempt to house and manipulate descriptive metadata. As noted above, however, a possible future development is for `FileLingR` to link filenames or abbreviations to a table with explanations, thus augmenting the material in the file structure and making information in collections more searchable and filterable.

Currently, `FileLingR` is implemented in RStudio, and so some familiarity with R and RStudio is required in order to run the program. Users need to be able to identify the relevant directory and knit the RStudio document. They also need to be able to understand the R code enough to make modifications to instructions about what output should be generated if they do not wish to compile all the results that `FileLingR` does by default. We recognize that this may be a hurdle to use for some who would like to use this program.

In the long term, we plan to migrate `FileLingR` to a Shiny app that can be run with more graphical user interaction and that requires little to no familiarity with R. However, given that technical expertise with R is increasingly common in linguistics, we also consider `FileLingR` as a potential entry point for fieldworkers who are seeking further familiarity with R and learn from existing scripts.

We hope that `FileLingR` will assist depositors in preparing their collections for deposit. We also hope it will assist users of archival collections in rapidly inventorying collections so they can find the materials they wish to prioritize.

Ethics Statement

We view accurate archiving as an ethical issue. Particularly for endangered languages, it is a matter of ethics that collections be as complete as possible, particularly where communities and individuals rely on such collections for future language support, revitalization, and reclamation. It is also a matter of good scholarship (Berez-Kroeker et al., 2017, 2018; Harris et al., 2015). As Rice (2022) and Perley (2012) among others have pointed out, the history of academic language documentation has involved extractive practices where linguistic recordings are made, removed from communities, and decontextualized. Metadata and collection structure is crucial to restoring and retaining that context. While language recordings are made and compiled for many purposes, none of these purposes can be met appropriately without sustainable metadocumentation of collections on the behalf of people working with language materials.

Acknowledgements

Thank you to the Yale fieldwork group (particularly Sunkulp Ananthanarayan and Coralie Cram, and anonymous reviewers for ACL who provided helpful comments.

References

Sarah Babinski, Jeremiah Jewell, Kassandra Haakman, Juhyae Kim, Amelia Lake, Irene Yi, and Claire Bowern. 2022. How usable are digital collections for endangered languages? a review. *Proceedings of the Linguistic Society of America*, 7(11):5219.

Stefan Milton Bache and Hadley Wickham. 2022. *magrittr: A Forward-Pipe Operator for R*. Https://magrittr.tidyverse.org, https://github.com/tidyverse/magrittr.

Dale Barr. 2015. elan. `https://github.com/dalejbarr/elan`.

Andrea Berez-Kroeker, Gary Holton, Susan Kung, and Peter Pulsifer. 2017. Developing standards for data citation and attribution for reproducible research in linguistics: Project summary and next steps. *Presentations from the Linguistic Society of America symposium and poster session on Data Citation and Attribution in Linguistics, 5-9 January 2017, Austin TX*.

Andrea L. Berez-Kroeker, Lauren Gawne, Susan Smythe Kung, Barbara F. Kelly, Tyler Heston, Gary Holton, Peter Pulsifer, David I. Beaver, Shobhana Chelliah, and Stanley Dubinsky. 2018. Reproducible research in linguistics: A position statement on data citation and attribution in our field. *Linguistics*, 56(1):1–18.

Steven Bird and Gary Simons. 2003. Seven dimensions of portability for language documentation and description. *Language*, page 557–582.

Claire Bowern. 2015. *Linguistic fieldwork: A practical guide*. Springer. Citation Key Alias: bowern2015b, bowern2015c.

Claire Bowern, Irene Yi, and Sarah Babinski. 2022. How usable are digital collections for endangered languages? a review. Presented at the "In Case You Missed It" series of the Linguistic Society of America.

Shawn Garbett, Jeremy Stephens, Kirill Simonov, Yihui Xie, Zhuoer Dong, Hadley Wickham, Jeffrey Horner, Will Beasley, Brendan O'Connor, Gregory Warnes, Michael Quinn, and Zhian Kamvar. 2023. yaml: Methods to convert r data to yaml and back. `https://CRAN.R-project.org/package=yaml`.

Amanda Harris, Nick Thieberger, and Linda Barwick. 2015. *Research, Records and Responsibility: Introduction*. Sydney University Press. Accepted: 2015-10-07.

John Hatton, Gary Holton, Mandana Seyfeddinipur, and Nick Thieberger. 2021. Lameta [software].

Ryan E Henke and Andrea L Berez-Kroeker. 2016. A brief history of archiving in language documentation, with an annotated bibliography. *Language Documentation*, 10:47.

Felicity Meakins, Jennifer Green, and Myfany Turpin. 2018. *Understanding linguistic fieldwork*. Routledge.

David Nathan. 2010. Archives 2.0 for endangered languages: From disk space to myspace. *International Journal of Humanities and Arts Computing*, 4(1–2):111–124.

Bernard C. Perley. 2012. Zombie linguistics: Experts, endangered languages and the curse of undead voices. *Anthropological Forum*, 22(2):133–149.

R Core Team. 2017. *R: A language and environment for statistical computing*. Vienna, Austria. 00000.

Mskwaankwad Rice. 2022. Power and positionality: A case study of linguistics' relationship to indigenous peoples. *Proceedings of the Linguistic Society of America*, 7(11):5295.

Ryan Sullivant. 2020. Archival description for language documentation collections. *Language Documentation & Conservation*, 14:520–578.

Kevin Ushey, JJ Allaire, and Yuan Tang. 2023. *reticulate: Interface to 'Python'*. Https://rstudio.github.io/reticulate/, https://github.com/rstudio/reticulate.

Hadley Wickham. 2011. The Split-Apply-Combine strategy for data analysis.

Hadley Wickham, Jim Hester, Winston Chang, and Jennifer Bryan. 2022. *devtools: Tools to Make Developing R Packages Easier*. Https://devtools.r-lib.org/, https://github.com/r-lib/devtools.

P Wittenburg, H Brugman, A Russel, A Klassman, and H Sloetjes. 2006. Elan: a professional framework for multimodality research. *Proceedings of LREC 2006, Fifth International Conference on Language Resources and Evaluation.*, page 1556–1559. 00216.

Yihui Xie. 2018. xfun: Miscellaneous r functions. `https://CRAN.R-project.org/package=xfun`.

Irene Yi, Amelia Lake, Juhyae Kim, Kassandra Haakman, Jeremiah Jewell, Sarah Babinski, and Claire Bowern. 2022. Accessibility, discoverability, and functionality: An audit of and recommendations for digital language archives. *Journal of Open Humanities Data*, 8(00):10.

An Empirical Study on Gender Bias within an Indigenous Language Revitalization Perspective and an Inclusive NMT

Ngoc Tan Le
Université du Québec à Montréal
le.ngoc_tan@uqam.ca

Oussama Hansal
Université du Québec à Montréal
Oussama.Hansal@courrier.uqam.ca

Fatiha Sadat
Université du Québec à Montréal
sadat.fatiha@uqam.ca

Abstract

Natural Language Processing applications, such as Neural Machine Translation, typically exhibit substantial biases toward sensitive factors such as gender or race. This degrades the performance of machine translation and promotes unfavorable preconceptions. The current paper examines the issues and challenges of gender bias within Inuktitut, an under-represented Indigenous language of Canada, and discusses how to enhance the performance of Inuktitut-English NMT; all with the aim of revitalizing the Indigenous language and considering an inclusive NMT. Firstly, we performed the detection of gender bias in word embeddings in Inuktitut and English. Secondly, we compared the debiasing effect with the traditional word to vectors and also based on a dictionary. Then, we adopted a strategy, within the Inuktitut-English NMT, using the two bilingual debiased word embeddings.

1 Introduction

In recent years, studies on under-represented languages within NLP and AI, such as the Indigenous and Endangered languages have drawn a number of scholars. For example, some researchers have focused their studies on new conceptualisation of language revitalisation (Grenoble and Whaley, 2006; Pine and Turin, 2017) and others proposed revitalisation strategies to strengthen communities and promote commitment (Wiltshire et al., 2022).

This can be considered as a promising factor for the development of language technologies for this category of languages. However, the complex morphology of these under-represented languages, as well as lack of resources and the presence of biases, have been regarded as serious barriers.

Gender bias, in particular, may be described as a prejudice toward one gender over the other. Bias can vary from the usage of gender defaults to the association between occupation and gender. Since language technologies become more widely used and implemented, their social influence creates issues both intrinsically and extrinsically (Hovy and Spruit, 2016; Dastin, 2018; Sun et al., 2019).

Many NLP tasks are trained using collected human language data. These applications are likely to display biases in various ways such as data, annotation, input representations, models, and research design (Hovy and Prabhumoy, 2021). To analyze the context, NLP research was investigated by Sun et al. (2019). Their research, however, is centred on monolingual applications, and the underlying hypothesis and method may not be applicable to languages other than English. Gender stereotypes have therefore been defined differently from research to study, depending on the language used and the elements considered.

As an illustration, Google Translate can translate the following statement from English to French [1], and to Inuktitut[2] :

(en) **The developer** disagreed with **the designer** because **she** did not like **her** design.

(fr) **Le développeur** n'était pas d'accord avec **le concepteur** car **elle** n'aimait pas **son** design.

(iu) **Sanaji** angiqatiqalaut**tuq titiraujaqtimit** piugilaum**magu** titiraujaqsimaninga.

We observe gender stereotypes that classified the first subject "*developer*" and the second subject "*designer*" in the masculine category, despite the fact that we used *she, her* to focus on the feminine gender. Such flaws not only challenge the development of NLP applications for under-represented languages, but they also intensify existing biases.

In Inuktitut, we notice another linguistic problem in terms of gender, since the language is gender-

[1] https://translate.google.ca/, consulted on November 18th, 2022

[2] https://www.bing.com/translator?from=pt-pt&to=iu&setlang=be, consulted on November 18th, 2022

less and does not identify a masculine or feminine category, compared to European languages.

Actually, Inuktitut people determine rather another concept of animacy, which means whether a noun is considered animate or inanimate[3]. For example, animate nouns are most obviously related to humans and animals, but other objects, such as river, tree, are considered inanimate (Hassan, 2015).

Given that word embeddings are often employed in NLP tasks, understanding how human biases are absorbed into them might help us understand bias in NLP models.

This study aims to investigate the gender bias challenges by assessing current efforts to identify and minimise gender stereotypes. Furthermore, we present an empirical case study of Inuktitut-English NMT, in which Inuktitut is considered as an under-represented language. Inuktitut is considered as an Indigenous language of Eastern Canada and also the official language of the Nunavut government. The main goal also contributes to the efforts on the revitalization and preservation of Indigenous languages.

This paper is organised as follows: Section 2 presents the relevant work. Section 3 introduces linguistic challenges in Indigenous languages, especially in Inuktitut. Sections 4 presents several detection and mitigation methods to deal with gender bias. Sections 5 presents an empirical case study of the Machine Translation downstream task on gender bias. The experiments and evaluations are presented in Sections 6 and 7 with other state-of-the-art approaches; following an error analysis and a discussion. Finally, Section 8 gives some conclusions and presents future research directions.

2 Related work

Interest in identifying, measuring, and mitigating gender bias in NLP continues to grow, with recent research demonstrating how gender differences influence language technology (Cislak et al., 2018). Recently, several approaches have been proposed in order to identify gender bias in NLP. They are classified in two main approaches, depending on what they are based on; (1) traditional word embeddings or (2) dictionary-based embeddings. In the following subsections, we give some details on the state-of-the-art of these two approaches and also that of methods for measuring gender bias.

Approach of using traditional embeddings

This technique uses some term list, i.e. occupation for male and female. The main component of a word vector consisting of gender defining word pairs defines gender directions, such as *she* and *he* (Bolukbasi et al., 2016). Besides the use of monolingual word embeddings, bilingual word embeddings are used for gender bias identification task (Liu et al., 2019), to map with similar words in related languages in the same task (Alipour et al., 2022); multilingual word embeddings (Zhao et al., 2020; Bansal et al., 2021); and contextual word embeddings with ELMo or BERT (Kurita et al., 2019; Zhao et al., 2019).

Approach of using dictionary-based embeddings

Existing debiasing algorithms usually need a precompiled list of seed words to indicate the bias direction, which is followed by the removal of biased information. Kaneko and Bollegala (2021) proposed a method for debiasing pre-trained word embeddings using dictionaries, without requiring access to the original training resources or any knowledge regarding the word embedding algorithms that was used. An et al. (2022) developed dictionary-guided loss functions, which promote word embeddings to be comparable to their relatively neutral Dictionary Definition (DD) representations. The authors proposed DD-GloVe, a train-time debiasing algorithm to learn word embeddings by leveraging dictionary definitions.

Besides, Ding et al. (2022) proposed a causal inference framework to leverage causal structure among bias and semantic components in order to remove gender bias.

Methods for measuring gender bias

In terms of measuring gender bias in NLP, the calculation is usually done at the profession level and at the corpus level for English, and then applied to other languages (Chaloner and Maldonado, 2019; Fabris et al., 2020; Gezici and Saygin, 2022; Jentzsch and Turan, 2022). Among other researches, Chen et al. (2021) reported measurements of gender bias in the Wikipedia corpora for nine languages, such as Chinese, Spanish, English, Arabic, German, French, Farsi, Urdu, and Wolof, in the NLP pipeline.

[3]https://linguisticmaps.tumblr.com/post/169273617313/grammatical-gender-or-noun-class-categories-new

In terms of mitigating gender bias in NLP, especially in the downstream tasks, i.e. Machine Translation, the main goal consists of reducing the reliance on gender stereotypes, and also improving the translation quality (Sun et al., 2019; Stafanovičs et al., 2020; Liao, 2021; Chen et al., 2022; Kirtane and Anand, 2022).

In order to evaluate gender bias in NLP, multiple methods are proposed such as hard debias and soft debias (Bolukbasi et al., 2016). Moreover, Ravfogel et al. (2020) proposed iterative nullspace projection to evaluate on bias and fairness. Their proposed algorithm could mitigate bias in word embeddings. On the other hand, the WEAT (Word Embedding Association Test) bias detection method is usually performed for assessing word embedding bias (Caliskan et al., 2017).

3 Linguistic challenges of Inuktitut

3.1 Morphological segmentation in Inuktitut

The morphology of Indigenous languages in the Americas is very complex, with the majority being polysynthetic or agglutinative (Gasser, 2011; Littell et al., 2018; Joanis et al., 2020; Le and Sadat, 2020, 2022b).

Morphology segmentation is important in the learning of these languages. In this paper, we focus on Inuktitut, the most popular polysynthetic Indigenous language in Northern Canada, in the context of NLP research.

Polysynthetic languages, in principle, have lengthy sentence-words and a regular agglutinative and strongly suffixing morphology, which causes words to be exceedingly long and potentially unique (Lowe, 1985; Mithun, 2015). Besides, Inuktitut's morphophonemics are quite complicated.

In the following example, in Nunavut Inuktitut (Lowe, 1985), we observe no gender, only one long word corresponding to one sentence in English translation, and the verb root in the first position:

(iu) **tusaa**tsiarunnanngittualuu**JUNGA**

(en) **I** can't **hear** very well.

where *tusaa* means to *hear*, and *junga* means *I*.

We may highlight two relevant works in terms of developing a morphological segmenter for Inuktitut: (1) Uqailaut morphological analyzer (Farley, 2012), and (2) an Inuktitut Neural Network-based (NN) word segmenter (Le and Sadat, 2020).

The Uqailaut tool used a Finite-State Transducer-based method by combining several techniques such as grammar rules, linguistic knowledge and heuristics; while the NN word segmenter is trained using a set of rich features and by leveraging bicharacter-based and word-based pretrained embeddings from large-scale raw corpora. When used to perform word segmentation along with pretrained embeddings, NN-based techniques have demonstrated their usefulness. Thus, we adopted the second segmentation approach in order to prepare the experimental training data in Inuktitut.

4 Word embeddings for debiasing

Inspired by (Hansal et al., 2022) to analyse and mitigate bias in word embeddings, we adopted the three following methods to measure bias in word embeddings:

Hard debiasing (Bolukbasi et al., 2016)

The hard debiasing method aims to detect and reduce bias in word embeddings. Bolukbasi et al. (2016) presented a post-processing strategy for projecting gender-neutral words into a subspace orthogonal to the gender dimension specified by a list of gender-definitional terms (e.g., she, her, him, actor, driver), as cited in (Kaneko and Bollegala, 2021).

In particularly, it needs a set of gender-specific word pairs. Then the gender direction is computed as the difference vectors between the embeddings of the corresponding gender-definitional words.

Sent-Debias (Liang et al., 2020)

This method consists of the main following processes: (1) define bias attributes as a set of relevant words; (2) transform sentence representations using bias attributes; (3) compute bias subspace; and (4) project onto bias subspace, then remove biased sentences. As a result, the output is the general sentences debiased.

The Sent-Debias algorithm1 is described below.

Dictionary-based debiasing (Kaneko and Bollegala, 2021)

This method aims to debias pretrained word embeddings using a monolingual dictionary. It does not require the bias attributes to be annotated in the word pair lists or any prior knowledge.

Given a dictionary D containing the definition, and n-dimensional pretrained word embedding, the debiasing process is considered as the task of learning an encoder, $E(w; \theta_e)$, such that w desribes all

Algorithm 1 Sent-Debias algorithm (Liang et al., 2020).

To initialize pretrained sentence encoder M_θ
To define bias attributes
To obtain words D indicative of bias attributes
$S = Contextualize(D)$ ▷ words into sentences
for each element in D **do**
    To get sentence representations
end for
To compute bias subspace V
for each new sentence representation h **do**
    To project onto bias subspace h_V
    To subtract the projection $\widehat{h} = h - h_V$
end for

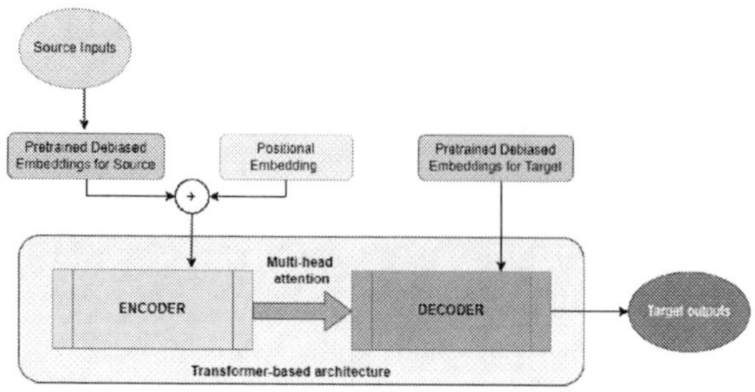

Figure 1: Architecture of our framework: Deep Learning-based debiased NMT for Indigenous language, with pretrained debiased word-based embedding for both source and target, combining with positional embedding.

words in the vocabulary, that is trained to generate a debiased version of an input embedding. A loss function is computed in order to optimize the learning process. This computation is based both on the pre-trained word embeddings and on the unbiased dictionary definition of the term.

A decoder D_d allows to compute the encoded version of w, $E(w;\theta_e)$, using a parameter of θ_d and an objective function $J_d(w)$, as described in the following equation 1:

$$J_d(w) = \|s(w) - D_d(E(w;\theta_e);\theta_d)\|_2^2 \quad (1)$$

where $s(w)$ represents the dictionary-definitional vectors.

5 Methodology

5.1 Machine Translation downstream task

The purpose of this paper aims to investigate the impact of pretrained debiased word embeddings into an Inuktitut-English NMT system based on the Transformer encoder-decoder architecture (Vaswani et al., 2017).

5.2 The framework

Inspired by (Font and Costa-Jussa, 2019), we built an NMT framework by taking advantage of pretrained debiased word embeddings, and also source-target alignment information as an additional feature. Figure1 shows the architecture of the proposed architecture.

First, the pretrained debiased word embeddings are used to initialize the embedding layers of the NMT model, both in the encoder and the decoder. We deal with the morphology complexity by applying the morpheme segmentation for Inuktitut (Le and Sadat, 2020, 2022a). Second, source-target alignment information are incorporated in the training step. We apply an unsupervised word aligner (Dyer et al., 2013) to generate symmetrical source-target alignments. Third, we inject in the decoding, the source-target morphological information, such as a bilingual lexicon. We apply lexicon extractor from Moses (Koehn et al., 2007) to prepare a bilingual lexical shortlist which is passed to the decoder.

We hypothesize that an ensemble of all the models of different types and architectures, with weights, could lead to an improved NMT performance. The following equation 2 of the objective function $f(x)$ helps in weighting all possible NMT models.

$$f(x) = \alpha Model_1 + \beta Model_2 + \theta Model_3 \quad (2)$$

where, $\alpha + \beta + \theta = 1$.

6 Evaluations

6.1 Data preparation

We performed experiments on gender bias mitigation in Inuktitut. The Nunavut Hansard Inuktitut–English Parallel Corpus 3.0 (Joanis et al., 2020) is used to train and to evaluate our proposal.

As described in Table 1, the Inuktitut-English corpus contains 1,293,348 sentences pairs, 5,433 sentences pairs and 6,139 sentences pairs for the training, development and testing sets, respectively. Regarding the pretraining of word embeddings, we applied a setting of the hyper-parameters, as described in Table 2, and used *fastText* toolkit to pretrain them, as proposed by Bojanowski et al. (2017).

Dataset	Train set	Dev set	Test set
Inuktitut (iu)	1,293,348	5,433	6,139
English (en)	1,293,348	5,433	6,139

Table 1: Statistics of Nunavut Hansard for Inuktitut-English (Joanis et al., 2020).

Hyper-parameters
Epochs = *50*
Dimension size = *300*
Window size = *2*
Alpha value = *0.03*
Loss function = *softmax*

Table 2: Setting of the hyper-parameters for embedding pretraining.

6.2 Neural Machine Translation

Our experiments on NMT using the Transformer-based architecture (Vaswani et al., 2017) are described as follows:

(1) System 1: Baseline of Joanis et al. (2020) without pretrained debiased embeddings.

(2) System 2: Transformer-based model with only word alignment information as additional feature.

(3) System 3: Transformer-based model with only pretrained debiased embeddings.

(4) System 4: Transformer-based model with debiased embeddings and word alignment information as additional feature.

The configuration of the experimental environment is described in Table 3 and the relevant hyper-parameters of the NMT models are shown in Table 4.

Environment	Configuration
Operating platform	CUDA 11
Operating System	Ubuntu
Memory	32 GB
multi-GPU	6 cores
Python version	python 3.8
Tensorflow version	v2.10.0

Table 3: Configuration of the experimental environment

Hyper-parameter	Value
Maximum sentence length	128
Batch size	64
Transformer layers	12
Transformer hidden layers	768
Learning rate	0.0001
Epoch	50
Optimizer	adam

Table 4: Setting of hyper-parameters for NMT models

7 Evaluations

7.1 Results on bias mitigation

The WEAT evaluation is performed on the altered terms list which is translated into Inuktitut. We observe strong impact sizes across all standard word embeddings and several tests are significant at various levels. The WEAT results shows impact sizes on gendered tests, where a large impact size on debiased word embeddings is observed from the original models. Moreover, our evaluations show that the dictionary-based debiasing method outperforms other methods, as shown in Table 5. It effectively removes unfair biases encoded in pre-trained word embeddings, while retaining meaningful semantics.

Method	Debiased WEAT
Baseline	0.034
Hard debiasing	0.385
Sent debiasing	0.377
Dictionary-based debiasing	0.527

Table 5: The evaluation of WEAT using fastText toolkit, with significance of p-value < 0.05, against the WEAT baseline value = 0.034.

As Inuktitut is a complex-gender language, using pronouns might be challenging. Common names are utilised for males and females rather than particularly gendered terminology to identify the male and female groups (Goldfarb-Tarrant et al., 2020). We performed three tests to examine male and female name correlations to job occupations and family, art words and science.

In accordance with the projection in Figure 2, we notice that the significant association between the groups is no longer present in the tests. The experimental results show that the classes are no longer sequentially separated. This behaviour differs significantly from the sent debias and hard debias approaches, which have been found to preserve a significant amount of the closeness between female and male-biased vectors.

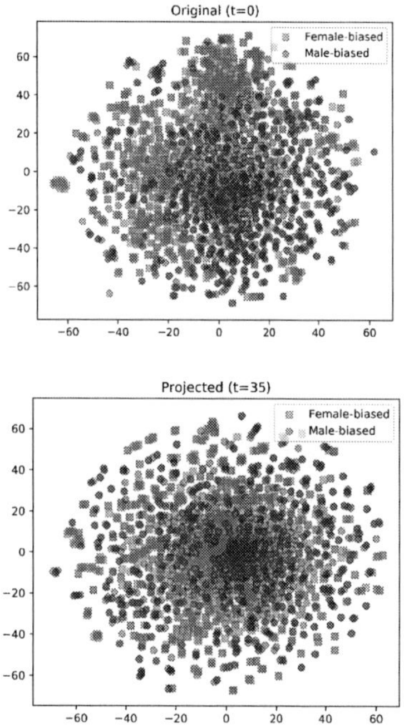

Figure 2: Projection with t-distributed stochastic neighbor embedding about different clusters between female and male biased states, at t=0 for original state and t=35 for projected state.

7.2 Results on Neural Machine Translation

We used automatic evaluation metrics such as SacreBLEU (Post, 2018) [4] for BiLingual Evaluation Understudy (BLEU) (Papineni et al., 2002), chrF++ (Popović, 2015) [5] for calculating character n-gram F-score, and translation error rate (TER).

As shown in Table 6, in the Inuktitut-English direction, systems 1, 2, and 4 outperformed the base system, with significant gains from $+0.93$ to $+3.03$ points BLEU. In the other hand, Table 7, which related to the English-Inuktitut direction, shows the best scores for System 4, with 20.5, 48, and 62.3 in terms of BLEU, chrF++, and 62.3 respectively. In both directions, we notice negative impacts on the use of debiased word embedding while injecting into NMT models. Especially, the system 3 (Table 6), with only pretrained debiased word embeddings for initialization phase, obtained 32.76 BLEU point against 35.00 BLEU point of the baseline, so a decrease of -2.24 point.

[4]https://github.com/mjpost/sacrebleu

[5]https://github.com/m-popovic/chrF

Experiment	BLEU	chrF++	TER
System 1 (base)	35.00	63.1	53.3
System 2	35.93	64.2	53.2
System 3	32.76	55.3	56.3
System 4	36.61	67.5	52.6

Table 6: Performances on Inuktitut-English NMT in terms of lowercase word BLEU score.

Experiment	BLEU	chrF++	TER
System 1	16.5	30.5	70.4
System 2	19.30	42.2	66.5
System 3	18.34	34.6	68.1
System 4	20.5	48.0	62.3

Table 7: Performances on English-Inuktitut NMT in terms of lowercase word BLEU score. We consider the system 1 as baseline.

On the other hand, with an ensemble of others models, combining both the alignment feature and debiased word embeddings, BLEU score has been improved, in all the systems, with 1.61 BLEU more, and 4 BLEU compared to the baseline, in the direction of Inuktitut-English and in the direction of English-Inuktitut, respectively.

Comparing the evaluation at the n-gram character level (Tables 6 and 7), we notice a similarity between the models, with regard to the chrF++ scores, that seems slightly more efficient than the baseline, except for System 3 that shows a drop of 0.55 point (Tables 6).

Additionally, in terms of translation error rate (TER) reductions, all systems performed better than the baseline, while applying alignment information as an additional feature, or combining both alignment information and pre-trained debiased embeddings. In the next subsection, we discuss error analysis and all possible causes.

7.3 Error analysis and discussion

Identifying the true gender direction in word embeddings is always challenging. We found a significant effect in traditional embeddings, which can be considered positive if the embeddings used ensure a more gender-neutral approach.

In addition, we have noticed, in the context of gender bias, a drawback which consists in the dependence of all 3 debiasing methods presented, like other machine learning approaches for that matter, on the data provided to it.This assumes that the training data is large enough and sampled from the same distribution as the test data.

Another finding we made is that a large omission of masculine pronouns (less) is present in the MT outputs, compared to feminine pronouns (many). Alternatively, we notice that Inuktitut is a non-gendered language as pronouns might be dropped in translation outputs. This phenomenon makes the issue of gender or racial bias more difficult to manage in NMT systems in conjunction with underrepresented polysynthetic languages.

Statistics of errors found in accordance with the pronouns including *he, him, his, she, her* are shown in Tables 8 and 9 below.

For the NMT downstream task, we observed a decrease in the performance when initializing embedding layers with pretrained debiased embeddings. The plausible causes are related to the limited vocabulary size of pretrained embeddings. In contrast, using an ensemble of all the models outperformed all other NMT systems, with 36.61 BLEU score, and could have a better coverage of vocabulary for the model training.

Exp	he	him	his	she	her
System 1	46.79	26.32	62.04	13.89	16.13
System 2	41.28	15.79	62.04	19.44	14.52
System 3	45.87	42.11	58.33	22.22	11.29
System 4	48.62	31.58	59.26	8.33	14.52

Table 8: Precision on Inuktitut-English NMT in terms of pronouns found in accordance with {he, him, his, she, her}.

Exp	he	him	his	she	her
System 1	27.52	15.79	35.19	13.89	9.68
System 2	45.87	42.11	59.26	19.44	14.52
System 3	41.28	26.32	58.33	22.22	11.29
System 4	48.62	47.37	59.26	22.22	30.65

Table 9: Precision on English-Inuktitut NMT in terms of pronouns found in accordance with {he, him, his, she, her}.

8 Conclusion and perspectives

This research reveals that gender prejudice occurs in Inuktitut as in other languages. In this empirical study, we demonstrated how methodologies used to measure and minimise biases in English embeddings can be adapted to Inuktitut embeddings by accurately translating the data and taking into consideration the language's distinctive features. Furthermore, in Inuktitut-English NMT framework, we suggested a technique that combines bilingual debiased word embeddings with source-target alignment information.

As a future direction, we intend to examine other types of biases in Inuktitut, in close collaboration and in partnership with the indigenous community. Our primary goal is to help revitalize and preserve Indigenous languages in Canada through the use of NLP and machine learning technology and thus contribute to the effort of an inclusive AI. We hope that these preliminary results will inspire future studies on Indigenous and Endangered languages.

Acknowledgements

The authors wish to acknowledge the time and effort devoted by members of the Indigenous communities for their guidance in this research effort. We are also grateful to the anonymous reviewers for their valuable comments and feedbacks.

References

Ghafour Alipour, Jamshid Bagherzadeh Mohasefi, and Mohammad-Reza Feizi-Derakhshi. 2022. Learning bilingual word embedding mappings with similar words in related languages using gan. *Applied Artificial Intelligence*, pages 1–20.

Haozhe An, Xiaojiang Liu, and Donald Zhang. 2022. Learning bias-reduced word embeddings using dictionary definitions. In *Findings of the Association for Computational Linguistics: ACL 2022*, pages 1139–1152, Dublin, Ireland. Association for Computational Linguistics.

Srijan Bansal, Vishal Garimella, Ayush Suhane, and Animesh Mukherjee. 2021. Debiasing multilingual word embeddings: A case study of three indian languages. In *Proceedings of the 32nd ACM Conference on Hypertext and Social Media*, pages 27–34.

Piotr Bojanowski, Edouard Grave, Armand Joulin, and Tomas Mikolov. 2017. Enriching word vectors with subword information. *Transactions of the Association for Computational Linguistics*, 5:135–146.

Tolga Bolukbasi, Kai-Wei Chang, James Zou, Venkatesh Saligrama, and Adam Kalai. 2016. Man is to computer programmer as woman is to homemaker? debiasing word embeddings.

Aylin Caliskan, Joanna J Bryson, and Arvind Narayanan. 2017. Semantics derived automatically from language corpora contain human-like biases. *Science*, 356(6334):183–186.

Kaytlin Chaloner and Alfredo Maldonado. 2019. Measuring gender bias in word embeddings across domains and discovering new gender bias word categories. In *Proceedings of the First Workshop on Gender Bias in Natural Language Processing*, pages 25–

32, Florence, Italy. Association for Computational Linguistics.

Xiuying Chen, Mingzhe Li, Rui Yan, Xin Gao, and Xiangliang Zhang. 2022. Unsupervised mitigating gender bias by character components: A case study of chinese word embedding. In *Proceedings of the 4th Workshop on Gender Bias in Natural Language Processing (GeBNLP)*, pages 121–128.

Yan Chen, Christopher Mahoney, Isabella Grasso, Esma Wali, Abigail Matthews, Thomas Middleton, Mariama Njie, and Jeanna Matthews. 2021. Gender bias and under-representation in natural language processing across human languages. In *Proceedings of the 2021 AAAI/ACM Conference on AI, Ethics, and Society*, pages 24–34.

Aleksandra Cislak, Magdalena Formanowicz, and Tamar Saguy. 2018. Bias against research on gender bias. *Scientometrics*, 115(1):189–200.

Jeffrey Dastin. 2018. Amazon scraps secret ai recruiting tool that showed bias against women. In *Ethics of Data and Analytics*, pages 296–299. Auerbach Publications.

Lei Ding, Dengdeng Yu, Jinhan Xie, Wenxing Guo, Shenggang Hu, Meichen Liu, Linglong Kong, Hongsheng Dai, Yanchun Bao, and Bei Jiang. 2022. Word embeddings via causal inference: Gender bias reducing and semantic information preserving. In *Proceedings of the AAAI Conference on Artificial Intelligence*, volume 36, pages 11864–11872.

Chris Dyer, Victor Chahuneau, and Noah A Smith. 2013. A simple, fast, and effective reparameterization of ibm model 2. In *Proceedings of the 2013 Conference of the North American Chapter of the Association for Computational Linguistics: Human Language Technologies*, pages 644–648.

Alessandro Fabris, Alberto Purpura, Gianmaria Silvello, and Gian Antonio Susto. 2020. Gender stereotype reinforcement: Measuring the gender bias conveyed by ranking algorithms. *Information Processing & Management*, 57(6):102377.

Benoit Farley. 2012. The uqailaut project. *URL http://www. inuktitutcomputing. ca.*

Joel Escudé Font and Marta R Costa-Jussa. 2019. Equalizing gender biases in neural machine translation with word embeddings techniques. *arXiv preprint arXiv:1901.03116.*

Michael Gasser. 2011. Computational morphology and the teaching of indigenous languages. In *Indigenous Languages of Latin America Actas del Primer Simposio sobre Enseñanza de Lenguas Indígenas de América Latina*, page 52.

Gizem Gezici and Yucel Saygin. 2022. Measuring gender bias in educational videos: A case study on youtube. *arXiv preprint arXiv:2206.09987.*

Seraphina Goldfarb-Tarrant, Rebecca Marchant, Ricardo Muñoz Sánchez, Mugdha Pandya, and Adam Lopez. 2020. Intrinsic bias metrics do not correlate with application bias. *arXiv preprint arXiv:2012.15859.*

Lenore A. Grenoble and Lindsay J. Whaley. 2006. Saving languages: An introduction to language revitalization. In *Cambridge: Cambridge University Press.*

Oussama Hansal, Ngoc Tan Le, and Fatiha Sadat. 2022. Indigenous language revitalization and the dilemma of gender bias. In *Proceedings of the 4th Workshop on Gender Bias in Natural Language Processing (GeBNLP)*, pages 244–254, Seattle, Washington. Association for Computational Linguistics.

Jenna Hassan. 2015. De-colonizing gender in indigenous language revitalization efforts. In *Western Papers in Linguistics*, volume 1, Issue 2. Master's Major Research Papers and Proceedings of WISSLR 2015.

Dirk Hovy and Shrimai Prabhumoy. 2021. Five sources of bias in natural language processing. *Language and Linguistics Compass.*

Dirk Hovy and Shannon L Spruit. 2016. The social impact of natural language processing. In *Proceedings of the 54th Annual Meeting of the Association for Computational Linguistics (Volume 2: Short Papers)*, pages 591–598.

Sophie Jentzsch and Cigdem Turan. 2022. Gender bias in bert-measuring and analysing biases through sentiment rating in a realistic downstream classification task. In *Proceedings of the 4th Workshop on Gender Bias in Natural Language Processing (GeBNLP)*, pages 184–199.

Eric Joanis, Rebecca Knowles, Roland Kuhn, Samuel Larkin, Patrick Littell, Chi-kiu Lo, Darlene Stewart, and Jeffrey Micher. 2020. The nunavut hansard inuktitut english parallel corpus 3.0 with preliminary machine translation results. In *Proceedings of The 12th Language Resources and Evaluation Conference*, pages 2562–2572, Marseille, France. European Language Resources Association.

Masahiro Kaneko and Danushka Bollegala. 2021. Dictionary-based debiasing of pre-trained word embeddings. In *Proceedings of the 16th Conference of the European Chapter of the Association for Computational Linguistics: Main Volume*, pages 212–223, Online. Association for Computational Linguistics.

Neeraja Kirtane and Tanvi Anand. 2022. Mitigating gender stereotypes in hindi and marathi. *arXiv preprint arXiv:2205.05901.*

Philipp Koehn, Hieu Hoang, Alexandra Birch, Chris Callison-Burch, Marcello Federico, Nicola Bertoldi, Brooke Cowan, Wade Shen, Christine Moran, Richard Zens, et al. 2007. Moses: Open source toolkit for statistical machine translation. In *Proceedings of the 45th annual meeting of the association for computational linguistics companion volume proceedings of the demo and poster sessions*, pages 177–180.

Keita Kurita, Nidhi Vyas, Ayush Pareek, Alan W Black, and Yulia Tsvetkov. 2019. Measuring bias in contextualized word representations. In *Proceedings of the First Workshop on Gender Bias in Natural Language Processing*, pages 166–172, Florence, Italy. Association for Computational Linguistics.

Ngoc Tan Le and Fatiha Sadat. 2020. Low-resource NMT: an empirical study on the effect of rich morphological word segmentation on Inuktitut. In *Proceedings of the 14th Conference of the Association for Machine Translation in the Americas (Volume 1: Research Track)*, pages 165–172, Virtual. Association for Machine Translation in the Americas.

Ngoc Tan Le and Fatiha Sadat. 2022a. Towards a low-resource neural machine translation for indigenous languages in Canada. *Journal TAL, special issue on Language Diversity*, 62:3:39–63.

Tan Ngoc Le and Fatiha Sadat. 2022b. Towards a low-resource neural machine translation for indigenous languages in canada. In *Journal TAL, special issue on Language Diversity*, volume 62, pages 39–63.

Paul Pu Liang, Irene Mengze Li, Emily Zheng, Yao Chong Lim, Ruslan Salakhutdinov, and Louis-Philippe Morency. 2020. Towards debiasing sentence representations. *arXiv preprint arXiv:2007.08100*.

Yuxin Liao. 2021. *Gender Bias in Neural Machine Translation*. Ph.D. thesis, University of Pennsylvania.

Patrick Littell, Anna Kazantseva, Roland Kuhn, Aidan Pine, Antti Arppe, Christopher Cox, and Marie-Odile Junker. 2018. Indigenous language technologies in Canada: Assessment, challenges, and successes. In *Proceedings of the 27th International Conference on Computational Linguistics*, pages 2620–2632, Santa Fe, New Mexico, USA. Association for Computational Linguistics.

Xuebo Liu, Derek F. Wong, Yang Liu, Lidia S. Chao, Tong Xiao, and Jingbo Zhu. 2019. Shared-private bilingual word embeddings for neural machine translation. In *Proceedings of the 57th Annual Meeting of the Association for Computational Linguistics*, pages 3613–3622, Florence, Italy. Association for Computational Linguistics.

Ronald Lowe. 1985. *Basic Siglit Inuvialuit Eskimo Grammar*, volume 6. Inuvik, NWT: Committee for Original Peoples Entitlement.

Marianne Mithun. 2015. Morphological complexity and language contact in languages indigenous to north america. *Linguistic Discovery*, 13(2):37–59.

Kishore Papineni, Salim Roukos, Todd Ward, and Wei-Jing Zhu. 2002. Bleu: a method for automatic evaluation of machine translation. In *Proceedings of the 40th annual meeting on association for computational linguistics*, pages 311–318. Association for Computational Linguistics.

Aidan Pine and Mark Turin. 2017. Language revitalization. In *Oxford research encyclopedia of linguistics, Oxford. University Press*.

Maja Popović. 2015. chrf: character n-gram f-score for automatic mt evaluation. In *Proceedings of the Tenth Workshop on Statistical Machine Translation*, pages 392–395.

Matt Post. 2018. A call for clarity in reporting BLEU scores. In *Proceedings of the Third Conference on Machine Translation: Research Papers*, pages 186–191, Brussels, Belgium. Association for Computational Linguistics.

Shauli Ravfogel, Yanai Elazar, Hila Gonen, Michael Twiton, and Yoav Goldberg. 2020. Null it out: Guarding protected attributes by iterative nullspace projection. In *Proceedings of the 58th Annual Meeting of the Association for Computational Linguistics*, pages 7237–7256, Online. Association for Computational Linguistics.

Arturs Stafanovičs, Toms Bergmanis, and Mārcis Pinnis. 2020. Mitigating gender bias in machine translation with target gender annotations. In *Proceedings of the Fifth Conference on Machine Translation*, pages 629–638.

Tony Sun, Andrew Gaut, Shirlyn Tang, Yuxin Huang, Mai ElSherief, Jieyu Zhao, Diba Mirza, Elizabeth Belding, Kai-Wei Chang, and William Yang Wang. 2019. Mitigating gender bias in natural language processing: Literature review. *arXiv preprint arXiv:1906.08976*.

Ashish Vaswani, Noam Shazeer, Niki Parmar, Jakob Uszkoreit, Llion Jones, Aidan N Gomez, Łukasz Kaiser, and Illia Polosukhin. 2017. Attention is all you need. In *Advances in neural information processing systems*, pages 5998–6008.

Brandon Wiltshire, Steven Bird, and Rebecca Hardwick. 2022. Understanding how language revitalisation works: a realist synthesis. pages 1–17. Journal of Multilingual and Multicultural Development.

Jieyu Zhao, Subhabrata Mukherjee, Saghar Hosseini, Kai-Wei Chang, and Ahmed Hassan Awadallah. 2020. Gender bias in multilingual embeddings and cross-lingual transfer. In *Proceedings of the 58th Annual Meeting of the Association for Computational Linguistics*, pages 2896–2907, Online. Association for Computational Linguistics.

Jieyu Zhao, Tianlu Wang, Mark Yatskar, Ryan Cotterell, Vicente Ordonez, and Kai-Wei Chang. 2019. Gender bias in contextualized word embeddings. In *Proceedings of the 2019 NAACL: Human Language Technology Conference, Volume 1*, pages 629–634, Minneapolis, Minnesota. Association for Computational Linguistics.

Text normalization for low-resource languages: the case of Ligurian

Stefano Lusito[*†]
Universität Innsbruck,
Institut für Romanistik

Edoardo Ferrante[†]
Conseggio pe-o Patrimònio
Linguistico Ligure

Jean Maillard[‡]
Meta AI

Abstract

Text normalization is a crucial technology for low-resource languages which lack rigid spelling conventions or that have undergone multiple spelling reforms. Low-resource text normalization has so far relied upon hand-crafted rules, which are perceived to be more data efficient than neural methods.

In this paper we examine the case of text normalization for Ligurian, an endangered Romance language. We collect 4,394 Ligurian sentences paired with their normalized versions, as well as the first open source monolingual corpus for Ligurian. We show that, in spite of the small amounts of data available, a compact transformer-based model can be trained to achieve very low error rates by the use of backtranslation and appropriate tokenization.

Scintexi

A normalizzaçion da grafia a l'é unna tecnologia d'importansa primmäia pe-e lengue con pöche resorse che mancan de regole fisse à sto reguardo ò ch'en passæ pe varie reforme de scrittua. Fin à oua st'operaçion, pe-e lengue de sta categoria, a l'é stæta basâ ciù che tutto in sce de regole mecaniche, tegnue pe ciù efficaçe che l'utilizzaçion di metodi neurali.

Inte ste pagine analizzemmo o caxo da normalizzaçion pe-o ligure zeneise, unna lengua romansa à reisego de scentâ. Da unna parte emmo arrecuggeito 4.394 frase in ligure e ê emmo accobbiæ co-a seu verscion in grafia normalizzâ; da l'atra, emmo creou o primmo corpus monolingue pe-o ligure à liçensa averta. Into studio demostremmo che, pe quante i dati à dispoxiçion seggian scarsci, l'é poscibile allenâ un modello compatto basou in sciô transformer pe razzonze di basci tasci d'errô, pe mezo da backtranslation e de unna tokenizzaçion appropiâ.

1 Introduction

Many recent advances in the field of NLP rely on large-scale textual corpora. Low-resource languages are typically excluded from such developments due to data scarcity issues. To exacerbate the problem, many low-resource languages suffer from noisy data, due to factors such as the absence of rigid spelling conventions or the lack of user-friendly input methods for special characters (Nekoto et al., 2020; Riabi et al., 2021). Text normalization can be a crucial tool to address these issues and enable the creation of corpora from noisy sources (Zupon et al., 2021).

Just as importantly, such technologies can be directly applied to speed up orthographic leveling operations in the field of publishing. Orthographic editing may be desirable when republishing older literary works written according to spelling rules which are no longer in use, or to canonicalize variant forms that may be inadvertently employed even within the same manuscript. This work was born out of such editorial needs for the case of Ligurian, an endangered language spoken within the homonymous region of Liguria in Northern Italy and neighboring territories. The orthographic leveling of historical texts in Ligurian has so far been performed by hand (see e.g. Toso, 1992). The approach presented in this paper represents work conducted by members of the Ligurian linguistic community aiming to largely automate this tedious and time-consuming task with a neural model.

The application of neural methods to text normalization has been limited to high-resource languages (Nguyen and Cavallari, 2020; Wu et al., 2021; Wu and Cotterell, 2019; Tang et al., 2018). Instead, previous work on low-resource text normalization has relied upon hand-crafted rules (Pretorius and Bosch, 2003; Hurskainen, 2004; Asahiah et al., 2017), often perceived as being more data efficient. Indeed the survey by Bollmann (2019)

[*] stefano.lusito@uibk.ac.at.
[†] Equal contribution.
[‡] Work conducted in a personal capacity, independently of the author's affiliation.

recommended the use of substitution lists for low-resource languages and suggested reserving statistical and neural approaches for datasets with at least ~10k entries.

In this paper we reassess this belief, looking specifically at the case of Ligurian. We show that, by combining modern data augmentation techniques with a neural model, we are able to achieve average character error rates as low as 2.64 when normalizing texts from a wide range of domains and with a high degree of spelling variation. We achieve this without needing a large-scale annotated corpus: the only resources used are 4.4k unnormalized short sentences (38.1k tokens), manually normalized to produce a parallel corpus (requiring a single native speaker less than five hours of work) and a small unannotated corpus of text (6.7k sentences, 347.5 tokens) which was already in normalized form. We contribute the following:

1. A recipe for training a transformer-based text normalization model for an endangered language, showing how backtranslation (Sennrich et al., 2016a), a commonly applied technique in machine translation, can help boost performance in low-resource scenarios. The model and code are released publicly.[1]

2. A study of the importance of tokenization for neural-based text normalization, showing the effect of varying the vocabulary size for byte-pair encoding (Sennrich et al., 2016b).

3. The creation and public release of the first dataset for Ligurian text normalization as well as the first monolingual corpus for Ligurian.[2]

2 Background

The variety of Ligurian we consider in this paper is Genoese, spoken in the capital and neighboring regions (Toso, 2002). It is not only the most widespread dialect in terms of geographical area and number of speakers, but also the only one to possess a written literary tradition that has developed without interruption from the 13th century to the present day (Toso, 2009).

The spelling system of Genoese has developed over the centuries hand in hand with the evolution of the language itself (Toso, 2009, p. 27-32). A high degree of variation in spelling can still be observed today, due in part to the absence of regulatory bodies and to the lack of keyboard support for several special characters. However, the traditional spelling conventions as formalized by Toso (1997) and recently revised by a group of writers and researchers (Acquarone, 2015) are seeing increasing adoption in the publishing and academic worlds (Toso, 2015; Autelli et al., 2019; Lusito and Maillard, 2021; Lusito, 2022).

In this work, we train models capable of normalizing a variety of Ligurian texts according to the set of spelling conventions mentioned above.

3 Data collection

The texts used for this study were chosen to provide a heterogeneous dataset of variously relevant spellings in Genoese literature. They are:

1. 1,000 sentences and short examples extracted from Casaccia (1876), the most important Genoese-Italian dictionary of the 19th century.

2. Two poems by Piaggio (1846), the most prolific Genoese poet of the first half of the 19th century (1,240 verses).

3. Two issues of *O Balilla* (1,108 sentences in total), one of the main Genoese bi-weekly papers of the 19th and 20th century. Typographical errors were particularly frequent in this newspaper, making it a perfect source of data for this study.

4. Five cantos from Gazzo (1909)'s Genoese translation of Dante's *Comedy* (1,046 verses).

While the first three sources have a similar spelling model[3], Gazzo adopts an extremely complex spelling system, somewhere between the traditional model and a para-phonetic approach (Lusito, 2019, p. 173-175). Unlike the other data sources, Gazzo's spelling system strongly deviates from contemporary Ligurian spelling and does not reflect current usage or even past adoption beyond the author's own work. We nevertheless include it in our analysis to illustrate the model's ability to adapt to strong outliers.

Each one of the datasets above was manually normalized by a native speaker, leading to four parallel corpora which match unnormalized sentences to their normalized versions. For brevity, in experiments we will be referring to these four datasets

[1] https://github.com/fleanend/fairseq-text-normalizer

[2] https://github.com/ConseggioLigure/normalized_ligurian_corpus

[3] See Boano (1997, p. 104-114) for an outline of Casaccia's spelling choices.

as *C*, *P*, *B* and *G* respectively. We use a 70/20/10 training/test/validation split throughout this work.

Additionally, we also use a small monolingual corpus of 6,723 sentences of Ligurian, made up of excerpts from the following sources: *O Stafî*, a contemporary magazine devoted to sociopolitical discussions, a novel (Lusito, 2020), and a dozen articles from Ligurian Wikipedia. These texts are largely already in normalized form, apart from a few simple aspects which were fixed in an automated manner.

The divergences between the different spelling systems of the texts considered in this study are illustrated in figure 1, showing the target normalized form at the top.

Unna rondaniña affammâ a s' é pösâ in sciô teito de coppi

Ûnn-a rõndaninn-a affammâ a s' é pösâ in sciö teito de cõppi
Ûnn-a rondaninn-a affammâ a s' è pösâ in sciö teito de coppi
Ûnn-a rondaninn-a affamâ a s' è pösâ in sce-o teito de coppi
Ûña rundaniña affammä' a s' é pösä in sce o téyto de cuppi

Figure 1: A sample sentence (*A hungry swallow rests on the tiled roof*) in normalized form (top), compared with how it might have appeared in the unnormalized datasets **C**, **P**, **B** and **G**.

4 Experiments

4.1 Baseline

Our baseline is the transformer architecture used to perform historical text normalization by Wu et al. (2021). After conducting some preliminary experiments to determine if their hyperparameters would be applicable in our highly data scarce setting, we settled upon a much smaller batch size. The resulting architecture, which was trained on `fairseq` (Ott et al., 2019), is made up of 4 encoder and decoder layers with 4 attention heads, embeddings of size 256, a hidden size of 1024, dropout of 0.3 and label smoothing with a factor of 0.1. The model was trained with Adam (Kingma and Ba, 2015) with an inverse square root scheduler, a learning rate of 10^{-3}, 4000 warmup updates, and a batch size of 20.

We train one model per each of the four parallel datasets described in section 3. We then also train one more model on the union of all datasets, with the aim of producing a normalization model capable of working with a wide range of texts.

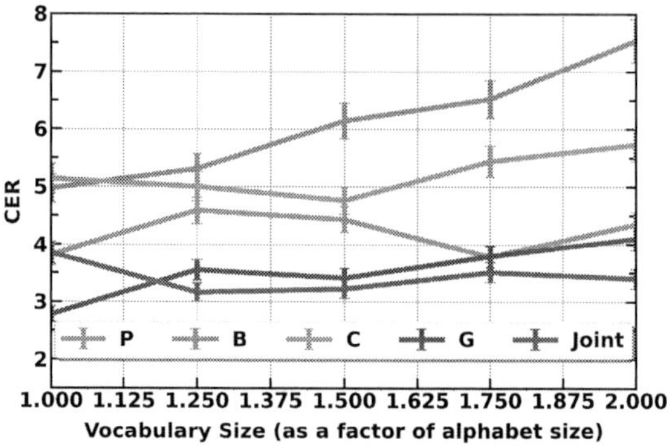

Figure 2: Effect of tokenizer vocabulary size on the validation performance of baseline models. We report the average of three runs and standard error.

4.2 Tokenization

As is common with transformer-based NLP models we apply subword tokenization to our data (Kudo and Richardson, 2018). We hypothesize that vocabulary size might play an important role in a normalization model's performance. We tested several vocabulary sizes, to check whether the tokenization of digraph and initial, medial or caudal position of a grapheme can help or hinder learning. We measure vocabulary size as a factor of the total alphabet size of a dataset, and experiment with values of 1 (corresponding to a character-level model), 1.25, 1.5, 1.75 and 2. Alphabet sizes for the four datasets are 66, 63 , 50 and 78 for the *P*, *B*, *C* and *G* datasets respectively; their union has size 82.

As shown in figure 2, we see that, especially for the spelling systems with the least resources, the level of tokenization (determined by the vocabulary size) has a noticeable impact on the model performance. We suspect the optimal number is highly dependent on the number of unigraph $\leftrightarrow$ multigraph alignment pairs in each parallel dataset: having a multigraph tokenized as a single unit should aid in the task of mapping it to a monograph, while having it split up into multiple tokens should make the model's task harder.

We select vocabulary sizes for each setup based on this validation performance and keep them fixed for the remaining experiments.

4.3 Joint model

A normalization model is most useful if it can operate on texts regardless of their domain or the nature of their spelling variation, and without the need to tag them as being from specific sources. We attempt to create a universal normalizer by merging

	Dataset				
	P	*B*	*C*	*G*	Joint
Specific	3.78	4.97	5.14	**2.78**	4.42
Joint	**2.57**	**3.29**	**2.28**	4.32	**3.16**
Copy	9.54	8.24	21.05	14.59	12.76

Table 1: Test set performance (CER) of the dataset-specific and joint models of section 4.1, compared to a naive "copy" baseline. Best of three runs based on validation performance.

	Dataset				
	P	*B*	*C*	*G*	Joint
Specific+BN	2.26	4.95	2.32	**2.39**	3.11
Joint+BN	2.80	2.96	1.67	4.42	2.98
Specific+BN'	2.28	2.45	2.52	2.44	**2.47**
Joint+BN'	**1.91**	**2.38**	**1.36**	4.55	2.64

Table 2: Test set performance (CER) of the dataset-specific and joint models when augmenting training data via "backnormalization" (section 4.4) of 3.7k sentences (+BN) and all 6.7k sentences (+BN') from an unannotated corpus. Best of three runs based on validation performance.

all datasets described in section 3 and training one more model on this unified parallel corpus.

Table 1 compares the results of the joint and dataset-specific models. For reference, we additionally report the performance of a naive "copy" baseline, which simply leaves text as-is. We also report the performance on the joint dataset of the dataset-specific models, which consists in sending each sample to the appropriate dataset-specific model depending on its origin.

We find from these results that the joint model still manages to achieve sub-5 CER on all datasets, even outperforming the dataset-specific models in a majority of cases. We believe that concatenating all data helps the model learn the target spelling system better, while consolidating any grapheme normalization rules in common among the sources. On the other hand, the joint model also learns on contrasting evidence for several graphemes, favoring thus the spelling systems with the most features in common (*B* and *C*) and punishing the most eclectic ones. This is particularly evident for the case of *G* which, as already noted in section 3, is by far the most complex to deal with.

4.4 "Backnormalization"

Backtranslation (Sennrich et al., 2016a) is an extremely effective approach used in machine translation to benefit from unannotated, monolingual data (Edunov et al., 2018). We adapt this method to the task of text normalization as follows. We train an additional set of dataset-specific baseline models as in section 4.1, but this time on the reverse task, going from normalized to unnormalized text ("backnormalization" for brevity). We then take our unannotated corpus, which is already in normalized form, and run it through these four backnormalization models. The result of this procedure are four new pseudo-parallel corpora, the target side being our unannotated corpus, and the source side being our backnormalization models' attempts at reconstructing how this text might have been written in unnormalized form, with the spelling variations typical of the four sources of data under study in this paper.

These backnormalized datasets were then used in addition to our original training data. Due to the noisy nature of backnormalized data, which is half-synthetic, in training we upsample the original parallel datasets with a factor of $\lfloor N_{\text{backnormalized}}/N_{\text{original}} \rfloor$ (where N is the length in tokens of a corpus). This is so that in training the model would learn from an equal number of human-normalized and backnormalized data.

To study the effectiveness of backnormalization as well as the effect of the size of the unannotated corpus, we repeat this experiment twice. First using a 3.7k-sized portion of the unannotated corpus, then using the full dataset. The results in table 2 confirm that backnormalization is indeed effective, showing a noticeable reduction in character error rate overall for the models trained on the augmented data. We also a fairly clear trend of improvement in the error rate when more unannotated data is used via backnormalization.

One notable case is performance on dataset *G*, which shows mild improvement in the dataset-specific models but degradation for the joint model. As previously discussed, the spelling system of this dataset represents a clear outlier, deviating strongly from actual contemporary usage. We note that in any kind of real-world use case such type of data would be considered out-of-scope.

5 Conclusion

In this paper we have tackled the issue of text normalization for Ligurian, an endangered low-resource language. We did so by collecting and releasing a dataset of 4,394 Ligurian sentences in different spelling systems paired with normalized versions. We further gathered and released the first open source digital monolingual corpus of contemporary Ligurian, consisting of 6,723 sentences, and showed its potential despite its modest size.

We have shown that in low-resource settings a compact transformer-based model with the appropriate choice of hyperparameters and tokenization, combined with "backnormalization", can achieve CER under 3 points on average, even when the model is given no information on the provenance and spelling conventions of the source text. By varying the size of the corpus used with backnormalization we have further shown that performance is likely to improve even further, should more unannotated data be collected.

There are multiple practical applications of such a model. First of all, it could allow the general public – which tends to experiences difficulties entering Ligurian characters by means of the Italian keyboard – to publish texts in a relatively uniform spelling. Second, on the editorial side, it would greatly speed up orthographic leveling operations, not just of contemporary material but also for the republishing of older literary works written according to spelling rules which are no longer in use. Finally, the normalization of corpora with noisy spelling is especially important for a low-resource language, as it would make more data available for downstream tasks such as language modelling and machine translation which are reliant upon the availability of large corpora.

In conclusion, we consider neural text normalization combined with backnormalization to be a particularly useful tool to promote the preservation as well as the revival of the Ligurian language. The present work only focuses on the case of Ligurian. However, due to the low amount of data needed to train a normalization system, we hope that other researchers and members of language communities in analogous situations will be able to adapt and apply this approach.

References

Andrea Acquarone. 2015. Scrivere la lingua. In Andrea Acquarone, editor, *Parlo Ciæo. La lingua della Liguria*, pages 87–94. De Ferrari / Il Secolo XIX, Genoa, Italy.

Franklin Asahiah, Odejobi Odetunji, and Emmanuel Adagunodo. 2017. Restoring tone-marks in standard yorùbá electronic text: Improved model. *Computer Science*, 18.

Erica Autelli, Konecny Christine, and Stefano Lusito. 2019. GEPHRAS: il primo dizionario combinatorio genovese-italiano online. In Fiorenzo Toso, editor, *Il patrimonio linguistico storico della Liguria: attualità e futuro. Raccolta di Studi*. InSedicesimo, Savona, Italy.

Attilio Giuseppe Boano. 1997. L'alfabeto genovese: dalla codificazione di Giovanni Casaccia alla normalizzazione grafica in atto. *Bollettino dell'Atlante linguistico italiano*, 21:99–133.

Marcel Bollmann. 2019. A large-scale comparison of historical text normalization systems. In *Proceedings of the 2019 Conference of the North American Chapter of the Association for Computational Linguistics: Human Language Technologies, Volume 1 (Long and Short Papers)*, pages 3885–3898, Minneapolis, Minnesota. Association for Computational Linguistics.

Giovanni Casaccia. 1876. *Dizionario genovese-italiano. Seconda edizione accresciuta del doppio e quasi tutta rifatta*. Franchielli, Genoa, Italy.

Sergey Edunov, Myle Ott, Michael Auli, and David Grangier. 2018. Understanding back-translation at scale. In *Proceedings of the 2018 Conference on Empirical Methods in Natural Language Processing*, pages 489–500, Brussels, Belgium. Association for Computational Linguistics.

Angelico Federico Gazzo. 1909. *A Diviña comédia de Dante di Ardighê tradûta in léngua zeneyze cu 'i segni da pronúnçia*. Stampaya da Zoventù, Genoa, Italy.

Arvi Hurskainen. 2004. Swahili language manager: A storehouse for developing multiple computational applications. *Nordic Journal of African Studies*, 13.

Diederik P Kingma and Jimmy Ba. 2015. Adam: A method for stochastic optimization. In *ICLR (Poster)*.

Taku Kudo and John Richardson. 2018. SentencePiece: A simple and language independent subword tokenizer and detokenizer for neural text processing. In *Proceedings of the 2018 Conference on Empirical Methods in Natural Language Processing: System Demonstrations*, pages 66–71, Brussels, Belgium. Association for Computational Linguistics.

Stefano Lusito. 2019. La *Grammatica genovese* di Angelico Federico Gazzo. *Bollettino dell'Atlante linguistico italiano*, 43:155–177.

Stefano Lusito. 2020. Lazarillo de Tormes. In *Cabirda. Lengue e lettiatue romanse*, volume 5. Zona, Genoa, Italy. Translation of an anonymous Spanish novella from 1554.

Stefano Lusito. 2022. *Dizionario italiano-genovese. O diçionäio ch'o mostra o zeneise d'ancheu*. Editrice Programma, Treviso, Italy.

Stefano Lusito and Jean Maillard. 2021. A Universal Dependencies corpus for Ligurian. In *Proceedings of the Fifth Workshop on Universal Dependencies (UDW, SyntaxFest 2021)*.

Wilhelmina Nekoto, Vukosi Marivate, Tshinondiwa Matsila, Timi Fasubaa, Taiwo Fagbohungbe, Solomon Oluwole Akinola, Shamsuddeen Muhammad, Salomon Kabongo Kabenamualu, Salomey Osei, Freshia Sackey, Rubungo Andre Niyongabo, Ricky Macharm, Perez Ogayo, Orevaoghene Ahia, Musie Meressa Berhe, Mofetoluwa Adeyemi, Masabata Mokgesi-Selinga, Lawrence Okegbemi, Laura Martinus, Kolawole Tajudeen, Kevin Degila, Kelechi Ogueji, Kathleen Siminyu, Julia Kreutzer, Jason Webster, Jamiil Toure Ali, Jade Abbott, Iroro Orife, Ignatius Ezeani, Idris Abdulkadir Dangana, Herman Kamper, Hady Elsahar, Goodness Duru, Ghollah Kioko, Murhabazi Espoir, Elan van Biljon, Daniel Whitenack, Christopher Onyefuluchi, Chris Chinenye Emezue, Bonaventure F. P. Dossou, Blessing Sibanda, Blessing Bassey, Ayodele Olabiyi, Arshath Ramkilowan, Alp Öktem, Adewale Akinfaderin, and Abdallah Bashir. 2020. Participatory research for low-resourced machine translation: A case study in African languages. In *Findings of the Association for Computational Linguistics: EMNLP 2020*, pages 2144–2160, Online. Association for Computational Linguistics.

Hoang Nguyen and Sandro Cavallari. 2020. Neural multi-task text normalization and sanitization with pointer-generator. In *Proceedings of the First Workshop on Natural Language Interfaces*, pages 37–47, Online. Association for Computational Linguistics.

Myle Ott, Sergey Edunov, Alexei Baevski, Angela Fan, Sam Gross, Nathan Ng, David Grangier, and Michael Auli. 2019. fairseq: A fast, extensible toolkit for sequence modeling. In *Proceedings of the 2019 Conference of the North American Chapter of the Association for Computational Linguistics (Demonstrations)*, pages 48–53, Minneapolis, Minnesota. Association for Computational Linguistics.

Martin Piaggio. 1846. *Raccolta delle migliori poesie edite e inedite*. Fratelli Pagano, Genoa, Italy.

Laurette Pretorius and Sonja E Bosch. 2003. Exact hard monotonic attention for character-level transduction. *Southern African Linguistics and Applied Language Studies*, 21.

Arij Riabi, Benoît Sagot, and Djamé Seddah. 2021. Can character-based language models improve downstream task performances in low-resource and noisy language scenarios? In *Proceedings of the Seventh Workshop on Noisy User-generated Text (W-NUT 2021)*, pages 423–436, Online. Association for Computational Linguistics.

Rico Sennrich, Barry Haddow, and Alexandra Birch. 2016a. Improving neural machine translation models with monolingual data. In *Proceedings of the 54th Annual Meeting of the Association for Computational Linguistics (Volume 1: Long Papers)*, pages 86–96, Berlin, Germany. Association for Computational Linguistics.

Rico Sennrich, Barry Haddow, and Alexandra Birch. 2016b. Neural machine translation of rare words with subword units. In *Proceedings of the 54th Annual Meeting of the Association for Computational Linguistics (Volume 1: Long Papers)*, pages 1715–1725, Berlin, Germany. Association for Computational Linguistics.

Gongbo Tang, Fabienne Cap, Eva Pettersson, and Joakim Nivre. 2018. An evaluation of neural machine translation models on historical spelling normalization. In *Proceedings of the 27th International Conference on Computational Linguistics*, pages 1320–1331, Santa Fe, New Mexico, USA. Association for Computational Linguistics.

Fiorenzo Toso. 1992. Nota al testo. In *Ginn-a de Sampedaenn-a*, pages 24–25. Microart's.

Fiorenzo Toso. 1997. *Grammatica del genovese*. Le Mani, Recco, Italy.

Fiorenzo Toso. 2002. Liguria. In Manlio Cortelazzo, Carla Marcato, and Nicola De Blasi, editors, *I dialetti italiani: storia, struttura, uso*, pages 245–252. UTET, Turin, Italy.

Fiorenzo Toso. 2009. *La letteratura ligure in genovese nei dialetti locali. Profilo storico e antologia*, volume 1. Le Mani, Recco, Italy.

Fiorenzo Toso. 2015. *Piccolo dizionario etimologico ligure. L'origine, la storia e il significato di quattrocento parole a Genova e in Liguria*. Zona, Lavagna, Italy.

Shijie Wu and Ryan Cotterell. 2019. Exact hard monotonic attention for character-level transduction. In *Proceedings of the 57th Annual Meeting of the Association for Computational Linguistics*, pages 1530–1537, Florence, Italy. Association for Computational Linguistics.

Shijie Wu, Ryan Cotterell, and Mans Hulden. 2021. Applying the transformer to character-level transduction. In *Proceedings of the 16th Conference of the European Chapter of the Association for Computational Linguistics: Main Volume*, pages 1901–1907, Online. Association for Computational Linguistics.

Andrew Zupon, Evan Crew, and Sandy Ritchie. 2021. Text normalization for low-resource languages of africa. In *AfricaNLP 2021*.

LSDT: a Dependency Treebank of Lombard Sinti

Marco Forlano
University of Bergamo/Pavia
marco.forlano@unibg.it

Luca Brigada Villa
University of Bergamo/Pavia
luca.brigadavilla@unibg.it

Abstract

Lombard Sinti is a variety of Romani spoken in Italy, in an area that can be identified with the Italian region of Lombardy. In this paper we present LSDT, a dependency treebank of Lombard Sinti consisting of 100 sentences manually annotated both morphologically and sintactically.

1 Introduction

Since its publication, Universal Dependencies (de Marneffe et al., 2021) provides annotated resources for 130 languages. The data comes in form of treebanks, that is, collections of sentences with morphological and syntactic annotation. For such annotation, UD has developed a scheme which has the goal to be cross-linguistically consistent in order to facilitate research from a typological perspective. Despite the amount of languages in UD, minority languages are still underrepresented in this project. This paper presents LSDT, a treebank of Lombard Sinti, a variety of Romani.

Romani is an Indo-Aryan language spoken across Europe by socio-ethnic communities whose members mostly call themselves *Roma* or *Sinte/i*. Nowadays, it is widely acknowledged that such groups have a common Indian origin (see Matras, 2002: 14-18 for an overview on the theories about the origin of Romani populations). According to scholars, their migration from India began by the first millennium AD, and after they arrived in Greece in the Middle Ages, they started to move all over Europe in different groups, slowly getting to those areas where they still largely reside (see Beníšek, 2020: 25-26). As a non-territorialized language, Romani shows a very high rate of geographic variation (see Matras et al., 1997; Matras, 2002: 5-13; Elšík and Beníšek, 2020 for an overview on Romani dialects and their classification criteria). Furthermore, all Romani varieties are affected in each country by asymmetric contact with their various co-territorial majority languages (Matras and Adamou, 2020), which ultimately leads to different degrees of language shift (see e.g. Adamou, 2010, 2016).

The paper is structured as follows: in Section 2 we introduce Lombard Sinti providing the typologycal classification of this language and its historical background; in Section 3 we present the data and how we converted the sentences to CoNLL-U format; in Section 4 we explain in detail the process of annotation of the treebank; finally, Section 5 concludes the paper and presents the work we plan to do in the future.

2 Lombard Sinti

Lombard Sinti (endonym: *sinto/sintu*[1]) is a variety of Romani spoken in Northern Italy. Its core area corresponds to the Italian region of Lombardy, though Lombard Sinti speakers are also found in the adjacent areas of Eastern Piedmont and Emilia. Lombard Sinti is commonly assigned by scholars to the Northern branch of Romani dialects (see Matras, 2002: 9). In this section, we discuss some typological features of Lombard Sinti and we offer a historical background of the variety.

2.1 Typological classification

Romani is a language with rich inflectional morphology; as for the nominal inflection, "lexical nouns inflect for the paradigmatic categories of nominal case and number and have an inherent gender, masculine vs feminine" (Elšík, 2020: 163). There are eight cases, commonly referred to as nominative, vocative, oblique, dative, locative, comitative/instrumental, and genitive. From a syntactic point of view, Romani shows several typological features that have been shaped through contact

[1]The alternation between the vowels -o e -u in Lombard Sinti should be probably understood as a free variation, although a preference for one vowel over the other in terms of norm and frequency seems to be partially linked to sub-group membership within Lombard Sinti.

with non-Indic languages, especially with Bizantine Greek (Adamou and Matras, 2020: 235). The most prominent is the nominative-accusative and neutral alignment, as opposed to the ergative one that is found in modern Indo-Aryan languages and that can be even reconstructed for Proto-Romani (Beníšek, 2020). Other innovations include the emergence of definite and indefinite articles and the development of an unmarked VO order, alongside some cross-linguistic tendencies associated with it, e.g., the presence of prepositions (Adamou and Matras, 2020). Furthermore, in all Romani varieties, subordinate clauses follow independent clauses. The outlined typological features are generally found in Lombard Sinti too. However, in Lombard Sinti, a complete loss of cases in the nominal inflection has occurred. Moreover, the variety shows a neutral morphosyntactic alignment, whereby A, S, and P arguments are expressed identically (i.e. with a zero-mark, see e.g. Malchukov et al., 2010), while in most Romani varieties, animated P arguments are expressed differently from A and S through a dedicated oblique suffix. From the above overview, it appears that Lombard Sinti and Italian are similar in many respects as far as typology is concerned (see also Sorrenti, 2014). Nonetheless, some major differences can be found. Just to mention a few, while pronominal clitics in Lombard Sinti are consistently placed after the verb, in Italian their positioning is constrained (and appear after the verb only when the mood is non-finite). Moreover, in Lombard Sinti, the rich inherited case system has been retained for personal pronouns, which limits the use of prepositions in such contexts. Finally, if compared to Italian, Lombard Sinti disposes of a smaller range of non-finite verbal moods, which tend to be expressed analytically.

2.2 Available sources on Lombard Sinti

The available sources on Lombard Sinti are rather scarce. The glossary by Partesani (1973) and the sketchy grammatical description by Soravia (1977) represent the first attempts in this direction. Moreover, Lombard Sinti lemmas appear in Soravia and Fochi (1995) *Dizionario Sinottico delle Parlate Zingare in Italia*[2], the only existing vocabulary on Romani varieties spoken in Italy. More recently, some research by Andrea Scala has focused on specific structural aspects of Lombard Sinti, such as the numeral system (Scala, 2017) or some morphosyntactic constructions, such as the negative one (Scala, 2020). The most complete work to date is perhaps Sorrenti (2014), which proposes a full grammatical description of Lombard Sinti, pointing out similarities and differences with Italian.

2.3 Historical background

As is often the case with Romani varieties, the history of Lombard Sinti and its speakers can be partially reconstructed on linguistic evidence. The high rate of borrowings from Germanic languages and, to a lesser extent, from Slavic languages, suggests that after the Greek diaspora Lombard Sinti speakers resided for some time in German-speaking areas via the Western Balkans. Their arrival in Italy is estimated during the Modern Era (Piasere, 2004).

Official data on Lombard Sinti speakers is not available. Indicatively, in Northern Italy, there are an estimated 30.000 Sinti[3], divided into different groups speaking different varieties, including the Lombard ones. In the panorama of the Sinti varieties spoken in Italy, Lombard Sinti appears to be one of the best preserved. Indeed, it is still learned as L1 by children and maintains strong identity functions. According to the Expanded Graded Intergenerational Disruption Scale (Lewis and Simons, 2010), a measure that is used to assess the vitality or endangerment rate of languages, Lombard Sinti might thus be classified as Vigorous. Currently, Lombard Sinti speakers exhibit a linguistic repertoire where Italian and Sinti are used together in informal domains, while in formal ones only Italian is used (Scala, 2012).

Lombard Sinti, as Romani varieties in general, is a non-standardized language, as its use is primarily oral. Therefore, neither normative grammar nor graphic standards are available in this variety, although some more or less spontaneous written productions exist (see the translation of the Gospel of Mark by don Mario Riboldi, or the use of Sinti on new media, cf. Scala, 2015). Among scholars, to transcribe Lombard Sinti data it is common to adopt a semi-conventionalized academic standard that promotes, for instance, the use of diacritics from Slavic alphabets to represent affricate sounds (Matras, 1999). Such a choice informs, among others, the *Dizionario Sinottico delle Parlate Zingare in Italia* (Soravia and Fochi, 1995) as well as

[2] Synoptic Dictionary of Gypsy Speeches in Italy.

[3] http://romafacts.uni-graz.at/

the Lombard Sinti sample in the Romani Morpho-Syntax Database (Matras et al., 2009).

Finally, it is worth mentioning that Romani varieties in Italy do not appear among the languages that enjoy the specific protection tools provided by national law 482/1999 on linguistic minorities (see e.g. Fiorentini, 2022). This inhibits the use of Roman Sinti in public domains, from schools to local and national media.

3 Data

The sentences included in the treebank[4] were collected from the Romani Morpho-Syntax Database (Matras et al., 2009) a resource that collects dictionaries, sentences and phrases from many Romani dialects.

We extracted the available data from the Lombard Sinti portion of the database[5], selecting 100 complete sentences from the sample. The goal of the selection was to include in our sample sentences that differ from each other for length, gender of the nominal elements, tenses of the verbs in order to obtain a diverse set.

num. tokens	num. sentences
4	1
5	4
6	9
7	14
8	11
9	13
10	11
11	11
12	6
13	5
14	5
15	2
16	2
17	3
18	1
19	1
20	1

Table 1: Distribution of the lengths of the sentences in the treebank in terms of number of tokens

After the selection of the sentences, we performed a shallow tokenization considering the spaces in the sentences which resulted in a CoNLL-U file with one token per line without annotation. Each sentence in the treebank was provided with a `sent_id` which contains a four-digit number that refers to the position of the sentence in the treebank and the number of the sample in the Lombard Sinti portion of the RMS Database (e.g. `sent_id = 0027@RMS-443` is the 27th sentence in the treebank and corresponds to sentence 443 in the RMS). Along with the `sent_id`, we included the text and the English translation in the metadata of each sentence.

4 Annotation

To annotate the treebank, we used UD Annotatrix (Tyers et al., 2017), a tool that allows to upload a file formatted in CoNLL-U and annotate it. First, we corrected the tokenization obtained considering the spaces between words, then we provided lemmatization and morphological features for each token. Finally, for each sentence, we annotated the syntactic dependencies.

In this Section we explain more in detail each phase of the annotation process.

4.1 Tokenization and lemmatization

The tokenization obtained considering the spaces between words was corrected by manually separating pronominal clitics from their host verbs (e.g. *selma* → *sel ma* '(he/she) visits us'; *dukadoma* → *dukadom ma* '(I) hurt myself') and articles from prepositions in case of articulated prepositions (e.g. *pur drom* → *par u drom* 'on the street'; *ki vierta* → *ka i vierta* 'to the pub') in order to adhere to Universal Dependencies' guidelines on tokenization[6].

number of tokens	990
number of unique lemmas	293

Table 2: Number of tokens and unique lemmas in the LSDT treebank

To carry out the lemmatization, we relied on the conventions that are used in Romani linguistics. Therefore, we considered the masculine singular forms as lemmas for nouns, adjectives and demonstrative pronouns and the third person of the present indicative for verbs. As for stressed personal pronouns, since in Lombard Sinti they are inflected by case and gender (only in the third person), we chose the nominative masculine as base form.

[4]https://github.com/unipv-larl/LSDT

[5]https://romani.humanities.manchester.ac.uk//rms/browse/phrases/phraselist

[6]https://universaldependencies.org/u/overview/tokenization.html

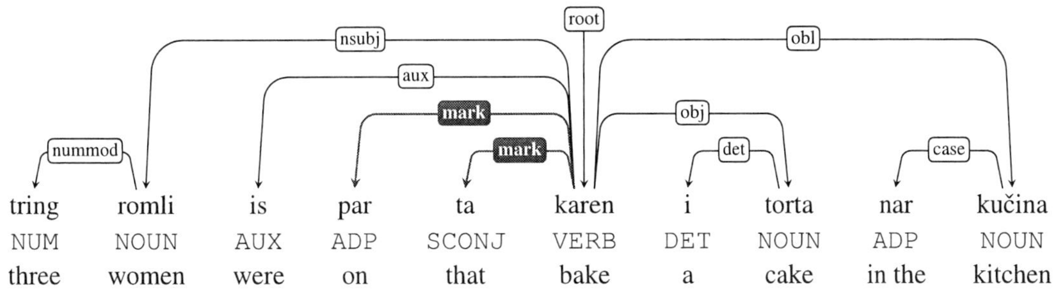

Figure 1: Dependecy tree of the sentence 'tring romli is par ta karen i torta nar kučina' ('three women were baking a cake in the kitchen').

4.2 POS tagging and morphological annotation

Each POS was then assigned the relevant morphological features (see Table 4 in the Appendix A for the complete list). Gender and number were annotated for nouns and adjectives, while verb form, mood, tense, and person were annotated for verbs. Among verbs, only past participles, which in Lombard Sinti have an adjectival meaning (Scala, 2011: 256), were also annotated for number and gender. In line with the literature on Romani linguistics, the feature `Mood=Subj` (subjunctive) was used to indicate the "subordinative mood" (Scala, 2011: 258; Sorrenti, 2014: 138), i.e., the mood of verbs in implicit completive clauses. As for personal pronouns, gender was annotated only for third-person singular, since a gender-based distinction is made in Lombardi Sinti only between the forms *joi* 'she' and *jo* 'he'. `Case` was annotated only for stressed personal pronouns, as unstressed clitics show one single morphological manifestation for the non-nominative case (Sorrenti, 2014: 135).

4.3 Syntactic annotation

Lombard Sinti shows some language-specific constructions. To express the progressive meaning, it uses a periphrasis where the verb 'to be' is followed by the preposition *par* 'on', by the complementizer *ta* (which is however optional) and the dependent subjunctive (e.g. *jom par ta sua*, 'I'm going to sleep', lit. 'I'm on that sleep'). In such constructions, we considered the dependent subjunctive as the root and annotated the relation between it and the two function words *par* and *ta* as `mark`, and the relation with the verb 'to be' as `aux` (as shown in Figure 1).

The label `fixed` was used to annotate, among others, the relation between the third person copula *i* 'is' and the oblique pronouns (Figure 2) that in Lombard Sinti are used together to form the paradigm of the verb *to have* (e.g. *i-ma* 'I have', lit. 'is-to-me').

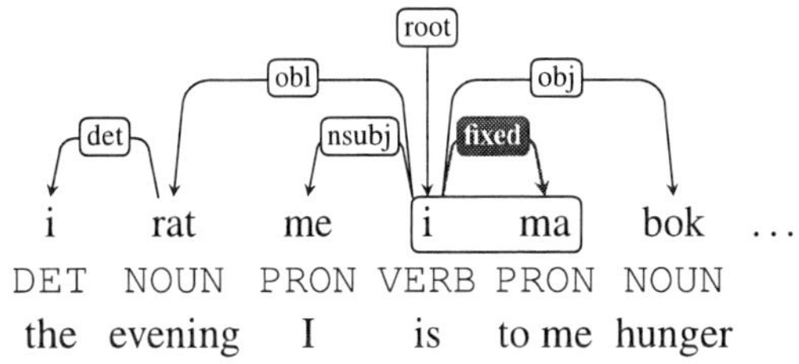

Figure 2: Dependecy tree of part of the sentence 'i rat me ima bok, ma se xava vava tulo' ('in the evening I get very hungry, but if I eat I'll get very fat').

Finally, in Lombard Sinti, third-person unstressed pronouns are used as clitics to (re)activate a reference to the subject of the sentence, that may be overtly expressed or not (e.g. *u ker i-lu nevo eta baro*, 'the house is-it new and big', see Figure 3 in Appendix B). In such constructions, we used the label `expl` to annotate the relation between the clitic and the verb.

5 Conclusion and future work

In this paper, we presented LSDT, a dependency treebank of Lombard Sinti which constitutes the first resource of this kind for this language. We showed the process we followed to annotate the sentences both morphologically and syntactically, dealing with the issues that this language presents.

In the future, we plan to enlarge the treebank with more sentences including different sources (speech, written documents). A language resource like this, if sufficiently expanded, might be also useful to train a parser to automatically annotate other texts in Lombard Sinti and to build models that can be used to transfer information and annotate texts in other Romani varieties.

Acknowledgments

We would like to thank the anonymous reviewers who provided great insights and suggestions. The paper is the result of close collaboration between the two authors. For academic purposes, Marco Forlano is responsible of the annotation of the treebank, Sections 2 and 4 and Luca Brigada Villa is responsible of Sections 1, 3 and 5.

References

Evangelia Adamou. 2010. Bilingual speech and language ecology in greek thrace: Romani and pomak in contact with turkish. *Language in society*, 39(2):147–171.

Evangelia Adamou. 2016. *A Corpus-Driven Approach to Language Contact*. De Gruyter Mouton, Berlin, Boston.

Evangelia Adamou and Yaron Matras. 2020. Romani syntactic typology. In Yaron Matras and Anton Tenser, editors, *The Palgrave Handbook of Romani Language and Linguistics*, pages 187–227. Palgrave Macmillan, London.

Michael Beníšek. 2020. The historical origins of romani. In Yaron Matras and Anton Tenser, editors, *The Palgrave Handbook of Romani Language and Linguistics*, pages 13–47. Palgrave Macmillan, London.

Marie-Catherine de Marneffe, Christopher D. Manning, Joakim Nivre, and Daniel Zeman. 2021. Universal Dependencies. *Computational Linguistics*, 47(2):255–308.

Viktor Elšík. 2020. Romanimorphology. In Yaron Matras and Anton Tenser, editors, *The Palgrave Handbook of Romani Language and Linguistics*, pages 155–186. Palgrave Macmillan, London.

Viktor Elšík and Michael Beníšek. 2020. Romani dialectology. In Yaron Matras and Anton Tenser, editors, *The Palgrave Handbook of Romani Language and Linguistics*, pages 389–417. Palgrave Macmillan, London.

Ilaria Fiorentini. 2022. *Socialinguistica delle minoranze in Italia: Un'introduzione*. Carocci, Rome.

Paul Lewis and Gary Simons. 2010. Assessing endangerment: Expanding Fishman's GIDS. *Revue Roumaine de Linguistique*, 55(2):103–120.

Andrej Malchukov, Martin Haspelmath, and Bernard Comrie. 2010. Ditransitive constructions: a typological overview. In Andrej Malchukov, Martin Haspelmath, and Bernard Comrie, editors, *Studies in ditransitive constructions: A comparative handbook*, pages 1–64. De Gruyter Mouton, Berlin, New York.

Yaron Matras. 1999. Writing romani: The pragmatics of codification in a stateless language. *Applied linguistics*, 20(4):481–502.

Yaron Matras. 2002. *Romani: A Linguistic Introduction*. Cambridge University Press, Cambridge.

Yaron Matras and Evangelia Adamou. 2020. Romani and contact linguistics. In Yaron Matras and Anton Tenser, editors, *The Palgrave Handbook of Romani Language and Linguistics*, pages 329–352. Palgrave Macmillan, London.

Yaron Matras, Peter Bakker, and Hristo Kyuchukov. 1997. *The typology and dialectology of Romani*, volume 156 of *Amsterdam studies in the theory and history of linguistic science : Series 4, Current issues in linguistic theory*. John Benjamins Publishing Company, Amsterdam.

Yaron Matras, Christopher White, and Viktor Elšík. 2009. The Romani Morpho-Syntax (RMS) Database. In Martin Everaert, Simon Musgrave, and Alexis Dimitriadis, editors, *The Use of Databases in Cross-Linguistic Studies*, pages 329–362. De Gruyter Mouton, Berlin, New York.

Sergio Partesani. 1973. Glossario del dialetto zingaro lombardo. *Lacio Drom*, 8(4):2–29.

Leonardo Piasere. 2004. *I Rom d'Europa*. Laterza, Rome, Bari.

Andrea Scala. 2011. Così vicini, così lontani: i parlanti romanì, l'italiano e la scuola. In Rosella Bozzone Costa, Luisa Antonietta Fumagalli, and Ada Valentini, editors, *Apprendere l'italiano da lingue lontane: prospettiva linguistica, pragmatica ed educativa*, pages 249–265. Guerra Edizioni, Perugia.

Andrea Scala. 2012. Purché la lingua non sia una sola. Trasformazione dei repertori e conservazione del plurilinguismo presso i sinti italiani dall'Unità ad oggi. In *Coesistenze linguistiche nell'Italia pre-e postunitaria, Congresso Internazionale di Studi della Società di Linguistica Italiana (SLI)*, pages 437–448, Rome. Bulzoni.

Andrea Scala. 2015. Se proprio dobbiamo scrivere, almeno facciamolo come gli altri italiani: i Sinti dell'Italia settentrionale e la grafizzazione della loro lingua. In Silvia Dal Negro, Federica Guerini, and Gabriele Iannaccaro, editors, *Elaborazione ortografica delle varietà non-standard. Esperienze spontanee in Italia e all'estero*. Bergamo University Press, Bergamo.

Andrea Scala. 2017. I numerali da 1 a 10 in sinto lombardo. In Giuseppe Sergio and Massimo Prada, editors, *Italiani di Milano. Studi in onore di Silvia Morgana*, pages 789–797. Ledizioni, Milano.

Andrea Scala. 2020. A lombard sinti ethno-text on mourning and marriage. *Eivista annuale dell'associazione Ethnorema*, 16:59–71.

Giulio Soravia. 1977. *Dialetti degli zingari italiani*. Pacini, Pisa.

Giulio Soravia and Camillo Fochi. 1995. *Vocabolario sinottico delle lingue zingare parlate in Italia*. Centro Studi Zingari, Rome.

Elena Sorrenti. 2014. Italiano e sinto lombardo a confronto: somiglianze, divergenze e prospettive didattiche. *Italiano LinguaDue*, 6(1):117–147.

Francis M. Tyers, Mariya Sheyanova, and Jonathan North Washington. 2017. UD annotatrix: An annotation tool for Universal Dependencies. In *Proceedings of the 16th International Workshop on Treebanks and Linguistic Theories*, pages 10–17, Prague, Czech Republic.

A Tags used in the treebank

part-of-speech	count
ADJ	32
ADP	90
ADV	72
AUX	20
CCONJ	17
DET	150
NOUN	172
NUM	9
PRON	101
PUNCT	109
SCONJ	49
VERB	168

Table 3: Parts-of-speech and their frequencies in the treebank.

deprel	count
ADJ	Gender, Number
ADP	Gender, Number
AUX	Mood, Person, Tense, VerbForm
DET	Definite, Gender, Number, Poss Pron-Type
NOUN	Gender, Number
NUM	NumType
PRON	Case, Clitic, Gender, Number, Person
	Poss, PronType, Reflex
PUNCT	Gender, Number, Person, PronType
VERB	Gender, Mood, Number, Person, Tense, VerbForm

Table 4: List of features annotated for each part-of-speech tag.

deprel	count
acl	14
advcl	35
advmod	57
amod	13
aux	13
case	70
cc	17
ccomp	9
conj	16
cop	14
csubj	1
det	147
expl	23
fixed	19
iobj	34
mark	81
nmod	9
nsubj	66
nummod	9
obj	60
obl	55
punct	108
root	100
xcomp	19

Table 5: Dependency relations and their frequencies in the treebank.

B Additional tree

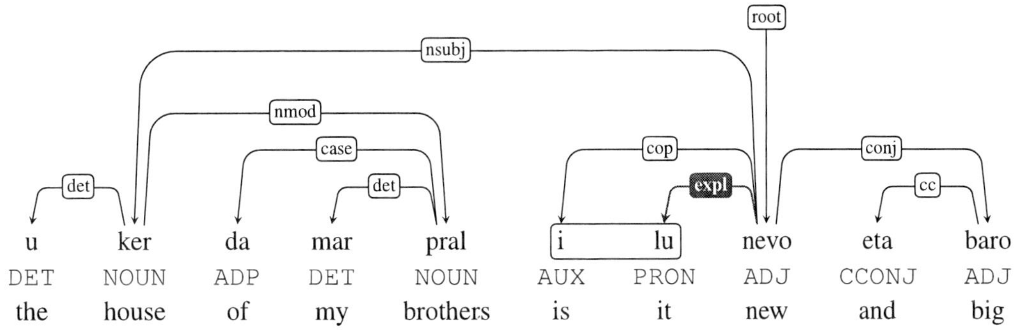

Figure 3: Dependecy tree of the sentence 'u ker da mar pral ilu nevo eta baro' ('my brother's house is new and big').

A morphological analyzer for Huasteca Nahuatl

Ana Tona and **Guillaume Thomas** and **Ewan Dunbar**
University of Toronto

Abstract

We present a morphological analyzer of Huastecan Nahuatl, which builds upon an existing analyzer of the Zacatlan-Ahuacatlán-Tepetzintla variety of Nahuatl (ZAT). We extend the range of morphological phenomena covered by the ZAT analyzer, and we adapt it to the Huastecan variety of Nahuatl, which broadens its potential userbase. The new analyzer has high coverage on a corpus of Huasteca Nahuatl texts (HN) and has improved coverage on a ZAT corpus.

1 Introduction

Nahuatl has been well documented by religious and academic institutions since colonial times, resulting in numerous descriptive and pedagogical grammars, dictionaries, published texts of various genres, and even digital resources. However, the overwhelming majority of these resources are for Classical Nahuatl, a prestige variety that is no longer spoken today. These resources are at best limited in their utility—and more often simply misleading—for native speakers, learners, and teachers, and for linguists interested in modern Nahuatl. While the situation is changing, the resources that exist for modern Nahuatl remain limited.

Modern Nahuatl consists of four dialectal areas: Western periphery, Huasteca, Center, and Eastern periphery. This paper presents an open-source morphological analyzer for Huasteca Nahuatl, one of the three modern varieties with a large number of speakers. Huasteca Nahuatl is spoken as a first language by over one million people in Mexico, and is often studied as a second language. The analyzer builds upon Pugh et al.'s (2021) analyzer of Zacatlan-Ahuacatlán-Tepetzintla (ZAT) Nahuatl, and accepts both the Huasteca and the ZAT varieties, while providing broader coverage of morphological phenomena than the previous analyzer.

2 Finite-state morphological analyzers

Digital resources facilitate access to language, creating opportunities for learners and providing rich supporting materials for teachers (Galla, 2021). Morphological analyzers play a key role in learning resources for morphologically-rich languages, as well as aiding in the construction of annotated textual corpora. Morphological analyzers built using finite-state transducers (FSTs) have the advantage of not requiring any training corpora, which, unlike Classical Nahuatl, are virtually non-existent for modern Nahuatl varieties. Although modern Nahuatl has some presence on the internet, the total amount of data available is not enough to use a data-driven approach. Our analyzer was developed with the HFST toolkit (Lindén et al., 2009). Morphotactic rules were described using a form of right-recursive grammar (Karttunen, 1993), while phonological and orthographical alternation rules were described using a declarative system of rule constraints (Karttunen et al., 1987). These descriptions are compiled out to FSTs by `lexc` (Lexicon Compiler) and `twolc` (Two-Level Compiler) respectively, and the resulting FSTs are composed and inverted to serve as an analyzer. Conversely, a morphological analysis can be given as input to generate the corresponding word form. An example is shown in 1.

(1) Input and parsed output:

a. `nicalchihqui`

b. `ni<Suj_sg1>calli<n><incrp> chihua<tv>qui<pret>`

3 Previous works

Several morphological analyzers exist for Classical Nahuatl, though not all are publicly available. These include *Chachalaca*[1] (Thouvenot,

[1] `http://www.sup-infor.com/program/Chachalaca/Chachalaca-txt.htm`

2011) and that of Martínez-Gil (1981). Relatedly, Escobar Farfán (2019) applies a morphological analyzer for Classical Nahuatl to modern Nahuatl varieties in order to assess overlap between modern varieties, and between modern varieties and Classical Nahuatl. For modern Nahuatl varieties, only the FST-based analyzer of Pugh et al. (2021) exists, which is open source and freely available. This analyzer is limited in three ways. First, it covers only Zacatlán-Ahuacatlán-Tepetzintla (ZAT) Nahuatl, a variety spoken in Western Puebla. Second, a number of common morphological phenomena are not handled, including causative and applicative suffixes and noun incorporation (see sections 4 and 5 below for more details). Finally, it accepts only the academic Andrews-Campbell-Karttunen orthography (ACK) orthography used for Classical Nahuatl, rather than that of the Secretaría de Educación Pública (SP) typically used in Mexico for modern varieties.

4 Features of Huasteca Nahuatl

General grammatical features are shared among Nahuatl varieties, but there are some phonological, morphosyntactic and lexical differences. Differences among varieties have not been thoroughly and systematically studied. The main resources consulted for the Huastecan variety were the grammatical descriptions of Hasler (2011) and Beller and Beller (1977), as well as Cruz (2018)'s dictionary and class notes from a Nahuatl course (Santos, 2019). Here we give a short summary of Huasteca Nahuatl morphology.

Nahuatl has a rich morphological system. As an omnipredicative language (Launey, 2004), Nahuatl verbs, nouns and adjectives can take subject prefixes to function as predicates, but other morphology is not shared among the three categories.

Non-possessed nouns obligatorily take a suffix called the *absolutive* which varies as a function of the noun class (e.g., *-li, -tli, -tl*).[2] Possessed nouns may take a *possessive* prefix indicating the possessor, which is in some cases obligatory (e.g., body parts). It is possible to form new nouns via compounding and derivational affixation (e.g., honorific, diminutive).

(2) *tepoz-toto-tl*
metal-bird-ABS
'airplane (lit. metal bird)'

(3) *pil-cone-tzi*
DIM-child-DIM
'baby (lit. little child)'

Verbs agree in number with the subject. Plural is marked as a suffix, while the singular is unmarked. Other verbal morphology includes subject (person) and object prefixes (person, plus undefined human and non-human object markers *te-* and *tla-*), a reflexive marker *mo-*, negative prefixes, and derivational prefixes. In non-Huastecan varieties (including ZATN), there is also a past-tense prefix (*o-*). Suffixes include tense and aspect markers. These are suffixed to the root or after causative/applicative suffixes, if they are present:

(4) *ø-cochi-qui*
3SG.SUBJ-sleep-PST
'(he/she) slept'

(5) *ø-tequiti-c*
3SG.SUBJ-work-PST
'(he/she) worked'

Tense and aspect markers are absent when there are directional affixes (which comprise aspect in their meaning) present. Unlike in other varieties, in Huastecan, directionals are suffixes. Deverbal nouns do not have tense and aspect markers, but do take object prefixes.

(6) *tla-mach-ti-quetl*
1OBJ.UNDEF.NH-learn-CAUS-NMLZR
'teacher'

Transitive and intransitive verbs may get (additional) objects by adding causative or applicative suffixes. The applicative marker does not always trigger a valency change, and may be used to focalize the (recipient) object (Peregrina et al., 2017).

Verbs may incorporate nouns and adverbs (Launey, 1999).

(7) *sesem-itta*
each-see
'watch closely'

It is also possible to incorporate other verbs, in which case the incorporating verb functions as an auxiliary.

(8) *ø-cochi-z-nequi*
3SUBJ-sleep-FUT-want
'he/she wants to sleep.'

Infrequently, verbs can be derived by partial reduplication of a verb root, or by adding causative morphology to a nominal root.

[2] Despite the name—an Uto-Aztecanist term—Nahuatl is not an ergative language.

(9) *ø-po-poca*
3SUBJ-RED-smoke
'to be smoking or giving off steam'

(10) *ni-h-xochi-tia*
1SG.SUBJ-3SG.OBJ-flower-CAUS
'I (put) flowers on it.'

Huastecan Nahuatl deletes final /n/ on nouns with absolutive *-in* and diminutive *-tzin* and deletes /j/ between vowels (e.g., *chiya* > *chia* 'wait'). The Huastecan variety does not show the extensive /i/-deletion nor the raising of /e/ to /i/ found in other varieties, including ZAT Nahuatl (Pugh et al., 2021).

Tense and aspect markers vary in form across varieties (notably for Huasteca, imperfect: *-yaya*, plural future: *-zeh*), as do pronominal forms (Huasteca, 1sg: *na*, 2sg: *ta*, 3sg: *ya*, 1pl: *tohuantih*, 2pl: *inmohuantih*, 3pl: *inihuantih*).

5 Implementation

Taking the system of Pugh et al. (2021) as a starting point, the new analyzer adds an analysis of reflexive/impersonal, causative, and applicative affixes—all of which typically change argument structure—nominalization, verb incorporation, noun incorporation, directional suffixes, noun-noun compounding, and the diminutive prefix. Because these features are common to many varieties, including ZAT, we chose to build an analyzer that would accept both Huasteca and ZAT forms. As with this earlier analyzer, ours accepts the ACK orthography.

As noted in section 2, the analyzer is implemented using HFST (Lindén et al., 2009) and consists of a morphotactic description in the `lexc` formalism and a morphophonological description in the `twolc` formalism. In `lexc`, morphotactics is described using a set of lexicons. Lexicons contain entries, each of which consists of a form and a continuation class. Figure 1 shows the lexical continuation classes for verbs and the graph that defines verb morphotactics. (In the interest of space, we do not detail the way the analyzer handles nouns here.) In order to handle valency-changing suffixes, the system weakens the traditional separation between inherently intransitive, transitive, and ditransitive verbs. There are no "intransitive" classes in which verbs are restricted to appearing without object prefixes. Rather a distinction is made between ditransitive (prefixed with **2-**) and transitive verbs, neither of which strictly enforces the presence of an object prefix. Similarly, ditransitive verbs can appear with only indirect object morphology, allowing more flexibility for valency changes (namely, reduction).

To handle noun and verb incorporation, additional lexicons were created for verbs that can incorporate other verbs, and for nouns as they appear in noun-incorporation (parallel to the main noun lexicon). The new lexicon of incorporating verbs also has access to the main verb list for incorporation.

Finally, two classes, **TAM-1** and **TAM-2,** allow us to distinguish two groups of inflectional suffixes marking tense, aspect, and mood, which require different verbal stems.

Differences between the Huastecan and the ZAT varieties are primarily in the realization of individual morphemes. Thus, to handle both varieties, we extended the lexicon of Pugh et al. (2021) to include Huastecan forms. The past tense prefix *o-* is not used in the Huastecan variety, and so, in our analyzer, this prefix is optional. ZAT also has several phonological rules which do not exist in the Huastecan variety, which we also made optional.[3]

6 Evaluation and performance

To evaluate coverage, a small corpus of short stories from the Huasteca region was collected and passed to the analyzer (285 tokens, 142 types). We calculate *token coverage* as the percentage of all tokens successfully parsed, and *type coverage* as the percentage of all types successfully parsed. As a baseline, we compare the system of Pugh et al. (2021). As many of the forms in our Huastecan corpus differ from their ZAT Nahuatl equivalents, we also assess performance of both systems on the ZAT corpus for which Pugh et al. (2021) report the best performance (*Omitlan*: 296 tokens, 168 types). In order to ensure the evaluation is of the analyzer, rather than of the lexicon, we add all morphemes in both corpora to the lexicon for the proposed analyzer. As the lexicon of Pugh et al. (2021) contains all of the types in the ZAT corpus, but not those of the new Huastecan corpus, we evaluate that system only on ZATN. Results are presented in Table 1.

As can be seen from Table 1, the proposed analyzer has high coverage on both Huastecan and ZAT Nahuatl. Comparison against the analyzer of

[3]The morphological tags used were also revised from the ZATN analyzer with Nahuatl- and Spanish-speaking users in mind and for consistency with modern grammatical descriptions of Nahuatl.

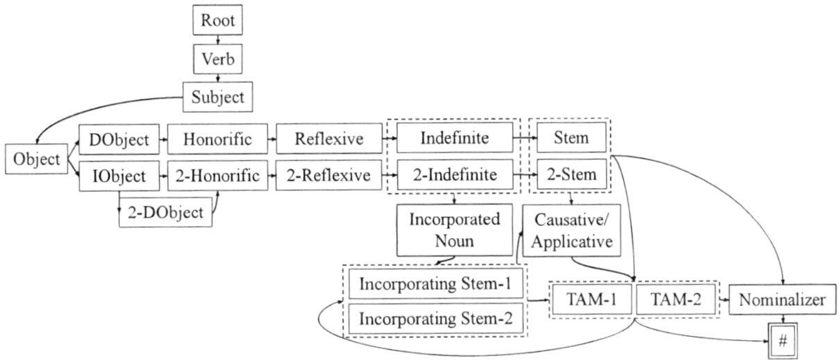

Figure 1: Morphotactics for verbs in terms of lexicon (LEXC) continuation classes. Arrows to (or from) the outside of dotted boxes indicate links to (or from) both of the classes inside the box.

	Huastecan		ZAT	
	Token	Type	Token	Type
Proposed	95.1%	90.8%	**92.6%**	**87.5%**
Pugh et al.	—		88.2%	80.9%

Table 1: Token- and type-level coverage of the proposed analyzer and that of Pugh et al. (2021) on Huastecan and Zacatlan-Ahuacatlán-Tepetzintla Nahuatl corpora.

Pugh et al. (2021) also demonstrates in improvement on ZAT, presumably due to the addition of novel morphological phenomena.

7 Limitations

This analyzer for Huasteca (and ZAT) Nahuatl is currently the broadest-coverage morphological analyzer for any modern variety of Nahuatl. Several phenomena are missing but are straightforward to add: verbal derivational prefixes such as *ix-* (e.g., *ix-ketsa* 'to build (lit. to make stand)') and the negative verbal prefix *ax-*, locative and other derivational suffixes attaching to nouns, and adverbial incorporation. Currently, the analyzer also fails to restrict plural markers to the appropriate noun/verb classes.

Other phenomena may require more reorganization, such as N+Adj/Adv compounds (*a-huelic* 'tasty water', *a-huehca-pan* 'sea bottom, abyss'), Adj/Adv+N compounds (*hueyi-cali* 'skyscraper (lit. big house)', *momoztla-moxtli* 'newspaper (lit. every-day book)'), denominal verbs (*ni-h-xochitia* 'I (put) flowers on it') and reduplication (*poctli* 'smoke' > *po-poca* 'smoking or giving off steam'). Since reduplication has limited productivity, with some instances being fossilized, reduplicated verbs may well be added into the lexicon.

The approach taken to incorporation introduces a cycle in the graph to avoid duplicating parts of the lexicon. As only one root can ever be incorporated, the system will accept unattested forms. The same is true for noun-noun compounds. Similarly, the approach taken to having a two-variety analyzer—by simply rendering variety-specific features optional—allows the analyzer to overgenerate, parsing forms that combine features in ways that would be ungrammatical in either variety. This approach was taken largely to be able to compare the coverage on variety-non-specific phenomena to the previously existing ZAT analyzer. Nevertheless, we believe that an FST-based morphological analyzer for Nahuatl should be multi-varietal, as many linguistic features are often subject to inter- and intra-speaker variation in a single text, and different varieties have overlapping features, as they form part of a continuum. Additionally, learners may not always know which variety they are dealing with and having a system that handles several varieties is helpful in such cases. Still, the problem of overgeneration brings up the question of whether having a multi-varietal system is the right approach. With this in mind, we believe that the current system would be best used for analysis rather than generation. A more robust system would be able to give information about which forms are typical of different varieties, which can be done using flags.

Three factors limit the usefulness of the current system for broad use. First, the current lexicon is limited to words needed to cover the corpora above. Second, it only accepts the ACK orthography, which is not widely used among speakers. Finally, it lacks an accessible and user-friendly interface that would allow the community to take advantage of it. We plan to make the system available via a web interface.

8 Summary of contributions

We have presented an open-source morphological analyzer for Huasteca Nahuatl, and which also accepts Zacatlan-Ahuacatlán-Tepetzintla (ZAT) forms. It has the broadest coverage of any existing modern Nahuatl analyzer, thus contributing to a small but growing body of resources for modern Nahuatl varieties.

References

Richard Beller and Patricia Beller. 1977. *Huasteca Nahuatl*. Modern Aztec Grammatical Sketches. Summer Institute of Linguistics, Dallas.

Marcos Hilario Cruz. 2018. *Diccionario bilingüe náhuatl-español. En defensa del náhuatl en el México moderno*.

Jonathan Escobar Farfán. 2019. *Publications Manual*. Ph.D. thesis, University of Sheffield.

Candace Galla. 2021. *Practical Educational Tools and Applications Used Within Native Communities*. Ph.D. thesis, University of Arizona.

Andres Hasler. 2011. *Gramática moderna del nahua de la Huasteca*.

Lauri Karttunen. 1993. Finite-state lexicon compiler. Technical Report ISTL-NLTT-1993-04-02, Xerox Palo Alto Research Center, Palo Alto, CA.

Lauri Karttunen, Kimmo Koskenniemi, and Ronald Kaplan. 1987. A compiler for two-level phonological rules. *Tools for morphological analysis*.

Michel Launey. 1999. Compound nouns vs. incorporation in classical nahuatl. *STUF - Language Typology and Universals*, 52(3-4):347–364.

Michel Launey. 2004. The features of omnipredicativity in classical nahuatl. *STUF - Language Typology and Universals*, 57(1):49–69.

Krister Lindén, Miikka Silfverberg, and Tommi Pirinen. 2009. HFST tools for morphology–an efficient open-source package for construction of morphological analyzers. In *International Workshop on Systems and Frameworks for Computational Morphology*, pages 28–47. Springer.

Martínez-Gil. 1981. Computer systems for analysis of nahuatl. *Research in Computing Science*, (47):11–16.

Manuel Peregrina, Albert Alvarez, and Zarina Estrada-Fernández. 2017. *Transitivity and valency-changing operations in Huasteca Nahuatl: Theoretical and typological perspectives*, pages 81–106.

Robert Pugh, Francis Tyers, and Maribel Huerta Mendez. 2021. Towards an open source finite-state morphological analyzer for Zacatlán-Ahuacatlán-Tepetzintla Nahuatl. In *Proceedings of the 4th Workshop on the Use of Computational Methods in the Study of Endangered Languages: Vol. 1*, pages 80–85.

Valeriano Santos. 2019. Nahuatl course notes. Taught at Centro Cultural de Tijuana, Mexico.

Marc Thouvenot. 2011. Chachalaca en cen, juntamente. *Compendio Enciclopedico del Nahuatl, DVD. INAH*.

Speech-to-text recognition for multilingual spoken data in language documentation

Lorena Martín Rodríguez and **Christopher Cox**
School of Linguistics and Language Studies / Carleton University
lorenamartinrodrigue@cmail.carleton.ca / christopher.cox@carleton.ca

Abstract

More than 85% of the languages spoken in Canada are deemed as vulnerable (Lewis, 2009). Efforts for language revitalization and maintenance are essential to maintain both the Indigenous knowledge and cultural diversity in the country. In this context, it is relevant to develop computational tools that may aid language communities and linguists involved in the process of language documentation and revitalization. One challenge of the documentation process is the existence of more than one language in spoken language materials. We propose a pipeline to handle multilingual spoken data using both custom-trained and commercial speech-to-text services. The main advantage of our approach is its user-friendly format as a recognizer for the audiovisual annotation application ELAN (Brugman and Russel, 2004), which facilitates its use in both community and university-based language work.

1 Introduction

Canada is the home of a wide language diversity, with almost 200 languages comprised in 11 Indigenous language families and isolates (Lewis, 2009). Many of these languages are spoken by First Nations, Inuit, and Métis peoples and are deemed as "fundamental to the identities, cultures, spirituality, relationships to the land, world views and self-determination of Indigenous peoples" (Branch, 2020). However, this linguistic diversity is endangered. More than 85% of the languages spoken in Canada are deemed as vulnerable (Lewis, 2009). Efforts for language revitalization and maintenance are essential to maintain Indigenous knowledge and cultural diversity in the country. In this context, it is relevant to develop computational tools that may aid language communities and linguists involved in the process of language documentation and revitalization.

One challenge of the documentation process is the existence of more than one language in the data. In many language documentation and revitalization initiatives, audiovisual recordings frequently include interactions that involve multiple varieties of languages. In projects focused on grammatical or lexical description, for instance, it is not uncommon for consultation sessions to feature bilingual (or, in some cases, multilingual) elicitation, interpretation, and/or translation involving both local languages and one or more languages of wider communication (e.g., lingue franche). In other cases, documentation of linguistic knowledge and practices may also feature multiple languages as a consequence of patterns of multilingualism that are part of the fabric of the local language ecology. Bilingual or multilingual documentation such as this poses additional challenges for annotation efforts that aim to make such resources more accessible for use in advocacy, revitalization, and research, beyond what has already commonly been reported as part of the broader "transcription bottleneck" (Reiman, 2010; Boerger, 2011) that current speech technologies applied in documentary linguistic contexts have generally sought to address (cf. Thieberger, 2016; Adams et al., 2018, inter alia).

We propose a solution for handling spoken multilingual data involving well-documented and under-resourced languages. We develop a modular speech-to-text pipeline to handle spoken multilingual data in English and Tsuut'ina (ISO 639-3: srs, Glottocode: sars1236), a Na-Dene language spoken by members of the Tsuut'ina Nation (Treaty 7, southern Alberta, Canada). Our approach makes use of existing speech-to-text services to provide automatic transcriptions of English utterances in tandem with a fine-tuned XLS-R model (Babu et al., 2022) to provide automatic transcriptions of Tsuut'ina utterances. These models are integrated into ELAN (Brugman and Russel, 2004), an open-source desktop application for audiovisual annotation widely used in language documentation and revitalization, to provide a user-friendly interface that may be employed by language workers without requiring extensive knowledge of computer science.

2 Literature Review

Extensive use of multilingual practices has been documented for speakers of minority languages belonging to a variety of language families and geographical areas. Research on under-researched languages has explored these code-mixing and code-switching practices in languages spoken in South America belonging to the Matacoan family (Campbell and Grondona, 2010) and the Eastern Tukanoan family (Silva, 2020); in Austronesian languages spoken in Vanuatu (Lindstrom, 2007); in Tibeto-Burman language spoken in Eastern Nepal (Stoll et al., 2015), as well as in Inuit languages in Canada (Allen et al., 2009). These multilingual practices do not conform to a homogeneous group of practices, but are realized differently for each language community and are shaped by language ideologies and cultural practices (Pakendorf et al., 2021). The documentation of these multilingual practices offers valuable insights into the linguistic practices and language ideologies of the communities, as well as into the status and vitality of languages by documenting possible cases of language-shifting. Therefore, it is relevant to develop computational tools to address multilingual practices present in the documentation.

A variety of approaches have been proposed for automatic speech recognition (ASR) of multilingual utterances in spoken data. Lin et al. (2009) defined a universal phone set across alphabets to improve their ASR model performance in multilingual contexts. In recent years, efforts have increased in developing quality multilingual models for ASR. Yadav and Sitaram (2022)'s survey of state-of-the-art models indicates that in certain models, multilingual pre-trained models outperform models pre-trained with monolingual data. Their survey highlights the relevance of the features selected in the models' general performance, as well as the choice of training languages. Although cross-lingual transfer methods generally perform better across languages of the same family, recent methods have achieved accurate results in languages that do not belong to the same language family as those in the training data, which indicates that the features selected may have more impact on the performance of the models than the choice of training languages.

One problem with several of the existing approaches for multilingual speech recognition is that they are not implemented in a user-friendly interface and require users with specialized knowledge in computer science. Recent efforts have started implementing state-of-the-art systems in user-friendly interfaces to promote wider access to these resources by non-specialized users and language communities. Foley et al. (2018) propose Elpis, a user-friendly pipeline that allows language documentation workers and language communities to develop their own speech recognition models. Other work has focused on incorporating resources into existing language documentation tools in the form of plugins. Adams et al. (2021) integrate a speech recognition toolkit, ESPNet, into Elpis to provide user-friendly access to readily available speech recognition technologies. Cox (2019) integrates an automatic phoneme transcription tool, Persephone (Adams et al., 2018), into ELAN, with Partanen et al. (2020) applying this extension to automatic phoneme recognition for Samoyedic languages. Our approach continues with these efforts of implementing speech recognition systems in user-friendly interfaces by integrating existing commercial and open-source models as extensions to ELAN.

3 Integrating speech technology into ELAN

This paper introduces the implementation of different models for speech detection and automatic speech recognition as extensions to ELAN. ELAN is widely adopted in language work involving audio and video recordings, serving as the current *de facto* standard for audiovisual annotation in documentary linguistics (Carreau et al., 2018). Its popularity among users involved in language documentation and revitalization, in particular, motivates the creation of tools that contribute to speed the task of language annotation, such as those presented in the current paper. By integrating existing models into the software, our proposal aims to make state-of-the-art speech recognition systems more widely available to language communities.

Since ELAN is open-source software, it is possible to incorporate new features by editing and recompiling the Java source code for the application itself. This has been the approach taken to date with import and export options within ELAN, for instance, with each supported format implemented as hard-coded Java classes that provide both the application logic and necessary user interface components. While this method of integration offers ready access to data structures internal to ELAN that may be helpful for conversion between file formats, it requires a degree of familiarity with both the ELAN code base and with Java software development practices, and may not always be amenable to integrating features from third-party packages that have not been developed in Java.

As an alternative to this approach, the AVATecH project (Tschöpel et al., 2011) developed an API within ELAN that aimed to facilitate the integration of free-standing audio and video analysis components as extensions, or 'recognizers'. Within this framework, recognizers could be developed either in Java, thereby having the ability to access data structures internal to ELAN and implement custom user interface components; or as an external, executable application developed in any programming language, interacting with ELAN via an XML-based protocol and exposing any user-defined input and output parameters via the ELAN user interface through a static, CMDI-based metadata definitions. Both 'native' (i.e., Java-based) and 'local' (non-Java-based) recognizers allow for external services to interact with ELAN without requiring changes to the ELAN source code itself. Importantly, from the perspective of ELAN users who may not have a background in language technology or software development, recognizers such as these provide a straightforward means of applying speech and language technologies to textual annotations and audiovisual materials represented in their ELAN documents from directly within the ELAN user interface, without having to learn how to use another application or service and import its results into ELAN.

The current paper presents a set of ELAN recognizers publicly available that automatizes parts of the annotation process for multilingual data. These recognizers can be used as stand-alone services or in combination with each other to generate linguistic outputs as ELAN tiers. The collection of multilingual audio data in Tsuut'ina and English provides a case study of how these recognizers are used in real linguistic documentation work and how they handle multilingual data in the context of elicitation sessions.

3.1 Voxseg-ELAN and SileroVAD-ELAN

As Hjortnæs et al. (2020, 36) note, applying speech recognition and other commonly targeted forms of language technology to new audiovisual recordings in language documentation also requires segmentation (and, for recordings involving more than one recorded participant, often speaker diarization, as well). Fundamental annotation tasks such as these are often still accomplished manually in language documentation, and contribute to the challenge of working with such materials.

As an initial step towards addressing this aspect of the annotation bottleneck beyond the silence vs. non-silence audio event detection provided by the Silence Recognizer bundled with ELAN[1], we have sought to integrate two current, DNN-based voice activity detection (VAD) models into ELAN, which distinguish speech from non-speech segments in unannotated audio recordings. This includes both the Voxseg voice activity detection (VAD) package (Wilkinson and Niesler, 2021), which provides a full VAD pipeline and pre-trained VAD model implemented in Python; and Silero-VAD (Silero Team, 2021), a model for voice activity detection pre-trained on extensive multilingual corpora.

Voxseg-ELAN[2] (Cox, 2022) and SileroVAD-ELAN[3] are local ELAN recognizers that allow users to apply VAD to a selected audio recording in the current ELAN transcript, returning a tier containing annotations representing any sections of speech detected by the underlying model. Figure 1 shows the Voxseg-ELAN recognizer user interface in ELAN, exposing both parameters to the VAD model itself (e.g., the speech vs. non-speech threshold value, which determines the sensitivity of VAD to possible speech events) and post-hoc adjustments made by the recognizer (e.g., fixed adjustments applied to the start and end times of all annotations returned by the model).

Both VAD models succeed in differentiating background noise from voice activity in most cases. However, it has been observed that sibilants placed at the beginning of words are not generally detected by the model. Therefore, the recognizer allows users to manually specify milliseconds of audio that should be added to the start and end of

[1] `https://www.mpi.nl/corpus/html/elan/ch05s04s03.html`

[2] `https://github.com/coxchristopher/voxseg-elan`

[3] `https://github.com/l12maro/SileroVAD-Elan`

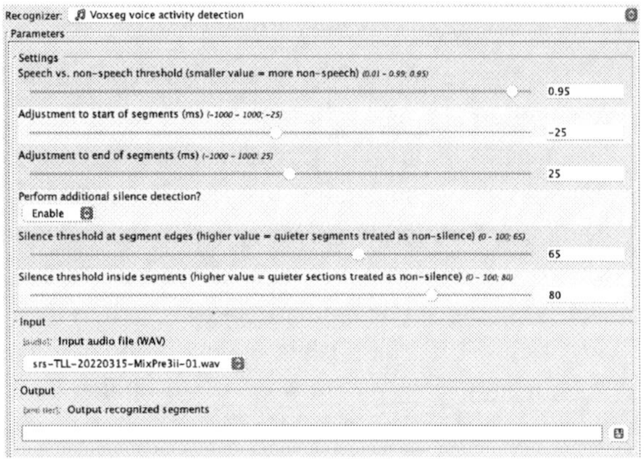

Figure 1: Parameters for Voxseg-ELAN

the outputted segments, and/or to apply silence vs. non-silence detection at the start and end of outputted segments to capture sibilants that may have been missed by the VAD model. This allows users to customize the output of the model according to the needs of their annotations. When applied to Tsuut'ina audio recordings in recent, community-based documentation, both VAD models generally produce acceptable results, although we note that some phonemes not found in the languages represented in these models' training data (e.g., ejective stops and affricates) are often not included in the output segments when appearing in utterance-initial position. It may be possible to address this through fine-tuning with Tsuut'ina training data, although this remains to be investigated in future work.

3.2 XLS-R-ELAN

XLS-R-ELAN[4] (Cox, 2023) presents a local recognizer that allows users to apply a fine-tuned XLS-R automatic speech recognition model (Babu et al., 2022) to an audio recording that has been segmented in ELAN. Input segments are taken from a user-specified tier, and may thus be manually created annotations or the output of one of the voice activity detection recognizers mentioned above. Internally, the recognizer converts the input segments into individual audio clips, applies the fine-tuned XLS-R to each one, and returns a new tier containing the recognized text.[5] In the case of Tsuut'ina, using XLS-R-ELAN to apply a XLS-R model that has been fine-tuned on a small audio corpus (14,144 tokens, 8,717 audio clips; 3h52m26s audio total) to segments produced automatically by one of the above VAD recognizers is generally sufficient to create usable first-pass transcriptions of Tsuut'ina speech (CER < 0.2), significantly reducing the overall workload required to annotate new recordings in ELAN.

3.3 Eng-ELAN

Eng-ELAN[6] comprises different state-of-the-art Speech-to-text models for the automatic transcription of English. Three models are made easily available through this recognizer: two commercial (provided by Amazon Web Services and Google Cloud) and one open-source model (Whisper AI). The recognizer incorporates different features, which allow the selection of an existing tier to annotate only certain audio segments or to provide annotations at the utterance or word level. Although the case study focuses on the transcription of English, all of the models provided have been trained with extensive multilingual data and provide support for several languages.

We integrate three existing speech-to-text models for the automatic transcription of well-resourced languages in multilingual corpora as an ELAN recognizer. These models include two commercial models (AWS, Google Cloud), and one open-source model (Whisper AI). Commercial models are chosen for their ready availability and support of quality transcription services for several languages (31 supported languages in AWS, 80 for Google Cloud). However, they provide barriers to user-friendly applications, since they require users to previously create an account and connect their profiles to their desktops using command-line instructions. Moreover, they are not free of cost and charge per transcribed audio second, which may affect the cost of documentation projects which include large quantities of audio data.

On the other hand, Whisper AI is an open-source model that provides quality transcriptions free of cost and does not require the usage of command-line instructions prior to its use. One disadvantage of this model over the commercial one is that it only

[4] `https://github.com/coxchristopher/xls-r-elan`

[5] Optionally, XLS-R-ELAN is also able to apply a CTC-based word beam search (Scheidl et al., 2018) to decode the predictions of the XLS-R model, drawing on a user-provided text corpus to derive a dictionary and language model that may help refine the XLS-R model's results. While not necessary for basic uses of XLS-R-ELAN, this feature proved useful in cases where written text was already available for a given audio recording (e.g., when the recording represented a reading of an existing written resource), improving the accuracy of the XLS-R model's results.

[6] `https://github.com/112maro/Eng-ELAN`

provides utterance-level transcriptions. Therefore, word-level annotations are currently unavailable using this model.

The possibility of specifying an existing ELAN tier as input facilitates the implementation of this recognizer along with the voice activity detection models previously described. In the event that a tier is provided as input, the existing segments are used for utterance-level annotation, and a transcription is provided only for segments with no existing annotations. Research suggests that the segmentation of multilingual audio in monolingual segments improves the performance of ASR models (Ramabhadran et al., 2003). Therefore, when a tier is provided as input, the original audio is split based on the existing spans within the tier.

4 Further improvements

The incorporation of state-of-the-art models into user-friendly interfaces includes numerous challenges. One of them is how to provide a user-friendly installation of the recognizers for their use by language documentation workers. The current installation process requires users to manually retrieve the recognizers from their respective GitHub repositories and perform a manual installation within the corresponding ELAN folder in the user's system. Moreover, additional libraries need to be installed by the user. In order to improve the accessibility of these resources, other options should be explored that do not place the responsibility of installing additional recognizers and libraries on the user side.

Similarly, the implementation of existing models presents new challenges for user-friendly interfaces. Commercial models such as Amazon Web Services or Google Cloud require a prior synchronization of the user accounts with the computer used for the annotations using the command line, which may not be accessible to users not familiar with this type of technology. Moreover, in order to use existing models that require fine-tuning, such as XLS-R for Tsuut'ina, prior knowledge of data management is needed. While other efforts in the area of language documentation technology have succeeded in easing the training process (cf. Foley et al., 2018), some of the recognizers presented in this article still need to overcome these difficulties.

In order to provide a service that can automatically handle multilingual data, a future improvement of this project is to train a language diarization model that may automatically classify the linguistic utterances according to the language spoken. This automatic classification could then be used to feed the segments to a transcription model tailored to the specific language.

In the implementation of models as ELAN recognizers, it is necessary to acknowledge the limitations of the software in terms of what can be automatized. While ELAN allows the creation of hierarchical tier structures and the modification of existing tiers, this must be done manually. Due to limitations in the current XML schema for tiers, hierarchical relations between tier structures cannot be automatically generated by recognizers. Similarly, while some of the current recognizers presented in this work allow the selection of a specific tier as input, it is not possible to return modifications within the specified tiers. Instead, a new tier is returned, which preserves the existing annotations. It is then still necessary that the user manually manipulates the tiers to reflect the desired hierarchical relations or modifications.

Another potential improvement of the present work would be to 'daisy-chain' recognizers, that is, for the output of one to be fed directly in as the input to the next. To our knowledge, this has not been done in ELAN before, but it could be potentially implemented with the creation of a Java-based recognizer in ELAN that connects the different recognizers linearly. Implementing this would automatize the language documentation process from the detection of voice activity to the transcription of linguistic data.

Moreover, language documentation projects generally comprise sets of recordings. However, recognizers in ELAN currently focus on individual recordings. Exploring options for batch processing outside of the software could extend the use of the recognizers to sets of transcripts and recordings, which would therefore speed the process of language documentation.

5 Conclusions

This paper has explored how existing speech technologies can be integrated into one of the most widely used annotation tools in language documentation. The aim of this contribution is to widen access to speech technologies by providing user-friendly interfaces to existing models. This would facilitate the contribution to tasks in language documentation by community members, language workers, and linguists alike.

Moreover, the recognizers shared in this paper provide a framework for the integration of models into ELAN. This framework can be easily adapted to other models and uses in ELAN, as illustrated by Partanen et al. (2020). With this contribution, we hope to encourage other initiatives for the implementation of speech technologies in user-friendly interfaces.

Acknowledgements

We gratefully acknowledge the ongoing contributions of the Tsuut'ina Nation to this work, in particular through the leadership of the Office of the Tsuut'ina Language Commissioner and the Tsuut'ina Gunaha Institute. This research has been funded by a Partnership Grant (895-2019-1012) from the Social Sciences and Humanities Research Council (SSHRC) of Canada.

References

Oliver Adams, Trevor Cohn, Graham Neubig, Hilaria Cruz, Steven Bird, and Alexis Michaud. 2018. Evaluation phonemic transcription of low-resource tonal languages for language documentation. In *Proceedings of the Eleventh International Conference on Language Resources and Evaluation (LREC 2018)*, Miyazaki, Japan. European Language Resources Association (ELRA).

Oliver Adams, Benjamin Galliot, Guillaume Wisniewski, Nicholas Lambourne, Ben Foley, Rahasya Sanders-Dwyer, Janet Wiles, Alexis Michaud, Séverine Guillaume, Laurent Besacier, Christopher Cox, Katya Aplonova, Guillaume Jacques, and Nathan Hill. 2021. User-friendly automatic transcription of low-resource languages: Plugging ESPnet into Elpis. *Proceedings of the Workshop on Computational Methods for Endangered Languages*, 1(2).

Shanley Allen, Fred Genesee, Sarah Fish, and Martha Crago. 2009. *Typological constraints on code mixing in Inuktitut–English bilingual adults*, volume 86, page 273–306. John Benjamins Publishing Company, Amsterdam.

Arun Babu, Changhan Wang, Andros Tjandra, Kushal Lakhotia, Qiantong Xu, Naman Goyal, Kritika Singh, Patrick von Platen, Yatharth Saraf, Juan Pino, Alexei Baevski, Alexis Conneau, and Michael Auli. 2022. XLS-R: Self-supervised cross-lingual speech representation learning at scale. In *Interspeech 2022*, page 2278–2282. ISCA.

Brenda H. Boerger. 2011. To BOLDly go where no one has gone before. *Language Documentation and Conservation*, 5:208–233.

Legislative Services Branch. 2020. Consolidated federal laws of Canada, Indigenous Languages Act.

Hennie Brugman and Albert Russel. 2004. Annotating multi-media/multi-modal resources with ELAN. In *Proceedings of the Fourth International Conference on Language Resources and Evaluation (LREC'04)*, Lisbon, Portugal. European Language Resources Association (ELRA).

Lyle Campbell and Verónica Grondona. 2010. Who speaks what to whom? multilingualism and language choice in Misión La Paz. *Language in Society*, 39(5):617–646.

Kathryn Carreau, Melissa Dane, Kat Klassen, Joanne Mitchell, and Christopher Cox. 2018. Integrating collaboration into the classroom: Connecting community service learning to language documentation training. In Wilson de Lima Silva and Katherine J. Riestenberg, editors, *Collaborative Approaches to the Challenges of Language Documentation and Conservation: Selected papers from the 2018 Symposium on American Indian Languages (SAIL)*, volume 20 of *Language Documentation & Conservation Special Publication*, pages 6–19. University of Hawai'i Press, Honolulu, HI.

Christopher Cox. 2019. *Persephone-ELAN: Automatic phoneme recognition for ELAN users*. Version 0.1.2.

Christopher Cox. 2022. *Voxseg-ELAN: Voice activity detection for ELAN users*. Version 0.1.1.

Christopher Cox. 2023. *XLS-R-ELAN: An implementation of XLS-R automatic speech recognition as a recognizer for ELAN*. Version 0.1.0.

Ben Foley, Joshua T. Arnold, Rolando Coto-Solano, Gautier Durantin, T. Mark Ellison, Daan van Esch, Scott Heath, František Kratochvil, Zara Maxwell-Smith, David Nash, Ola Olsson, Mark Richards, Nay San, Hywel M. Stoakes, N. Thieberger, and Janet Wiles. 2018. Building speech recognition systems for language documentation: The CoEDL Endangered Language Pipeline and Inference System (ELPIS). In *Workshop on Spoken Language Technologies for Under-resourced Languages*.

Nils Hjortnæs, Niko Partanen, Michael Rießler, and Francis M. Tyers. 2020. Towards a speech recognizer for Komi, an endangered and low-resource Uralic language. In *Proceedings of the Sixth International Workshop on Computational Linguistics of Uralic Languages*, pages 31–37, Wien, Austria. Association for Computational Linguistics.

M. Paul Lewis. 2009. *Ethnologue: Languages of the world*, 16. ed edition. SIL International, Dallas, Tex.

Hui Lin, Li Deng, Dong Yu, Yi-fan Gong, Alex Acero, and Chin-Hui Lee. 2009. A study on multilingual acoustic modeling for large vocabulary ASR. In *2009 IEEE International Conference on Acoustics, Speech and Signal Processing*, pages 4333–4336.

Lamont Lindstrom. 2007. Bislama into Kwamera: Code-mixing and language change on Tanna (Vanuatu).

Brigitte Pakendorf, Nina Dobrushina, and Olesya Khanina. 2021. A typology of small-scale multilingualism. *International Journal of Bilingualism*, 25(4):835–859.

Niko Partanen, Mika Hämäläinen, and Tiina Klooster. 2020. Speech recognition for endangered and extinct Samoyedic languages. In *Proceedings of the 34th Pacific Asia Conference on Language, Information and Computation*, pages 523–533, Hanoi, Vietnam. Association for Computational Linguistics.

B. Ramabhadran, Jing Huang, and M. Picheny. 2003. Towards automatic transcription of large spoken archives - english ASR for the MALACH project. In *2003 IEEE International Conference on Acoustics, Speech, and Signal Processing, 2003. Proceedings. (ICASSP '03).*, volume 1, pages I–216–I–219, Hong Kong, China. IEEE.

D. Will Reiman. 2010. Basic oral language documentation. *Language Documentation and Conservation*, 4:254–268.

H. Scheidl, S. Fiel, and R. Sablatnig. 2018. Word beam search: A Connectionist Temporal Classification decoding algorithm. In *16th International Conference on Frontiers in Handwriting Recognition*, pages 253–258. IEEE.

Silero Team. 2021. Silero VAD: pre-trained enterprise-grade Voice Activity Detector (VAD), number detector and language classifier. `https://github.com/snakers4/silero-vad`.

Wilson de Lima Silva. 2020. Multilingual interactions and code-mixing in northwest Amazonia. *International Journal of American Linguistics*, 86(1):133–154.

Sabine Stoll, Taras Zakharko, Steven Moran, Robert Schikowski, and Balthasar Bickel. 2015. Syntactic mixing across generations in an environment of community-wide bilingualism. *Frontiers in Psychology*, 6.

Nick Thieberger. 2016. Documentary linguistics: Methodological challenges and innovatory responses. *Applied Linguistics*, 37(1):88–99.

Sebastian Tschöpel, Daniel Schneider, Rolf Bardeli, Oliver Schreer, Stefano Masneri, Peter Wittenburg, Han Sloetjes, Przemek Lenkiewicz, and Eric Auer. 2011. AVATecH: Audio/Video Technology for Humanities Research. In *Proceedings of the Workshop on Language Technologies for Digital Humanities and Cultural Heritage*, pages 86–89, Hissar, Bulgaria. Association for Computational Linguistics.

Nicholas Wilkinson and Thomas Niesler. 2021. A hybrid CNN-BiLSTM voice activity detector. In *ICASSP 2021 - 2021 IEEE International Conference on Acoustics, Speech and Signal Processing (ICASSP)*, pages 6803–6807. ISSN: 2379-190X.

Hemant Yadav and Sunayana Sitaram. 2022. A survey of multilingual models for automatic speech recognition.

Towards Universal Dependencies in Cook Islands Māori

Sarah Karnes[1] **Rolando Coto-Solano**[1] **Sally Akevai Nicholas**[2]
[1]Department of Linguistics, Dartmouth College
[2]Waipapa Taumata Rau University of Auckland, New Zealand
sarah.r.karnes.23@dartmouth.edu
rolando.a.coto.solano@dartmouth.edu
ake.nicholas@auckland.ac.nz

Abstract

This paper presents a first attempt at applying Universal Dependencies (De Marneffe et al., 2021) to Cook Islands Māori, a Polynesian language from the Cook Islands. There is limited previous work on dependency parsing of Austronesian languages, and there are no existing treebanks for any Polynesian languages. This paper presents a treebank for Cook Islands Māori, with the goal of creating a syntactic resource for further research as well as language instruction. We also present a list of structures that have proved challenging or difficult to parse (e.g. negative sentences, equative sentences, spatial prepositional phrases, actor emphatic structures, and stative sentences with an agent). The treebank contains 126 sentences with 1035 tokens taken from Nicholas (2017), and annotated using UD v2 guidelines. We parsed the sentences using a context-free grammar and then generated dependency parses automatically by using the head-floating method of Xia and Palmer (2001). We are working to expand this treebank and use it to annotate existing corpora and create pedagogical tools for the community. Finally, we review some of the data sovereignty issues related to using Indigenous language data in large language models

1 Introduction

This paper presents the process of creation of a Universal Dependencies (De Marneffe et al., 2021) treebank for the Cook Islands Māori language (henceforth CIM). CIM is a Polynesian language, closely related but distinct from languages like te reo Māori, Samoan, Tongan and Tahitian. UD treebanks exist for other Austronesian languages such as Cebuano, Indonesian and Tagalog, but no previous work has been done on dependency parsing for the Polynesian branch of the Austronesian family.

CIM is spoken by approx 2,500 people in the Cook Islands (Ministry of Finance and Economic Management, Government of the Cook Islands, 2021), plus an additional 10,000 in Aotearoa New Zealand and Australia (Nicholas, 2018). Amongst the diaspora in New Zealand only 9% speak the language (Statistics New Zealand, 2018), and within the Cook Islands themselves familial transmission has decreased, especially on the more populated islands of Rarotonga and Aitutaki (Nicholas, 2018).

CIM is a predominantly isolating language, but it does present derivational morphology (e.g. *'aka-* 'causative' + *rongo* 'hear' = *'akarongo* "to cause to hear"; *tae* 'to reach a place' + *-'anga* 'nominalization' = *tae'anga* "reaching (of the place)"). The unmarked word order in CIM sentences is VSO, or more broadly, predicate initial, as many CIM sentences are nominal. CIM has several distinct dialects; this paper focuses on Southern CIM, spoken on the islands of Rarotonga, Aitutaki, Atiu, Ma'uke, Miti'aro and Mangaia.

There are no existing treebanks for Polynesian languages. There are a few for Austronesian languages, including Tagalog (Aquino and de Leon, 2020), Cebuano (Aranes, 2022) and Indonesian (Alfina et al., 2019). There are a number of Universal Dependency treebanks available for Indigenous languages. They exist for languages of the Americas like Yupik (Chen et al., 2020; Park et al., 2021), Maya Kiché (Tyers and Henderson, 2021), Bribri (Coto-Solano et al., 2021), Shipibo-Konibo (Vasquez et al., 2018), Guaraní (Thomas, 2019) and several other Tupí languages from Brazil (Ferraz Gerardi et al., 2021). They also exist for Australian languages like Warlpiri (Nivre et al., 2020), and Indigenous languages from Eurasia such as Sami (de Lhoneux et al., 2017) and Yakut (Merzhevich and Gerardi, 2022). In this paper we seek to start the creation of UD treebanks for Polynesian languages.

2 Methodology and Data Collection

We parsed 126 CIM sentences, with a total of 1035 tokens. On average the sentences were 8.2 tokens long, with a minimum of two tokens and a maximum of 21 tokens. The data consists of sentences from Nicholas (2017), which includes both isolated sentences from previously published material such as Buse's Dictionary of CIM (Buse and Taringa, 1995), as well as transcriptions of oral narrations gathered through linguistic fieldwork. Most of the sentences come from the Rarotonga and Ma'uke dialects. We used a two step process to parse these sentences: (1) First, we constructed a context-free grammar (CFG) to parse sentences that were manually tokenized and pre-labelled for part of speech. The CFG contains 163 rules: 7 for CPs, 40 for sentences, 15 for VPs, 32 for NPs, 44 for terminals, and 25 for other non-terminal structures. (2) With the CFG parse as a base, we used the method of Xia and Palmer (2001) to raise the heads of the CFG subtrees and establish dependencies between words. This part of our code also converts the XPOS used in the Nicholas (2017) linguistic description into UPOS and sets UD v2 relations between words.

Figure 1 shows an example CFG parse and its corresponding dependency structure. It shows elements that are common to other Polynesian languages. For example, the verb is preceded and followed by tense-aspect-mood (TAM) markers, which are labeled as auxiliaries.

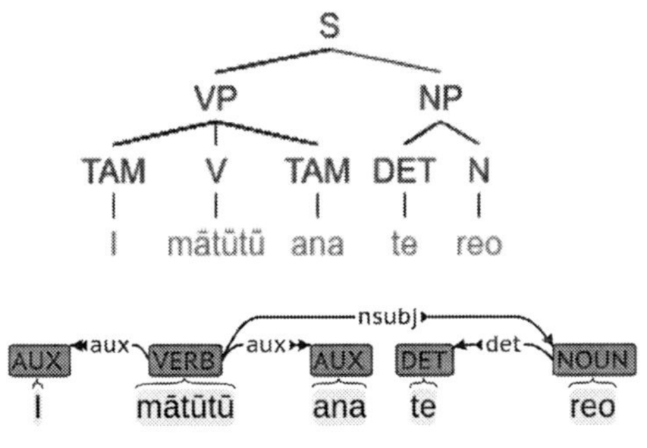

Figure 1: CFG and UD parses for *I mātūtū ana te reo* "The language was strong"

3 Results

Table 1 shows the UPOS in the existing dataset. The most common parts of speech are NOUN, DET, AUX and VERB, accounting for 61% of the tokens in the treebank.

NOUN	192 (19%)	ADV	72 (7%)
DET	149 (14%)	PROPN	46 (4%)
AUX	141 (14%)	PART	38 (4%)
VERB	139 (14%)	ADJ	18 (2%)
ADP	126 (12%)	PUNCT	14 (1%)
PRON	87 (8%)	Others	13 (1%)

Table 1: UPOS tags in CIM sentences.

Table 2 shows the relations used in the UD treebank. The most frequent relations are case, aux, nsubj, det and root, and they account for 65% of the labels in the dataset.

case	146 (14%)	nmod:poss	34 (3%)
aux	141 (14%)	nmod	28 (3%)
nsubj	130 (13%)	amod	26 (3%)
det	128 (12%)	det:poss	21 (2%)
root	126 (12%)	obl:agt	20 (2%)
advmod	62 (6%)	nummod	18 (2%)
obl	49 (5%)	punct	14 (1%)
dobj	46 (4%)	Others	46 (4%)

Table 2: Relations in CIM parsings

4 Challenging Structures

This treebank is a work in progress, but several issues have been observed which will also be found in other Polynesian languages.

4.1 Negative Sentences

The negative structures in CIM are different from those in most UD languages. Figure 2 has the word *kāre* "not" as the first in the structure. It might be tempting to tag this as a negative adverb, and have the verb *moe* "sleep" as the root. However, multiple analyses of Polynesian languages (Hohepa, 1969; Nicholas, 2017) have shown that *kāre* is actually a verb (diachronically the combination of the TAM *ka* and the adverb *kore* "not"). This should be the root of the structure, and have the second verb as its clausal complement (xcomp).

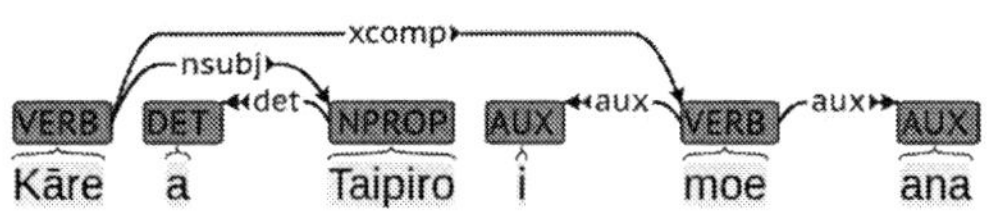

Figure 2: UD parse for the negative sentence "Taipiro didn't sleep"

4.2 Equative Sentences

Figure 3 shows examples of equative sentences. CIM does not have a copula, and therefore these are parsed similarly to their equivalent structure in languages like Russian: The predicate of the sentence, be it a noun or an adjective, is selected as the root. In figure 3a, the name *Mere* is the root, and it is marked as the predicate by the specifying word *ko*. This word "marks a phrase as nominal and specific" (Nicholas, 2017, 188). It usually marks the predicate of the equative, but it can also mark focused arguments

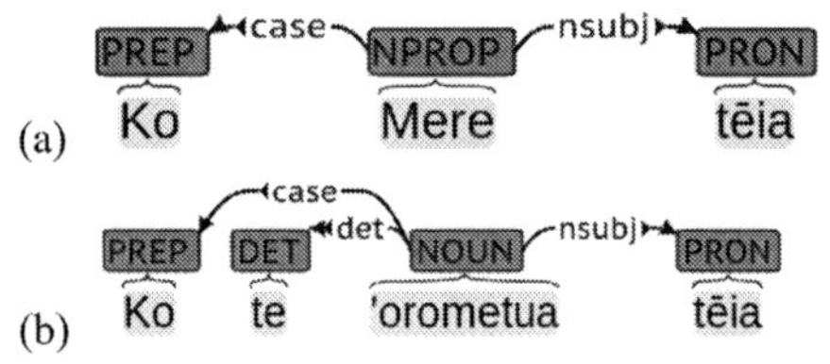

Figure 3: UD parse for (a) *Ko Mere tēia* "This is Mere" and (b) *Ko te 'orometua tēia* "This is the minister"

Given that this is a nominal construction, where the main element of *ko te 'orometua* in figure 3b is the noun *'orometua* "minister", and that there are no TAM markers in the sentence, there are no words that should be labeled as a VERB. The word *ko* is a function word, but it should not be labeled as a PART or an AUX (copula) because it doesn't have any TAM functions. There is research that has analyzed this as a preposition (Brown and Koch, 2016; Massam et al., 2006). If *ko* is a preposition, the relationship between *Mere* and *ko* would be case. This is a very desirable property; this is parallel to languages like Polish, where the predicate of an equative structure needs a particular case (e.g. the instrumental in the case of Polish).

4.3 Spatial prepositional phrases

Figure 4 shows the phrase *ki runga i tōna pona* "on her dress". The word *runga* means the surface of an object, and the preposition *ki* indicates that something is done in/on somewhere. The third word, *i*, usually works as a preposition for place (e.g. *i te kainga* "at home"). But, what is the role of the word *i* in the following parse?

This could be parsed in two ways. The first one is to see this as a sequence of prepositional phrases, whose literal translation would be "on the surface on her dress", and whose root would be *runga*. The second parse shows a potential, multi-

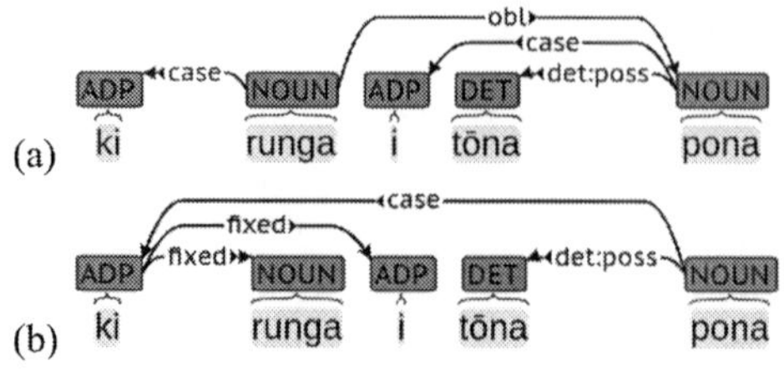

Figure 4: Two possible parses for *ki runga i tōna pona* "on her dress". The first one will be preferred.

word preposition *ki runga i* "on", whose root is the noun *pona* "dress". The literal translation of the second structure would be "on-top her dress". In our ongoing work we have chosen to use the first parse in order to keep the prepositions separate and gain in generalization.

4.4 Actor emphatic structures

CIM and other East Polynesian languages have a particular construction used for specifying the agent of a presupposed transitive event. Polynesianists have designated this the actor (or agent) emphatic construction (Nicholas, 2017, 239). Example 1 shows a typical example.

(1) *Nā Mere i tunu i tēia mānga.*
AEC mere TAM cook ACC DET food

"Mere cooked this food" or "It was Mere who cooked this food".

There are competing analyses for how this construction should be parsed, including differences in how many clauses it comprises, and the grammatical relationships between the constituent phrases (cf. Nicholas, 2017, ch7). Nicholas (2017, 259) analyses the agent phrase as the predicate (root) and the verb phrase as a subordinate clause. The status of the patient phrase is potentially unclear but, in examples such as 1 above, it is the object of the verb. We take it that these constructions are analogous to simple possessive constructions. In figure 5, the person *Mere* possesses the food, and therefore the sentence is translated as "The food is Mere's". In figure 6, the thing that *Mere* possesses is the action of "that [she] cooked the food".

The possessive *nā* phrase and the verb phrase function as two different clauses. The possessive phrase contains the root, just as it does in figure 5. The word *nā* is labeled here as an ADP, as its function is to express the grammatical/semantic relationship of the Nā phrase to the verb.

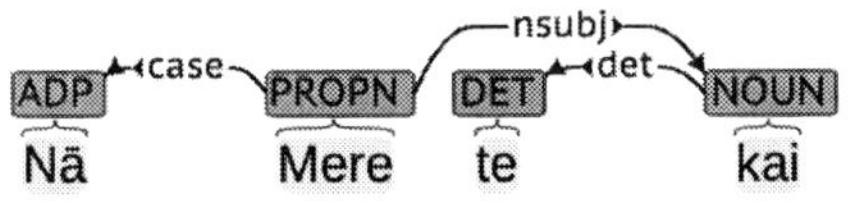

Figure 5: A possible parse for *nā Mere te kai* "The food is Mere's".

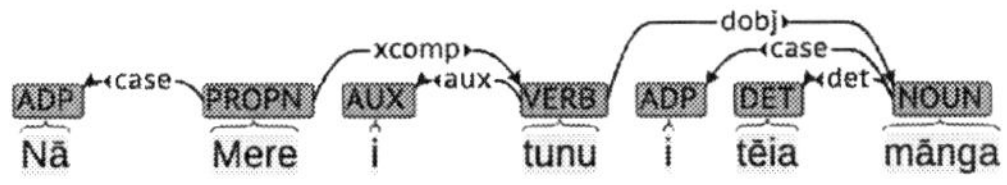

Figure 6: A possible parse for *nā Mere i tuna i tēia mānga* "Mere cooked this food for me".

4.5 Stative sentences with an agent

CIM has a subcategory of verbs commonly called *stative* that typically takes a theme as the subject and optionally includes an agent or cause NP introduced by the preposition *i*. The examples in 2 illustrate this.

(2) a. *Kua pou te taro*
TAM be-consumed DET taro
"The taro is all gone".

b. *Kua pou te taro i te puaka*
TAM be-consumed DET taro AGT DET pig
"The pigs ate all the taro" or "The taro has been consumed by the pigs".

c. *Kua pou te taro i te puaka te kai*
TAM be-consumed DET taro AGT DET pig DET eat
"The pigs ate all the taro by eating" or "By eating, the taro has been consumed by the pigs".

The sentence 2b is stative, but it has the same syntactic structure as a VSO active sentence. Furthermore, it has the same orthographic and phonetic characteristics as a regular transitive sentence. We predict that it will be very difficult for the parser to process these types of sentences without a deeper understanding of their semantics. This structure is only possible with a special lexical category of stative verbs. There are about 100 of these stative verbs, which do not take the -Cia passive suffix and which tend to have theme subjects. The system would need to learn to distinguish these verbs during the training process.

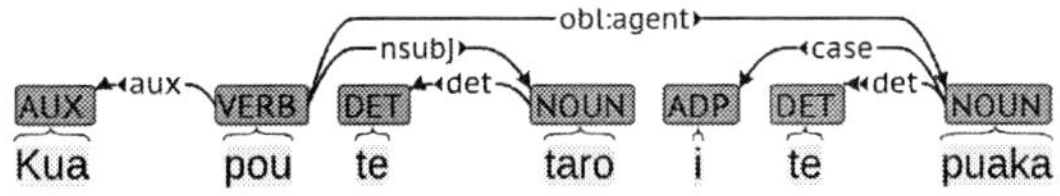

Figure 7: Parse for *Kua pou te taro i te puaka* "The pigs ate all the taro".

A further difficulty presents itself in examples like 2c. In the sentence "The pigs consumed all the taro by eating", the final clause *te kai* "by eating" can be analyzed in two different ways. The word *kai* could be analyzed as a bare VP within a verbal dependent clause, or it could be a bare nominal phrase akin to a gerund (Nicholas, 2017, 309).

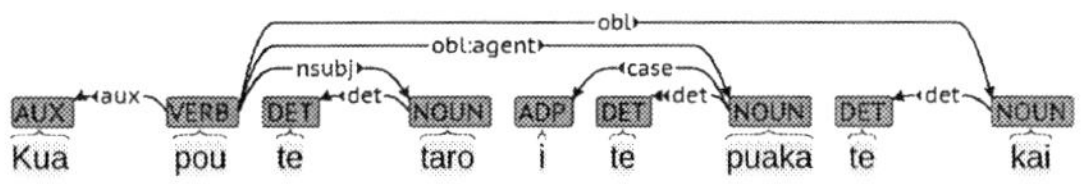

Figure 8: Parse for *Kua pou te taro i te puaka te kai* "The pigs consumed all the taro by eating".

We analyze this sentence in the manner demonstrated in figure 8. There, the word *kai* "food, eating" is marked as a nominal gerund, and is connected to the verb by the obl relation. While this captures the meaning of the structure, it will be a challenge for the parser because the majority of NPs without a preposition are subjects, and would be tagged as nsubj.

5 Data Sovereignty and Future Applications

One major consideration during this project is data sovereignty. As we make the treebank we are considering making it available through the Kaitiaki License from Te Hiku Media (2023). In this license, the mana (property, authority) of the data remains with the population of the Cook Islands, and the data itself is under the care of a Cook Islands researcher (author Nicholas). This means that, if the data were to be used by non Cook Islanders, for example to train a large-scale language model, the people seeking to use the treebank would need to ask permission from the Cook Islands author, as well as seek ways to contribute to the community. The Cook Islands author has a long history of work within her community, and has previously used corpora to create pedagogical tools. The treebank described here is intended to automate and accelerate the annotation of the corpus, but its use in other tools would be subject to approval by the Cook Islands researcher.

One of the main challenges during the process is to understand how contributors might potentially object to a usage of their data. We have solely used previously published materials for this treebank, but many of the sentences in Nicholas (2017) were uttered by Cook Islanders in direct interviews. We need to consider two components of this work: (i) the treebank itself, and (ii) the potential files where the trained parsing models (e.g. UDPipe models) are stored. In the treebank the people who uttered the sentences are credited, and it is easier for speakers of CIM to either approve the inclusion of their sentence, or to object to their data being part of the database. However, in the case of the model files, the data has been cut off from those who have uttered it. By the time the model receives these parsed sentences as input, the sentences are separated from their identifying metadata, and they become part of the numerical parameters of the model. Explaining this process to people is complex, and it makes it difficult for speakers to potentially object to certain ways of using their data (e.g. to augment a large-scale parsing database). We hope to use the aforementioned license to authorize projects which can have a positive impact on the community, and thereby allay potential objections of community members. However these relationships must be tended continuously by ongoing consultation, collaboration and responsiveness. We will communicate our results to the Cook Islands community through outreach at the University of the South Pacific, and through the connections of the research with the community.

There are two main goals of this work. The most immediate one is to create a fully parsed corpus for CIM, so that the grammatical structure of the language can be further studied. This corpus has been collected by the Cook Islands author, and has been used for creative pedagogical materials. The parser will accelerate the work of studying the grammar of CIM. We also have a further pedagogical goal: We are working to produce a web-based interface for the parser, so that school teachers and students of CIM can get grammatical information to assist them in their studies. Teachers currently take classes at the University of the South Pacific, where they study basic CIM grammar and parts-of-speech is one of their most challenging topics. We will train a POS tagger from the treebank and use this to help teachers in their training, and for them to become more involved in CIM NLP. The parsing model can also be used to build tools like question answering systems and chatbots, which would create a positive impact (Galla, 2016) and ultimately garner attention to the language, particularly from younger community members who might be drawn into the language through technology.

These difficult questions are of course not just part of the work with CIM, but should be incorporated in all NLP work with Indigenous languages. The challenge of balancing community benefit with data openness remains crucial to the progress of NLP for under-resourced languages.

6 Conclusions

In this paper we have presented the first steps towards the creation of a Universal Dependencies Treebank in the Cook Islands Māori language. This would be the first attempt to create such a treebank for a Polynesian language. We have tagged a total of 1035 words and we have plans to continue to expand it before releasing it to the public. We plan to release it under a license that privileges Cook Islander's decisions of how the data will be used. The overarching goal is to use this treebank to accelerate the tagging of CIM corpora and to create pedagogical tools to train teachers in CIM grammar.

7 Acknowledgments

Meitaki ma'ata ki te au tangata tei tuku mai tā rātou reo ki a mātou. Mē kāre kōtou kāre tēia 'anga'anga. Thank you so much to all the CIM speakers who shared their words with us and continue to collaborate in this project. Finally, this project is supported by the Marsden Fund Council from the Aotearoa New Zealand Government (21-MAU-018), managed by The Royal Society Te Apārangi.

References

Ika Alfina, Arawinda Dinakaramani, Mohamad Ivan Fanany, and Heru Suhartanto. 2019. A Gold Standard Dependency Treebank for Indonesian. In *the Proceedings of the 33rd Pacific Asia Conference on Language, Information and Computation (PACLIC 33)*.

Angelina Aquino and Franz de Leon. 2020. Parsing in the absence of related languages: Evaluating low-resource dependency parsers on Tagalog. In *Proceedings of the Fourth Workshop on Universal Dependencies (UDW 2020)*, pages 8–15.

Glyd Aranes. 2022. The GJA Cebuano Treebank: Creating a Cebuano Universal Dependencies Treebank. Master's thesis, Itä-Suomen yliopisto.

Jason Brown and Karsten Koch. 2016. Focus and change in Polynesian languages. *Australian Journal of Linguistics*, 36(3):304–349.

Jasper Buse and Raututi Taringa. 1995. *Cook Islands Maori Dictionary*, volume 123. Editorial of University of the South Pacific.

Emily Chen, Hyunji Hayley Park, and Lane Schwartz. 2020. Improved Finite-State Morphological Analysis for St. Lawrence Island Yupik using Paradigm Function Morphology. In *Proceedings of the 12th Language Resources and Evaluation Conference*, pages 2676–2684.

Rolando Coto-Solano, Sharid Loáiciga, and Sofía Flores-Solórzano. 2021. Towards Universal Dependencies for Bribri. In *Proceedings of the Fifth Workshop on Universal Dependencies (UDW, SyntaxFest 2021)*, pages 16–29.

Marie-Catherine De Marneffe, Christopher D Manning, Joakim Nivre, and Daniel Zeman. 2021. Universal dependencies. *Computational linguistics*, 47(2):255–308.

Fabrício Ferraz Gerardi, Stanislav Reichert, Carolina Aragon, Lorena Martín-Rodríguez, Gustavo Godoy, and Tatiana Merzhevich. 2021. TuDet: Tupían Dependency Treebank (version v0.2).

Candace Kaleimamoowahinekapu Galla. 2016. Indigenous language revitalization, promotion, and education: Function of digital technology. *Computer Assisted Language Learning*, 29(7):1137–1151.

Pat Hohepa. 1969. Not in English and Eehara in Maori. *Te Reo*, 12:1–33.

Miryam de Lhoneux, Yan Shao, Ali Basirat, Eliyahu Kiperwasser, Sara Stymne, Yoav Goldberg, and Joakim Nivre. 2017. From Raw Text to Universal Dependencies - Look, No Tags! In *Proceedings of the CoNLL 2017 Shared Task: Multilingual Parsing from Raw Text to Universal Dependencies*, pages 207–217.

Diane Massam, Josephine Lee, and Nicholas Rolle. 2006. Still a Preposition: The Category of Ko. *Te Reo*, 49.

Tatiana Merzhevich and Fabrício Ferraz Gerardi. 2022. Introducing Yakutoolkit. Yakut Treebank and Morphological Analyzer. In *Proceedings of the 1st Annual Meeting of the ELRA/ISCA Special Interest Group on Under-Resourced Languages*, pages 185–188.

Ministry of Finance and Economic Management, Government of the Cook Islands. 2021. Census 2021: Key findings. `https://www.mfem.gov.ck/statistics/census-and-surveys/census/267-census-2021`.

Sally Akevai Te Namu Nicholas. 2017. Ko te Karāma o te Reo Māori o te Pae Tonga o Te Kuki Airani: A Grammar of Southern Cook Islands Māori. *Doctoral Dissertation, University of Auckland*.

Sally Akevai Te Namu Nicholas. 2018. Language contexts: Te Reo Māori o te Pae Tonga o te Kuki Airani also known as Southern Cook Islands Māori. *Language Documentation and Description*, 15:64.

Joakim Nivre, Marie-Catherine de Marneffe, Filip Ginter, Jan Hajič, Christopher D Manning, Sampo Pyysalo, Sebastian Schuster, Francis Tyers, and Daniel Zeman. 2020. Universal Dependencies v2: An evergrowing multilingual treebank collection. *arXiv preprint arXiv:2004.10643*.

Hyunji Park, Lane Schwartz, and Francis Tyers. 2021. Expanding Universal dependencies for Polysynthetic Languages: A Case of St. Lawrence Island Yupik. In *Proceedings of the First Workshop on Natural Language Processing for Indigenous Languages of the Americas*, pages 131–142.

Statistics New Zealand. 2018. 2018 Census totals by topic – national highlights (updated). `(StatsNZWebsite)`.

Te Hiku Media. 2023. Kaitiakitanga License. `https://github.com/TeHikuMedia/Kaitiakitanga-License`.

Guillaume Thomas. 2019. Universal Dependencies for Mbyá Guaraní. In *Proceedings of the third workshop on universal dependencies (udw, syntaxfest 2019)*, pages 70–77.

Francis Tyers and Robert Henderson. 2021. A Corpus of K'iche' Annotated for Morphosyntactic Structure. In *Proceedings of the First Workshop on Natural Language Processing for Indigenous Languages of the Americas*, pages 10–20.

Alonso Vasquez, Renzo Ego Aguirre, Candy Angulo, John Miller, Claudia Villanueva, Željko Agić, Roberto Zariquiey, and Arturo Oncevay. 2018. Toward Universal Dependencies for Shipibo-Konibo. In *Proceedings of the Second Workshop on Universal Dependencies (UDW 2018)*, pages 151–161.

Fei Xia and Martha Palmer. 2001. Converting dependency structures to phrase structures. Technical report, Pennsylvania Univ Philadelphia.

Investigating Speaker Diarization of Endangered Language Data

Gina-Anne Levow
Department of Linguistics
University of Washington
Seattle, WA USA
levow@uw.edu

Abstract

The task of speaker diarization aims to determine which speakers spoke when in a recording. Such functionality could help to accelerate work in endangered languages by facilitating transcription and semi-automatically extracting useful meta-data to enrich language archives. However, there has been little work on speaker diarization for low-resource or endangered languages. This work explores three neural approaches to speaker diarization applied to data sets drawn from endangered language archives. We find consistent improvements for recent neural x-vector models over earlier approaches. We also assess the factors which impact performance across models and data sets, with a focus on the challenging characteristics of endangered language recordings.

1 Introduction

The task of speaker diarization aims to determine which speakers spoke when and for how long in a recording. Such functionality could facilitate work in endangered language documentation and revitalization by accelerating transcription and semi-automatically extracting useful meta-data to enrich language archives, making such materials more accessible to researchers and speaker communities. It could also help to alleviate the so-called "transcription bottleneck." The DIHARD series of shared task evaluations (Ryant et al., 2018) has brought renewed attention to the challenges of speaker diarization in a variety of interaction scenarios. However, there has been little work on speaker diarization for low-resource or endangered languages. This work explores three neural approaches to speaker diarization applied to data sets drawn from eight geographically and typologically diverse endangered language archives. We find consistent improvements for recent neural x-vector models over earlier approaches. We also assess the factors which impact performance across models and data sets, with a focus on the characteristics of endangered language recordings which prove challenging.

2 Related Work

Speaker diarization has been the subject of ongoing shared task evaluations (Ryant et al., 2018, 2019, 2020). Earlier work on diarization focused on telephone conversations (Godfrey et al., 1992), broadcast news, and multiparty meetings (Janin et al., 2003). Recent tasks and data sets have refocused attention on more varied and challenging interaction settings, such as child-directed speech, restaurant conversations, and courtroom speech, in the DIHARD (Ryant et al., 2018) task series. However, most diarization task data has been in English or other high resource languages, such as French or Chinese.

Some prior work has explored speaker diarization on endangered language data. Le Franc et al. (2018) investigated an easy-to-use diarization tool on child speech recordings, including datasets of Tsimane, an endangered Bolivian language, and Tseltal in Mexico. Both child speech data and recording environments posed challenges. Most closely related is work in Levow et al. (2021), which creates data sets and baselines for planned shared tasks on speech processing for endangered languages and reports diarization results from a LIUM (Rouvier et al., 2013) baseline. The current work investigates a range of stronger baselines and further analysis.

Endangered language data poses many challenges for speaker diarization. Diarization is sensitive to the style of interaction, e.g. broadcast news vs. courtroom vs. dinner-party conversation, and recordings collected by documentary linguists span diverse domains from structured elicitations to sermons and ceremonies. Recording conditions for documentary linguistic data are also potentially more variable than those in prior studies, many of which have focused on telephone or wideband laboratory recording settings. In addition, we consider endangered languages with areal and typological diversity. Finally and crucially, documentary linguistic data is typically much more limited in quantity, precluding techniques which rely on large amounts of in-language training data.

3 Data

Our experiments employ data following the language and data set selection and pre-processing of Levow et al. (2021), described briefly below. The data sets are drawn from eight different languages deposited in the Endangered Language Archive, now housed at `http://elararchive.org`. Recordings and accompanying time-aligned transcriptions in ELAN (Brugman and Russel, 2004) format form the basis for both the experimental data and the requisite gold-standard speaker segmentation for evaluation. For each language, we provide information about its language family, the ISO639-3 language codes where available[1], location of the fieldwork, and the genres represented in the collection. In addition, the total duration as well as the mean and standard deviation of turn lengths for recordings in the experimental data sets are presented.

Cicipu (ISO639-3:awc) The deposit for Cicipu a language of the Niger-Congo family, was collected in Nigeria and includes "greetings, conversations, hortative discourse, narratives, procedural, and ritual discourse" (McGill, 2012). The experimental data set comprises 3.3 hours of audio with an average turn length of 1.9 seconds, with a standard deviation of 1.3 seconds.

Effutu (ISO639-3:awu) The deposit for Effutu (Agyeman, 2016), a language of the Niger-Congo family, was collected in Ghana and includes interviews, prompted narratives, and elicitations, among others. The experimental data set comprises 2.0 hours of recordings, with mean turn length of 3.4 seconds, and standard deviation of 11.1s.

Mocho' (ISO639-3:mhc) The deposit for Mocho' (Pérez González, 2018), a Mayan family language, was recorded in Mexico and includes both biographical and non-biographical narratives (the latter including historical events, myths, etc.), a prayer, conversation, elicitation sessions, among others. The experimental set comprises 4.3 hours of recordings, with an average turn length of 2.0s (1.5s standard deviation).

Northern Prinmi (ISO639-3:pmi) The Northern Prinmi deposit aims to document oral art, including rituals, traditional songs, folktales and conversations (Daudey and Pincuo, 2018), from multiple locations. The data set used for experimentation includes 3.2 hours of audio, with turns averaging 3.2s, standard deviation of 19.0s.

Sakun (ISO639-3:syk) The Sakun deposit (Thomas, nd), of the Afro-Asiatic language family, is a collection of recordings of discourses typically among 2-5 participants relating to community cultural practices, collected in Nigeria. The experimental data set spans 9.2 hours, with mean turn length of 2.7s and standard deviation of 2.3s.

Upper Napo Kichwa The Upper Napo Kichwa deposit (Grzech, 2018) describes a Quechuan family language of Ecuador[2]. It includes grammatical elicitation and life interviews. The resulting experimental data set includes 10 hours of audio, with mean turn duration of 2.9s and standard deviation of 4.6s.

Toratán (ISO639-3:rth) The deposit for Toratán (Jukes, nd) (Austronesian, collected in Indonesia) spans conversational data, elicitation sessions, and various narratives. The experimental data set covers 14.5 hours of audio recordings, with mean turn lengths of 2.1s and standard deviation of 2.2s.

Ulwa (ISO639-3:yla) The deposit for Ulwa (Barlow, 2018), a Keram family language of Papua New Guinea, includes conversational data as well as traditional and personal stories. The experimental dataset comprises 3.2 hours of audio, with mean turn length of 3.6s and standard deviation of 5.1s.

4 Diarization Models

We compare three recent, high performing neural diarization models: the speaker diarization recipes (Snyder et al., 2018; Sell et al., 2018) for Kaldi (Povey et al., 2011), pyannote.audio (Bredin et al., 2020; Bredin and Laurent, 2021), and VBx (Landini et al., 2022). All models leverage a pre-trained neural network model to compute a so-called "x-vector" embedding representation of the

[1] https://www.iso.org/standard/39534.htm

[2] It is likely closely related to Tena Quechua (ISO639-3:quw).

audio. These x-vectors are then employed in subsequent clustering stages to produce a global segmentation and assignment of speakers to segments. In all cases, we used the system's included or publicly released x-vector models, without additional task-specific fine-tuning or adaptation. Furthermore, all models were run with default hyperparameters in a fully unsupervised mode, where the true segmentation, voice activity detection, and number of speakers were unknown and needed to be determined by the model. Additional model details are below.

Kaldi The Kaldi toolkit (Povey et al., 2011) provides reference implementations for a range of state-of-the-art models for speech processing, in the form of "recipes" to reproduce published approaches. For the speaker diarization task, we use the pre-trained x-vector models (Callhome Diarization Xvector Model 1a) (Snyder et al., 2018) available from the Kaldi site [3] with the DIHARD_2018 (Sell et al., 2018) recipe [4]. After creating x-vector representations of spans of the audio stream, the recipe uses a probabilistic linear discriminant analysis (PLDA) backend to score the similarity between spans after which clustering is performed to produce the final diarization output.

pyannote.audio The `pyannote.audio` package (Bredin et al., 2020; Bredin and Laurent, 2021) provides a neural speaker diarization pipeline, which is available through Hugging Face [5]. The pipeline leverages the SpeechBrain (Ravanelli et al., 2021) implementation of the ECAPA-TDNN (Desplanques et al., 2020) model, based on its superior performance within this pipeline. The approach applies a local neural speaker segmentation over 5 second windows of speech, from which local speaker embeddings are computed for each speaker in the window. A global agglomerative hierarchical clustering is then performed prior to a final aggregation phase which yields the full diarization.

VBx The VBx (VBHMM x-vectors Diarization) model (Landini et al., 2022) also computes x-vector representations over input audio spans. It then performs agglomerative hierarchical clustering over those representations as an initialization phase for a Variational Bayes (VB) Hidden Markov Model over the x-vectors to create final diarization output. This approach requires a preliminary segmentation created using voice activity detection (VAD) to distinguish speech and non-speech regions; we employ the Kaldi VAD scripts for this purpose.

4.1 Baseline Diarization Model: LIUM

We contrast the three neural diarization models above with the LIUM (Rouvier et al., 2013) system baseline presented in Levow et al. (2021), applied to the same data sets as in the current work. LIUM employs the previously popular i-vector model to represent speech spans and an Integer Linear Programming (ILP) approach to globally optimize the assignment of speech spans to particular speakers. LIUM's publicly available Java implementation [6] was used in an unsupervised setting, so that none of the endangered language data was used for tuning or training, and was all treated as test data.

5 Experiments & Results

All three neural speaker diarization models were applied to the eight endangered language data sets. The standard evaluation metric for speaker diarization is Diarization Error Rate (DER), which combines: 1) speaker error: the portion of scored time assigned to the wrong speaker, 2) false alarm speech: portion of scored time incorrectly labeled as speech, and 3) missed speech: portion of scored time incorrectly labeled as non-speech. All measures were computed with the `dscore` package [7].

5.1 Overall findings

Results are shown in Table 1. We can observe that all three neural diarization models outperform the LIUM i-vector baseline system. All pairwise system differences are significant by Wilcoxon signed rank test ($p < 0.05$), except for Pyannote/VBx. In addition, the best effectiveness for each of the languages is given either by Pyannote or VBx.

In addition to the overall differences in system effectiveness, there is also substantial variation across the different languages, with DER ranges of 25 or more across languages within each of the systems. The Sakun and Toratán data sets appear to be challenging for all of the systems, while Prinmi and Effutu conversely present less challenge overall.

[3] https://kaldi-asr.org/models/m6

[4] For simplicity, we employ the model without Variational Bayes inference, though we expect that better effectiveness would be achieved with it as in prior work.

[5] https://huggingface.co/pyannote/speaker-diarization

[6] `https://github.com/StevenLOL/LIUM`

[7] `https://github.com/nryant/dscore`

	LIUM	Kaldi	Pyannote	VBx
Cicipu	44.5	43.78	**32.45**	33.31
Effutu	34.7	31.46	34.88	**26.55**
Mocho'	60.2	51.85	**27.37**	33.36
Northern Prinmi	37.8	29.10	23.3	**22.97**
Sakun	62.6	57.37	**48.8**	52.45
Upper Napo Kichwa	43.7	35.26	**26.15**	30.34
Toratán	55.6	44.46	**40.13**	44.16
Ulwa	57.9	37.94	41.04	**29.23**

Table 1: Diarization Error Rates for Kaldi (DER), Pyannote, and VBx compared to a baseline LIUM system for eight endangered language data sets. Lower scores are better; best results for each language are in bold.

Mocho' and Ulwa yield quite variable performance across systems.

5.2 Analysis

Since we observe substantial variation in DER across languages and across files within languages, we investigate factors which might contribute to this disparity. One dimension of variation across datasets and recordings is the number of speakers per recording, ranging between 1 and 18, with a mean of 2.55. Speaker error is also a significant element of DER. So, we assess correlation between number of speakers and per-recording DER. For all systems, there was a highly significant ($p < 0.0001$) positive correlation between the true number of speakers and DER (Spearman: Kaldi: 0.28; VBx, Pyannote: 0.42)[8]. Thus, having more speakers in a recording was associated with more errors. If we look further at how the difference between the predicted and true speaker counts relates to DER, we find a significant correlation between predicting too few speakers and increased DER for Pyannote (0.22, $p < 0.0001$), but conversely a significant correlation with over-predicting speakers and DER for Kaldi. No such correlation was found for VBx. It seems reasonable that distinguishing among larger numbers of speakers would be intrinsically more difficult, and that models also differ in terms of over- or under-segmenting speech. Further, this difficulty can be exacerbated in endangered language recordings where a single microphone is often used and the distance from the speaker to the microphone may vary substantially. If available, supervision in the form of the number of known speakers could help to mitigate this problem.

Missed and false alarm speech also contribute to DER, and, while the data sets were constructed to exclude particularly poor or noisy recordings, background and environmental noise are likely to be more prevalent and variable in endangered language recordings than in more typical diarization data. This is another dimension along which models may differ. To investigate the effects of voice activity detection, we compute, for each experimental file, the total speech duration in the diarization output for each system and for the reference segmentation. Then we compute the correlation between the disparity in the system and the reference durations with the DER score for each file. We find a highly significant correlation between missing speech and DER for Pyannote (0.31, $p < 0.0001$), while, for VBx and Kaldi, false alarm speech is associated with higher DER. These associations highlight the challenges of accurate speech detection in varied and variable fieldwork recordings, and point to the importance of developing better and more adaptable techniques.

6 Ethical considerations

Speech remains intrinsically personally identifying information and can also expose personal information in the spoken content. Data pre-processing removes individual speaker names from the experimental data. However, the potential still exists to link data with other, potentially identifying information elsewhere on the web. As a result, these systems do raise the risk to privacy or harm from use in deep fakes. Furthermore, while these tools are being developed to support language documentation and revitalization, the same speaker-linking that these models create could itself increase the potential privacy risks. It is important that researchers communicate these possibilities and work with language archives and communities to craft appropriate access and use.

7 Conclusion & Future Work

We have evaluated three recent neural models on a diverse suite of endangered language archive data, with no special tuning, demonstrating improvements over a baseline i-vector model and potential increases in utility for researchers, archivists and community members. Further analysis highlights

[8] All correlations are Spearman correlation in the `scipy.stats` package

the challenges of the variation in this data, and the differences in how the models address them. Future work will explore adaptation to the endangered language data, and overall improvements to speech detection in these sorts of varied environments.

Acknowledgements

This work has been supported by NSF: #1760475. The views and conclusions contained herein are those of the authors and should not be interpreted as necessarily representing the official policies or endorsements, either expressed or implied, of NSF or the U.S. Government. Many thanks to Emily M. Bender, Emily P. Ahn, Cassandra Maz, Siyu Liang, and Isaac Manrique for their valuable contributions this work and the broader Streamlined project.

References

Nana Ama Agyeman. 2016. Documentation of Efutu. https://elar.soas.ac.uk/Collection/MPI1029692, Accessed on 12 Oct 2020.

Russell Barlow. 2018. Documentation of Ulwa, an endangered language of Papua New Guinea. https://wurin.lis.soas.ac.uk/Collection/MPI1035105, Accessed on 12 Oct 2020.

Hervé Bredin and Antoine Laurent. 2021. End-to-end speaker segmentation for overlap-aware resegmentation. In *Proc. Interspeech 2021*, Brno, Czech Republic.

Hervé Bredin, Ruiqing Yin, Juan Manuel Coria, Gregory Gelly, Pavel Korshunov, Marvin Lavechin, Diego Fustes, Hadrien Titeux, Wassim Bouaziz, and Marie-Philippe Gill. 2020. pyannote.audio: neural building blocks for speaker diarization. In *ICASSP 2020, IEEE International Conference on Acoustics, Speech, and Signal Processing*, Barcelona, Spain.

H. Brugman and A. Russel. 2004. Annotating multimedia/ multi-modal resources with ELAN. In *Proceedings of LREC 2004, Fourth International Conference on Language Resources and Evaluation.*

Henriëtte Daudey and Gerong Pincuo. 2018. Documentation of Northern Prinmi oral art, with a special focus on ritual speech. https://elar.soas.ac.uk/Collection/MPI1083424, Accessed on 12 Oct 2020.

Brecht Desplanques, Jenthe Thienpondt, and Kris Demuynck. 2020. ECAPA-TDNN: Emphasized channel attention, propagation and aggregation in TDNN based speaker verification. In *Proceedings of Interspeech 2020.*

J. Godfrey, E. C. Holliman, and J. McDaniel. 1992. Switchboard: Telephone speech corpus for research and development. In *Proceedings of the IEEE International Conference on Acoustics,Speech and Signal Processing, vol. 1*, page 517–520.

Karolina Grzech. 2018. Upper Napo Kichwa: A documentation of linguistic and cultural practices. https://elar.soas.ac.uk/Collection/MPI849403, Accessed on 12 Oct 2020.

A. Janin, D. Baron, J. Edwards, D. Ellis, D. Gelbart, N. Morgan, B. Peskin, T. Pfau, E. Shriberg, and A. Stolcke. 2003. The ICSI meeting corpus. In *Proceedings of the IEEE International Conference on Acoustics, Speech and Signal Processing, vol. 1.*

Anthony Jukes. nd. Documentation of Toratán (Ratahan). https://elar.soas.ac.uk/Collection/MPI87803, Accessed on 12 Oct 2020.

Federico Landini, Ján Profant, Mireia Diez, and Lukáš Burget. 2022. Bayesian hmm clustering of x-vector sequences (VBx) in speaker diarization: theory, implementation and analysis on standard tasks. *Computer Speech & Language*, 71:101254.

Adrien Le Franc, Eric Riebling, Julien Karadayi, Yun Wang, Camila Scaff, Florian Metze, and Alejandrina Cristia. 2018. The ACLEW DiViMe: An Easy-to-use Diarization Tool. In *Proc. Interspeech 2018*, pages 1383–1387.

Gina-Anne Levow, Emily P. Ahn, and Emily M. Bender. 2021. Developing a shared task for speech processing on endangered languages. In *Proceedings of the 4th Workshop on the Use of Computational Methods in the Study of Endangered Languages.*

Stuart McGill. 2012. Cicipu documentation. https://elar.soas.ac.uk/Collection/MPI97667, Accessed on 12 Oct 2020.

Jaime Pérez González. 2018. Documentation of Mocho' (Mayan): Language preservation through community awareness and engagement. https://elar.soas.ac.uk/Collection/MPI1079685, Accessed on 12 Oct 2020.

Daniel Povey, Arnab Ghoshal, Gilles Boulianne, Lukas Burget, Ondrej Glembek, Nagendra Goel, Mirko Hannemann, Petr Motlicek, Yanmin Qian, Petr Schwarz, et al. 2011. The kaldi speech recognition toolkit. In *IEEE 2011 workshop on Automatic Speech Recognition and Understanding*, CONF, pages 1–4. IEEE Signal Processing Society.

Mirco Ravanelli, Titouan Parcollet, Peter Plantinga, Aku Rouhe, Samuele Cornell, Loren Lugosch, Cem Subakan, Nauman Dawalatabad, Abdelwahab Heba, Jianyuan Zhong, Ju-Chieh Chou, Sung-Lin Yeh, Szu-Wei Fu, Chien-Feng Liao, Elena Rastorgueva,

François Grondin, William Aris, Hwidong Na, Yan Gao, Renato De Mori, , and Yoshua Ben-gio. 2021. SpeechBrain: A general-purpose speech toolkit. ArXiv:2106.04624.

M. Rouvier, G. Dupuy, P. Gay, E. Khoury, T. Merlin, and S. Meignier. 2013. An open-source state-of-the-art toolbox for broadcast news diarization. In *Interspeech 2013*, pages 1477–1481.

Neville Ryant, Kenneth Church, Christopher Cieri, Alejandrina Cristia, Jun Du, Sriram Ganapathy, and Mark Liberman. 2018. First DIHARD challenge evaluation plan. *2018, tech. Rep.*

Neville Ryant, Kenneth Church, Christopher Cieri, Alejandrina Cristia, Jun Du, Sriram Ganapathy, and Mark Liberman. 2019. The second DIHARD diarization challenge: Dataset, task, and baselines. In *Proceedings of Interspeech 2019*, pages 978–982.

Neville Ryant, Prachi Singh, Venkat Krishnamohan, Rajat Varma, Kenneth Church, Christopher Cieri, Jun Du, Sriram Ganapathy, and Mark Liberman. 2020. The third dihard diarization challenge.

G. Sell, D. Snyder, A. McCree, D. Garcia-Romero, M. Villalba, J. a nd Maciejewski, V. Manohar, N. Dehak, D. Povey, S. Watanabe, and J. Khuda npur. 2018. Diarization is hard: Some experiences and lessons learned for the jhu team in th e inaugural dihard challenge. *Interspeech.*

D. Snyder, D. Garcia-Romero, G. Sell, D. Povey, and S. Khudanpur. 2018. X-vectors: Robust dnn embeddings for speaker recognition. In *2018 IEEE International Conference on Acoustics, Speech and Signal Processing (ICASSP)*. IEEE.

Michael Thomas. nd. Sakun (Sukur) language documentation. `https://elar.soas.ac.uk/Collection/MPI184105`, Accessed on 12 Oct 2020.

Association for Computational Linguistics
209 N. Eighth Street
Stroudsburg, Pennsylvania 18360

ISBN 978-1-7138-9029-4

9 781713 890294

CURRAN ASSOCIATES INC.
proceedings.com